Student Guide with Map Exercises

THE ENDURING VISION

Volume One

Student Guide with Map Exercises

THE ENDURING VISION

A HISTORY OF THE AMERICAN PEOPLE

FOURTH EDITION

Boyer • Clark • Kett
Salisbury • Sitkoff • Woloch

Volume One: To 1877

Barbara Blumberg

Pace University

HOUGHTON MIFFLIN COMPANY   BOSTON   NEW YORK

Sponsoring Editor: Jeffrey Greene
Editorial Assistant: Shoma Aditya
Senior Manufacturing Coordinator: Marie Barnes
Marketing Manager: Sandra McGuire

Printed in the U.S.A.

ISBN: 0-395-96082-7

23456789-VG-03 02 01 00 99

Contents

Preface   vii

Prologue   Enduring Vision, Enduring Land   1

Chapter 1   America Begins   9

Chapter 2   Transatlantic Encounters and Colonial Beginnings, 1492–1630   17

Chapter 3   Expansion and Diversity: The Rise of Colonial America   32

Chapter 4   The Bonds of Empire, 1660–1750   46

Chapter 5   Roads to Revolution, 1744–1776   55

Chapter 6   Securing Independence, Defining Nationhood, 1776–1788   67

Chapter 7   Launching the New Republic, 1789–1800   79

Chapter 8   Jeffersonianism and the Era of Good Feelings   90

Chapter 9   The Transformation of American Society, 1815–1840   100

Chapter 10   Politics, Religion, and Reform in the Age of Jackson   110

Chapter 11   Life, Leisure, and Culture, 1840–1860   120

Chapter 12   The Old South and Slavery, 1800–1860   130

Chapter 13   Immigration, Expansion, and Sectional Conflict, 1840–1848   140

Chapter 14   From Compromise to Secession, 1850–1861   150

Chapter 15   Freedom Reborn: Civil War, 1861–1865   161

Chapter 16   The Crises of Reconstruction, 1865–1877   172

Preparing for the Final Examination: Prologue, Chapters 1 to 16   182

Answers to Multiple-Choice Questions   187

Preface

The final Guide chapter is intended

This *Student Guide with Map Exercises to Accompany The Enduring Vision,* Fourth Edition, is intended to help you to master the history presented in *The Enduring Vision: A History of the American People.* It is *not* a substitute for reading the textbook. However, used properly as a *supplement* to the text, it should assist you in focusing on the important events, issues, and concepts in American history, as well as on the well-known figures and ordinary people alike whose ideas and actions help us to understand the past. It is also designed to build your vocabulary, improve your knowledge of geography, and enhance your understanding of how the historian learns about the past.

Each chapter in the *Student Guide* corresponds to a chapter in *The Enduring Vision* and is divided into the following sections:

- *Outline and Summary.* This follows the outline of the textbook chapter and summarizes the material discussed under each text heading. You should read it quickly before reading the textbook chapter to give yourself an overview of the contents. Then carefully read the text chapter. After completing the text chapter, reread the outline and summary as a review.

- *Vocabulary.* In this section social-science terms and other words used in the text chapter that may be new to you are defined. Look over the list before you read the textbook chapter. Familiarize yourself with any words that you do not already know.

- *Identifications.* Here you will find the important persons, laws, terms, groups, and events covered in *The Enduring Vision.* After reading the text chapter, test yourself by identifying who or what each item was and how this person or thing fits into the overall story. That is, what is its historical significance?

- *Skill Building.* In most of the chapters of the *Student Guide,* you will find either (a) a section designed to help you interpret charts and tables in the textbook or (b) a map exercise, asking you to locate places mentioned in the text chapter and to explain the historical significance of those geographical places. Some chapters contain both.

- *Historical Sources.* Too often we simply accept what we see in print as true and memorize it without stopping to ask how the author obtained the information and whether we should believe it. The purpose of the Historical Sources section found in most chapters is to explain where the historian gets his or her facts, and to assist you in evaluating the reliability of those sources and the conclusions based on them.

- *Multiple-Choice Questions, Short-Answer Questions, Essay Questions, and Answers to Multiple-Choice Questions.* After reading the corresponding chapter in *The Enduring Vision,* you should try to answer these questions. They are designed to help you review the significant material in the chapter; they will probably be similar to the kinds of questions and essays that your professor will give you to write on in papers, quizzes, and exams. Answers to the multiple-choice questions appear at the end of the *Student Guide.*

The last *Student Guide* chapter is intended to aid you in preparing for the final examination in your history course. It contains hints on studying, as well as multiple-choice and essay questions that ask you to consider and pull together the material presented in *all* of the chapters of *The Enduring Vision*.

For help in preparing the *Student Guide*, I would like to thank the authors of *The Enduring Vision* for writing a lucid, informative, political, social, and cultural history of the United States that is a pleasure to read and to write about. Second I appreciate the help of the editors at Houghton Mifflin who made valuable suggestions. I am grateful to my husband, Alan Krumholz, and to my son, Mark, for their patience and support while I worked on this project.

—Barbara Blumberg

Student Guide with Map Exercises

THE ENDURING VISION

Volume One

PROLOGUE

Enduring Vision, Enduring Land

Outline and Summary

I. Introduction

America's "enduring vision" has constituted (1) a vision of the land itself in which the land offers a "haven for new beginnings" and opportunities, and (2) a search for a just social order that has constantly sought to balance individual freedom with obligations to the social group, or "community." Many times in our past we have not lived up to our ideals of freedom and social responsibility, but those who have tried to bring us back to the vision, along with most other Americans, have shared a hopefulness about progress.

II. An Ancient Heritage

The oldest rocks on the North American continent are 3 billion years old. By the Paleozoic era (around 250 million years ago), forests covered much of what would eventually be the United States, and the organic matter of these ancient forests was to provide America with its abundant coal deposits. About 180 million years ago, earth's one big landmass, Pangaea, began to split apart into separate continents. Millions of years later, violent movements of the earth's crust created the Pacific Coastal, Sierra Nevada, and Cascade mountain ranges on the western edge of the continent. Between 65 and 70 million years ago the shallow sea that covered much of west-central North America disappeared and was replaced by the Rocky Mountains. The decay and fossilization of plant and animal organisms in these regions had already started to form America's oil deposits.

  The four glaciations of the Ice Age, between 2 million and 10,000 years ago, reshaped much of Canada, New England, New York, and the Midwest. The first Americans were hunting bands who crossed the then-existing land bridge between Siberia and Alaska between 40,000 and 15,000 years ago.

III. The Continent and Its Regions

A. Introduction

As the ice retreated, North America slowly warmed. The geological, geographical, and climatic diversity that followed has contributed to the regional cultural differences that have developed and to America's physical beauty, wealth of resources, and political preeminence.

B. The West

Lands in Alaska and Canada ranged from the treeless tundra of the Arctic to the heavily forested taiga of the subarctic. Farther south the Pacific Northwest had a temperate, rainy climate and many

1

resources, while the southern California coast offered a drier, warmer, Mediterranean climate. To the east of the fertile intermountain range valleys and the Sierra Nevada lay the Great Basin, an arid, formidable desert. The backbone of western North America is formed by the Rocky Mountains. Beyond the Rockies' front range is the Continental Divide, the watershed separating rivers flowing eastward into the Atlantic from those draining westward into the Pacific. In the hot southwestern deserts of Arizona, southern Utah, western New Mexico, and southeastern California, Native Americans cultivated the first crops in what is now the United States.

C. The Heartland

North America's heartland extends from the Rocky Mountains to the Appalachians. Over the millennia, the Mississippi-Missouri-Ohio river system that drains it has carried so much silt down to the Gulf of Mexico that a fertile delta capable of providing food for a large population has been built up. Most of the eastern and northern sections of the heartland were once covered with thick forests. To the west the trees give way gradually to grass-covered prairies. Beyond the Missouri River, these prairies become the Great Plains—treeless, an endless sea of grass, bitter cold in winter, blazing hot in summer, and often dry. In the nineteenth century, white settlers displaced the Indians in the American heartland—felled the trees, plowed up the grasses, and turned the Midwest into a breadbasket for the world, except during periodic droughts when it was subjected to severe dust storms.

D. The Atlantic Seaboard

East of the Appalachians lies the upland area known as the piedmont, extending from Alabama to Maryland. Once blessed with rich, red soil, its fertility in modern times has been ruined by excessive cotton and tobacco farming. The northward extension of the piedmont runs from Pennsylvania to southern New England. In contrast, the terrain of upstate New York and most of New England was sculpted by glaciation. Strewn with the rocks and boulders left behind by retreating ice, New England's soil is difficult to plow.

The fall line, a series of rapids in the rivers that block navigation upstream from the coast, separates the Atlantic coastal plain, or tidewater, from the interior. In the south the tidewater is cut by numerous small rivers. To the north it narrows and flattens to form the New Jersey Pine Barrens, Long Island, and Cape Cod. North of Massachusetts Bay, the shoreline becomes mountainous. North America's true eastern edge, the continental shelf, is an area of relatively shallow water that extends as much as 250 miles into the Atlantic.

Some ten thousand years ago, Indians followed a warming climate eastward over the Appalachians to the coast. They found the waters of the Grand Banks and Cape Cod teeming with fish and the hardwood forests abundant with berries and game. Carrying Woodland culture with them, they also engaged in agriculture.

IV. A Legacy and a Challenge

Geographical isolation and ecological variety characterized the New World before the arrival of Europeans. Until the early twentieth century Americans hoped that separation would isolate them from Europe and its problems. Modern technology has killed that dream and posed another challenge—how to stop destruction of the very environment that has sustained us. Here we could well draw on the legacy of the Native Americans and reestablish a sense of historical and cultural continuity with our predecessors on the land. In this way we might recapture the Indians' sense "that the land—its life-sustaining bounty and its soul-sustaining beauty—is itself of inestimable value and not merely a means to the end of material growth."

Vocabulary

The following terms are used in the Prologue. To understand it fully, it is important that you know what each of them means.

eon   an indefinitely long period of time; an age; the largest division of geologic time, composing two or more eras

ephemeral   fleeting, impermanent, short-lived

geology   the scientific study of the earth, rocks, and the changes that the earth has undergone or is undergoing

exploitation   unfair or reckless use of people, animals, and/or the environment to profit materially from them

tundra   nearly level, treeless plain with sparse, stunted vegetation of the kind found in the arctic regions of Europe, Asia, and North America

taiga   the evergreen forests of subarctic lands covering vast areas of northern North America and Eurasia

anchorage   harbor

steppe   dry, grassy land or plains

delta   a nearly flat plain of river-deposited silt and soil between diverging branches of the mouth of a river

bayou   a sluggish tributary or a swampy arm of a lake or river

millennium (plural: millennia)   a period of a thousand years

pristine   of or pertaining to the earliest period or state; original, primitive, or having its original purity

ecologist   one who studies the interaction between plants and animals and their environment

Identifications

After reading the Prologue, you should be able to identify and explain the historical significance of each of the following:

New World

Pangaea and continental drift

Precambrian era

Paleozoic era

Mesozoic era

Ice Age

Continental Divide

breadbasket

fall line

continental shelf

Grand Banks

Skill Building: Maps

1. On the map of North America, locate each of the following and explain its geologic origins:

    continental shelf
    Appalachians
    Pacific Coastal, Sierra Nevada, and Cascade mountain ranges
    Rocky Mountains and Continental Divide
    Great Lakes
    Great Basin and Utah's Great Salt Lake
    southwestern desert, Colorado River, and Grand Canyon
    Mississippi Delta
    Great Plains
    tidewater region and fall line
    piedmont

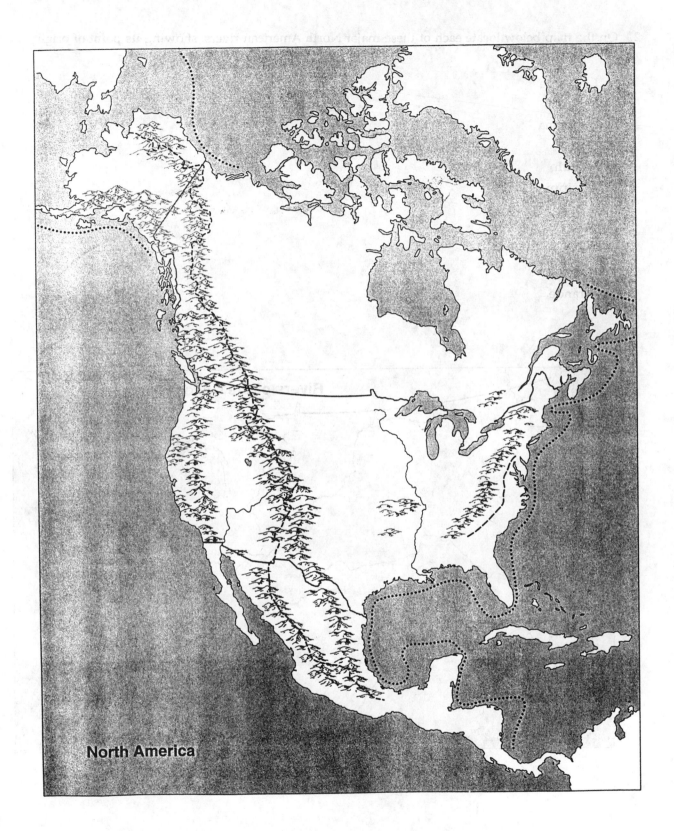

North America

2. On the map below locate each of these major North American rivers, showing its point of origin and its mouth:

St. Lawrence

Hudson

Susquehanna

Potomac

Savannah

Mississippi

Missouri

Ohio

Snake

Columbia

Rio Grande

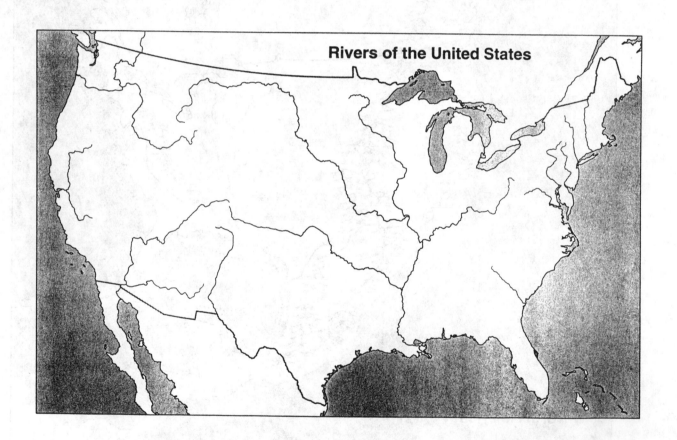

Rivers of the United States

Multiple-Choice Questions

Circle the letter of the item that best completes each statement or answers the question.

1. The fall line is
   a. the edge of the continental shelf where the Atlantic Ocean suddenly becomes much deeper.
   b. the mountain ranges of California over which Pacific air masses drop their moisture in the form of heavy rainfall.
   c. the divide between the treeless Great Plains and the more forested Mississippi-Ohio Valley.
   d. the series of rapids in rivers where hard continental rock meets the sedimentary plains along the Atlantic.

2. About how long ago did the last glacial expansion in North America occur?
   a. no one knows
   b. 50,000 years
   c. 10,000 years
   d. 2 million years

3. Agriculture was first practiced by the Indians of the
   a. Pacific Northwest.
   b. desert Southwest.
   c. midwestern heartland.
   d. Atlantic seaboard.

4. The Continental Divide is found in the
   a. Sierra Nevada.
   b. fall line.
   c. Ohio Valley.
   d. Rocky Mountains.

5. All of the following were created by glaciation *except*
   a. the Great Lakes.
   b. New England's rocky soil.
   c. the Grand Canyon.
   d. the coastline of Alaska.

6. Because of its geological and ecological history, North America has to this day the world's largest deposits of
   a. bauxite.
   b. coal.
   c. iron ore.
   d. oil.

7. Since the nineteenth century the geographical region that has become America's breadbasket is
   a. the Midwest.
   b. the Far West.
   c. the Atlantic seaboard.
   d. the Great Basin.

8. The region with the greatest annual temperature range in the United States is
   a. New England.
   b. the Southeast.
   c. the Pacific Northwest and Alaskan panhandle.
   d. the Great Plains.

9. An environmental historian has stated, "The ancestors of American buffaloes, Eurasian cattle, and Australian kangaroos shambled and hopped down diverging paths of evolution." Why did that happen?
   a. The plants and animals on each continent were virtually isolated from those on other continents for 180 million years.
   b. Agriculture and hunting patterns brought great changes to the plant and animal kingdoms.
   c. It was so cold in the northern hemisphere that the animals which survived there were very different from those of the southern hemisphere.
   d. No one knows the reasons for this diversity.

10. All of the following states have a portion of the piedmont running through them *except*
    a. Alabama.
    b. Pennsylvania.
    c. Rhode Island.
    d. North Carolina.

Short-Answer Questions

1. What was Pangaea? What happened to it about 180 million years ago? What were the consequences?

2. Describe the climate and terrain of each of the following regions: the West, the heartland, the Atlantic seaboard.

3. How was the fertile Mississippi Delta created?

4. Why was much of New England's soil rocky and difficult to plow?

Essay Questions

1. According to the Prologue, what has been the enduring vision of Americans? What have been some of the problems and contradictions within that vision?

2. "Geology, geography, and environment are among the fundamental building blocks of human history." Explain the meaning of this statement, and illustrate it with as many specific examples from the Prologue as possible.

CHAPTER 1
America Begins

Outline and Summary

I. Introduction

American history began more than ten thousand years before Columbus's first voyage. Here Native Americans developed diverse cultures, but with much interaction among the different groups.

This chapter focuses on these questions: (1) How did environmental changes produce transitions in Indian Cultures? (2) How did Indian cultures affect each other? (3) What values, if any, did all Native Americans share, and how did these differ from values of Europeans arriving after 1500?

II. The First Americans

A. Introduction

The most accepted theory about the origins of America's people is that during the last Ice Age bands of hunters from Siberia crossed the then-existing land bridge into Alaska. Most Native Americans descended from these first migrants, called Paleo-Indians by archaeologists.

B. The Peopling of North America

These Paleo-Indians lived in small hunting bands that moved constantly in pursuit of mammoths, mastodons and other big game. Groups came together briefly at quarries, where they obtained flint for spear points and tools. By way of these encounters the bands intermarried, traded, and came to share some culture in common. About 9000 B.C. the mammoths and mastodons became extinct because of climatic warming and relentless hunting.

C. Archaic Societies

As the earth's atmosphere warmed, a tremendous range of plants and animals flourished on the North American continent and in its waters. This enabled archaic peoples (North Americans of the period 8000 B.C. to 1500 B.C.) to broaden their diets to include small mammals, fish, and wild plants. This abundance was especially apparent in parts of the East and Midwest, allowing larger groups of people to live in a smaller area and establish permanent villages. Archaic peoples learned how to make tools, weapons, and utensils from materials such as stone, bone, shell, clay, and leather. They also started extensive trade networks to obtain items not available in their own area. Ideas and religious beliefs, as well as material goods, spread along these networks. These people distinguished sharply between men's and women's roles: men hunted and fished; women harvested and prepared wild plants.

III. *The Indians' Continent*

A. The Northern and Western Perimeters

In western Alaska a new arctic way of life was emerging. The Eskimos and Aleuts were making and using the first bows and arrows, ceramic pottery, and pit houses. The Eskimos spread across the tundra regions as far east as Greenland. They received some metal tools from trade with Siberia and the Norsemen in Newfoundland.

Along the Pacific coast, from southern Alaska to northern California, Indians fished for salmon and learned to dry and store their catch year-round, making possible the establishment of permanent villages of several hundred people. Farther south California Indians also resided in permanent villages and sustained themselves by collecting and grinding acorns into meal. Both groups engaged in trade and warfare and, as a result, united under the leadership of chiefs. Because the climate of the Great Basin was so warm and dry, Indians of that area could not settle in one region but continued to roam, hunting small mammals and foraging for wild seeds and nuts.

B. The Southwest

In the Southwest, Indians turned slowly to farming, creating sophisticated systems of irrigation. Farming in the Western Hemisphere began in about 5000 B.C. in central Mexico, and the techniques of plant domestication spread to western New Mexico. By the third century B.C. the Hohokam people of southern Arizona had built extensive canal systems for irrigation that allowed them to harvest two crops a year. They also resided in permanent villages of several hundred people. The Anasazi people of the Southwest lived primarily by farming, too. These ancestors of the modern Pueblo Indians dominated the Southwest for almost 600 years, founding towns such as Chaco Canyon, New Mexico, inhabited by about fifteen thousand persons. By the thirteenth century, however, the Anasazi and Hohokam cultures declined, and these peoples abandoned their large settlements because of prolonged periods of drought. At roughly the same time the foraging Apaches and Navajos arrived in the Southwest.

C. The Eastern Woodlands

Many tribes in the Eastern Woodlands (the area from the Mississippi Valley to the Atlantic coast) experimented with village life and political centralization even before they started farming. As early as 1200 B.C. five thousand people lived at Poverty Point on the shore of the Mississippi River in Louisiana. As Poverty Point declined in importance, a new mound-building culture, the Adena, emerged. Adena mounds, often containing graves and playing an essential role in the people's religion, were built all over the Mississippi Valley and Northeast. In the first century B.C. Adena culture evolved into the more complex and widespread Hopewell civilization, which built more elaborate mounds.

Agriculture did not become the primary source of food for Eastern Woodlands peoples until after the seventh century A.D. The first full-time farmers in the East lived on the flood plains of the Mississippi River, where, incorporating elements of Hopewell culture, they evolved into the still more sophisticated Mississippian civilization. Mississippian towns grew to have thousands of inhabitants. The most important town was Cahokia, near present-day St. Louis. Mississippian artists produced works of clay, stone, shell, and copper. Their religion was based on sun worship, and their political system was centralized and hierarchical. By the thirteenth century, Mississippian culture had declined and most Eastern Woodlands Indians had abandoned large settlements and centralized political power. However, they continued to engage in agriculture, using the ecologically sound slash-and-burn method of land clearing to grow their corn, beans and pumpkins.

Many different Indian cultures existed on the North American continent by 1500, but most shared certain characteristics: use of bows and arrows and ceramic pottery, belief in some common religious practices and rituals, preference for small kin-based communities, and rejection of political centralization.

IV. American Peoples on the Eve of European Contact

A. Introduction

By 1492 about 75 million people lived in the Western Hemisphere. Of these, 7 million to 10 million inhabited land north of Mexico. These peoples were divided into several hundred nations and tribes and spoke diverse languages. The most important social groupings were the family, the village, and, for many of the tribes, the clan.

B. Family and Community

Kinship held Indian societies together. The kinship group, or extended family, was far more important than the nuclear family of husband, wife, and young children. The men hunted, fished, traded, negotiated, and fought; the women did the farming (except among the tribes of the Southwest, where both sexes were cultivators).

C. Indian Spiritual and Social Values

Native Americans found all nature, including humanity, interrelated and suffused with spiritual powers or, in the language of the Algonquian, *manitou*. Indians sought to placate and be in tune with these spiritual forces. They did this through dreaming; altering their state of consciousness by acts of physical endurance and self-torture, such as the Sun Dance of the Plains Indians; and following the advice of shamans. To smooth relations between persons of unequal status and power and hold their societies together, Indians relied on reciprocity, which included the giving of gifts and trading of goods in return for receiving prestige, deference, and authority. Indian communities generally demanded conformity and close cooperation of their members.

V. Conclusion

Human history in the Western Hemisphere did not begin with the arrival of Columbus. For thousands of years before 1492 Native Americans hunted; gathered; farmed; built communities, roads, and trails; and created complex societies. While not always good conservationists, Indians did, for the most part, respect the land and use it in ways that allowed natural resources to renew themselves. Europeans arriving in North America after 1500 showed no such self-restraint.

Vocabulary

The following terms are used in Chapter 1. To understand the chapter fully, it is important that you know what each of them means.

archaeological   of or pertaining to the scientific study of any prehistoric culture by excavation and description of its remains

indigenous   native to a particular region

shaman   a medicine man; a worker with the supernatural

kiva   a large chamber, often wholly or partially underground, in a Pueblo Indian village; used for religious ceremonies and other purposes

deference   submission or yielding to the judgment, opinion, and/or will of another; respectful or courteous regard

clan   a group of families or households whose heads claim descent from a common ancestor

hierarchy   a system of placing persons or things in a graded order, from lower to higher, in wealth, power, status, and so on

reciprocity   a system of mutual give-and-take, allowing individuals or social groups of unequal power, wealth, or status to get along while preserving unequal power relationships; also, a system by which human beings can coexist with nature and the powerful supernatural forces in which they believe

consensus   agreement in opinion; collective opinion

Identifications

After reading Chapter 1, you should be able to identify and explain the historical significance of each of the following:

League of the Iroquois

Paleo-Indians

Archaic peoples

pit houses

Hohokam culture

Anasazi and Pueblo cultures

Chaco Canyon

Poverty Point, mound-building culture, and Adena culture

Hopewell and Mississippian cultures

Eastern Woodlands peoples

Cahokia

nuclear families versus extended families

manitou and the Sun Dance

Skill Building: Maps

On the map of North America on the following page, locate the regions where these Indian cultures and the sites associated with them existed:

Aleuts, Eskimos, and Arctic culture

Northwest Coast Indians

California Indians

hunting bands of the Great Basin

Hohokam culture

Anasazi and Pueblo cultures

Poverty Point

Adena culture

Hopewell and Mississippian cultures (Cahokia)

Eastern Woodlands culture (Iroquois Confederacy)

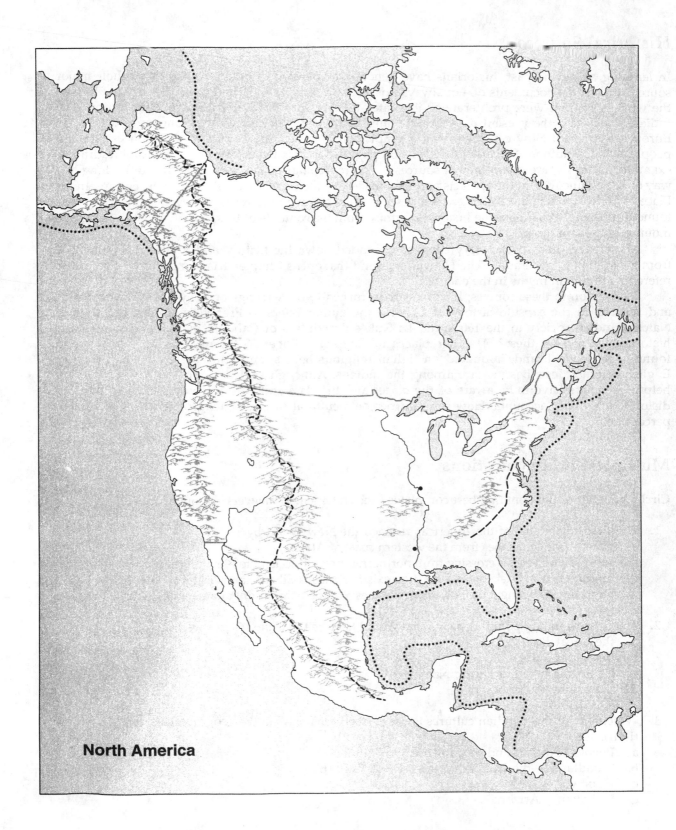

North America

Historical Sources

In learning about the past, historians have generally depended on written records as their major source. But written documents do not always exist for all places, groups, and times. For most of history the world's peoples were preliterate or illiterate and therefore left no written communication. The Indians inhabiting the present-day United States had not developed written languages before the Europeans arrived. How can historians attempt to reconstruct the lives and experiences of these peoples? As the author of Chapter 1 tells us on page 1, "archaeological evidence and oral traditions, examined critically, are our principal sources. . . ." Archaeologists can detect much about a long-lost way of life by uncovering the artifacts and remains left by the people who shared a past culture. In "A Place in Time: Cahokia in 1200" there is a description of a grave mount uncovered in a dig. What was found at that site? What does the historian surmise from the contents of this mound and of other grave mounds in the same area?

Many tribes had special storytellers who handed down the history and myths of their people from generation to generation. The Hiawatha legend that opens Chapter 1 is one example. Find other references to Indian myths in the chapter.

In addition to these sources, historians have turned to the writings of early European explorers and settlers. In the capsule history of Cahokia the author refers to French explorers' accounts of Natchez Indian society in the 1600s and La Salle's description of Cahokia in 1682. What does the historian learn from these? At other places in Chapter 1 Roger Williams, Puritan minister and founder of Rhode Island, is quoted on Indian religious beliefs, and another seventeenth-century English colonist describes warfare among the Indians. Although such written records can be very helpful, scholars have to be aware of the biases and the class and cultural points of view that can distort the writers' accounts. How might a person's cultural or class background color his or her perceptions?

Multiple-Choice Questions

Circle the letter of the item that best completes each statement or answers the question.

1. The first inhabitants of the Americas reached the New World by
   a. giant outrigger canoes from the western coast of Africa.
   b. swift sailing vessels crossing from northern Europe to Iceland to New England.
   c. migrating from Asia across the then existing Alaska-Siberia land bridge.
   d. migrating in outrigger canoes from Polynesia to the Isthmus of Panama and Central America.

2. The densest Indian populations in what would later be the United States were found in
   a. the Great Basin.
   b. the Great Plains.
   c. California and the Pacific Northwest.
   d. the southwestern desert.

3. Which one of these Indian cultures is *not* correctly matched to the geographical area in which it flourished?
   a. Pueblo—Arizona and New Mexico
   b. Woodlands—the Pacific Northwest and California
   c. Hopewell—the Midwest
   d. Hohokam—Arizona

4. All of the following helped shape Native Americans' social and cultural development before 1500 *except*
   a. geographical isolation.
   b. great climatic and geographical variations across America.
   c. contact with Asian and African cultures, from which they adopted many practices.
   d. long-term changes or cycles in weather, such as warming trends and extended droughts.

5. Which of the following tribes was the ancestor of the modern Pueblo Indians?
   a. Adenas
   b. Anasazis
   c. Aleuts
   d. Apaches

6. At the time of Columbus's first voyage to the New World, about how many native Americans lived on the continent north of present-day Mexico?
   a. 7 million to 10 million
   b. 75 million
   c. 50,000 to 100,000
   d. 1 million to 2 million

7. All of these were characteristics of Native American culture before contact with the Eastern Hemisphere *except*
   a. strong kinship or extended family ties.
   b. the belief that all nature was infused with spiritual power.
   c. the belief that property ownership gave the owner perpetual and exclusive control over the land.
   d. strong oral traditions but no written languages.

8. Cahokia was
   a. located near present-day New York City and reached its peak of glory in the 1700s.
   b. probably doomed by its primitive culture and lack of governmental institutions.
   c. destroyed by French explorers, who burned it in 1682.
   d. part of the mound-building Mississippian culture and grew to a population of 20,000 inhabitants.

9. Among North American Indians women alone did the farming *except* for in tribes in the
   a. Northeast.
   b. Great Basin.
   c. Southwest.
   d. Mississippi Valley.

10. The term *Archaic peoples* refers to
    a. native North Americans from about 8000 to 1500 B.C.
    b. the first nomadic hunters to reach North America.
    c. the mound builders of the Mississippi Valley.
    d. all Native Americans living here at the time of Columbus's voyage.

Short-Answer Questions

1. Where and when did the earliest direct contact between Europeans and Americans probably occur? What, if anything, resulted from the contact?
2. Where and how was agriculture first practiced in what is now the United States?

Essay Questions

1. Compare and contrast the development and later decline of each of these major Indian cultures: Hohokam and Anasazi; Adena, Hopewell, and Mississippian.

2. Discuss the differing ways of life of the Native Americans living in the Arctic, the Pacific Northwest, California, the Great Basin, the Southwest, the Mississippi Valley, and the Eastern Woodlands. Explain how the physical environment influenced each way of life.

3. Because the Indian peoples of the present-day United States had not developed written languages before the coming of Europeans, how have historians attempted to reconstruct Native American history? Give as many specific examples from Chapter 1 as possible.

4. Compare and contrast the descriptions of Native American culture presented in Chapter 1 with the impressions offered in movies and television.

CHAPTER 2

Transatlantic Encounters and Colonial Beginnings, 1492–1630

Outline and Summary

I. Introduction

Chapter 2 focuses on (1) how trade and war affected West Africa and Western Europe in the sixteenth century; (2) which developments in Europe facilitated its expansion to America; (3) why Spain outdistanced all European rivals for empire in the early sixteenth century only to be challenged by them in the early seventeenth; (4) why Native Americans sometimes welcomed, sometimes resisted European traders and colonists.

II. African and European Peoples

A. Mediterranean Crossroads

Peoples from Africa, Asia, and Europe have interacted around the Mediterranean since ancient times. They have traded, forged links, and sometimes engaged in holy wars to spread their religion and suppress others. By 1492, the Catholic kingdoms of Castile and Aragon had successfully driven Muslims and Jews from the Iberian peninsula, and Catholic Portugal had started sending ships down the Atlantic coast of Africa and was conquering Moroccan ports and Moroccan control of trade in gold and other items between Europe and West Africa.

B. West Africa and Its Peoples

In the grasslands south of the Sahara Desert and east of the West African coast, kingdoms arose that rivaled those in Europe in size and wealth. In the fourteenth century, one of these empires, Mali, dominated the whole region and carried on lucrative trade with Europe and the Middle East. Its leading city, Timbuktu, was an important center of Islamic learning. By the sixteenth century, however, most of Mali and the successor state, Songhai, had been conquered by Morocco. In the fifteenth century, the small states on the Guinea and Senegambian coast grew in population and importance because of the foreign demand for the gold that the Africans mined and traded. In the mid-1400s the Portuguese arrived on the coast, too, looking for gold and slaves. West African leaders ranged from powerful emperors, who claimed demigod status, to heads of small states, who ruled mainly by persuasion. Kinship groups formed the most important unit holding people together. Men could marry more than one woman, allowing high-status men to establish kinship networks with other important families through their several wives. Africans did not regard land as a commodity to be bought and sold. Rather, one honored one's ancestors and their spirits by proper land cultivation.

Agriculture was difficult in Africa and required the labor of both men and women, who grew yams, rice, and other grains. Religion and belief in magic permeated African culture and inspired artistic endeavors. West Africans developed sophisticated art and music, on which much of twentieth-century art and jazz are based. By the 1500s Islam was starting to spread beyond the kings and upper class to the common people of the grasslands. Christianity, introduced by the Portuguese in the 1400s and 1500s, made limited headway until the nineteenth century.

C. European Culture and Society

At the time of Columbus's first voyage to America, Europe was at the height of a great cultural revival, the Renaissance. Scholars were trying to map the world and to understand natural science, including astronomy. European society was hierarchical; at the top were the kings who governed most states and had been consolidating their power for a century. As a result of new economic forces, the power of the landed nobility was declining, while that of bankers, merchants, and the towns they dominated was climbing.

Exploited peasants comprised 70 percent to 80 percent of the people. Population increases in the sixteenth and seventeenth centuries made land in Europe scarce and valuable. That encouraged the upper classes to enclose more and more of the common fields, converting them to their private property, while displaced country people drifted to the small towns, which were crowded, dirty, and disease-ridden. Traditional European society, which like Native American and African cultures had been based on extended families and social reciprocity, was starting to change. Nuclear families were slowly replacing kinship networks. New business enterprises and organizations, like joint stock companies, broke the bonds of social reciprocity. Emerging entrepreneurs favored "unimpeded acquisition of wealth" and unregulated competition. They "insisted that individuals owed one another nothing but the money necessary to settle each market transaction."

D. Religious Upheavals

Except for small Jewish and Muslim minorities, all Europeans in 1492 were Christians. The Roman Catholic church was headed by a pope whose authority was acknowledged everywhere except in Russia and the Balkan peninsula, and it was administered by a hierarchy of clergy who did not marry. By the fifteenth century this powerful institution was selling indulgences (blessings that would shorten the repentant sinner's time in purgatory) for donations to the church.

In 1517 a German Friar, Martin Luther, denounced indulgences and other corrupt practices, broke with the pope, and initiated the Protestant Reformation. Luther and other Protestants preached that one could not buy or earn salvation by good works (or donations to the church) and that priests had no special powers of intervention. God alone decided who was saved and who was damned, and Christians must have faith in his love and justice. French Protestant leader John Calvin and his followers went a step further, emphasizing the doctrine of predestination—that is, God's foreknowledge of who was saved and who was damned.

The Protestant challenge led to the Counter-Reformation, in which the modern Roman Catholic church was born. The renewed church cleaned out corruption, stimulated religious zeal, and attempted to suppress Protestantism. Thereafter, European countries divided into rival Protestant and Catholic camps.

E. The Rise of Puritanism in England

The Reformation began in England when King Henry VIII (ruled 1509–1547) asked the pope to annul his marriage to Catherine of Aragon, who had not given birth to a male heir. After the pope refused, Henry pushed through Parliament the laws of 1533–1534, which dissolved his marriage and declared the king head of the Church of England (Anglican).

Religious strife continued in England for more than one hundred years after Henry's split with the Catholic church. Henry's son and successor, Edward VII, leaned toward Protestantism during his brief reign. He was followed by "Bloody Mary," who tried to restore Catholicism by burning Protestants at the stake. This persecution turned her successor and half-sister, Elizabeth I (1558–1603), and the majority of English people against Catholicism. But the English differed on how Protestant the Church of England should be. Those who wanted to remove all vestiges of Catholicism were called Puritans. These Calvinistic Puritans believed in predestination and felt that only the saved should belong to the church. They wanted each congregation to be self-governing and free from interference from bishops and a church hierarchy. Puritanism, with its message of righteousness and self-discipline, appealed particularly to England's landowning gentry, small farmers, university-educated clergy, intellectuals, merchants, shopkeepers, and artisans.

Elizabeth managed to satisfy most English Protestants (Puritan and Anglican), but her successor, James I (1603–1625) made clear his dislike of Puritans and his intentions to crack down on them. Charles I, who became king in 1625, increased the campaign to root Puritanism out of the Church of England. Under this repression and experiencing economic hard times, many English Puritans, after 1620, decided to move to New England

III. *European Expansion*

A. Seaborne Expansion

Portugal led the way in Europe's seaborne expansion. Because of advances in maritime technology, Prince Henry the Navigator was able to send Portuguese sailors farther and farther down the coast of Africa to fight Muslims and seek opportunities for profitable trade. Portugal established a gold-making factory at Arguin, rounded Africa's Cape of Good Hope, and developed valuable commercial links with India. These Portuguese voyages brought Europeans face to face with black-skinned Africans and the profits to be made in the already existing slave trade.

B. The "New Slavery" and Racism

Slavery existed in West African life before the arrival of Europeans, but it was not based on racial differences between masters and slaves, and the slaves were often absorbed eventually into the owners' families. First Muslims from North Africa, then Europeans turned African slavery into an "intercontinental business." Generally, European slavers bought war captives from African slave-trading kings, which encouraged those rulers to engage in constant warfare with their neighbors. Nearly 12 million Africans would be shipped across the Atlantic under terrible conditions to labor in the Western Hemisphere before the international slave trade finally ended, centuries later. The new slavery based on race would further dehumanize black Africans in the eyes of white Europeans.

C. Europeans Reach America

Christopher Columbus, like other educated men of the fifteenth century, believed that the world was round. Unlike others, however, he insisted that Europeans could reach Asia and its rich trading opportunities by sailing westward across the Atlantic. He convinced the king and queen of Spain, who were anxious to break Portugal's monopoly of trade via the route around Africa, to finance his voyages of discovery. On his 1492 trip he landed on the island of San Salvador, in the West Indies. On subsequent voyages he reached Hispaniola and the American mainland. He died never realizing he had discovered a new world. Others, however, soon suspected it, and most of the later explorers were bent on discovering a water route through or around the landmasses of the Americas to the beckoning trade of Asia. Balboa crossed the Isthmus of Panama and reached the Pacific in that quest. Magellan sailed around the tip of South America, getting as far as the Philippines before being killed. Verrazano explored the coast of North America, and Jacques Cartier sailed up the St. Lawrence, each looking for the supposed Northwest Passage to Asia.

D. Spain's Conquistadores

The early Spanish explorers soon became conquerors as well. Columbus exported Indian slaves from Hispaniola and gave grants to Spaniards to extract labor and other tribute from the native population there. In 1519 Hernán Cortés landed in Mexico and subjugated the mighty Aztec empire. During the rest of the sixteenth century, Spanish conquerors fanned out over the Caribbean and the Americas from Mexico to Chile, subduing and enslaving the native peoples and enriching themselves and Spain with fabulous finds of gold and silver. In their wake came 300,000 Spanish settlers, who developed West Indian sugar plantations, Mexican sheep and cattle ranches, and gold and silver mines, all worked with slave labor. The Indian population was nearly decimated by forced labor, warfare, starvation, and, above all, alien diseases to which the Indians lacked immunity. When shortages of Indian slaves developed, the Portuguese delivered African substitutes. The riches flowing to Spain enticed other Europeans to challenge her in the Americas.

IV. Footholds in North America

A. New Spain's Northern Frontier

In the 1500s a number of Spaniards, searching for gold, silver, and slaves, penetrated areas that would one day be the United States. Cabeza de Vaca and Estevanico traveled from Florida to Texas to New Mexico; de Soto's party went from Tampa Bay to the Appalachians and then to Texas. Although they found no gold, these and other expeditions spread European diseases that wiped out most of the surviving Mississippian communities. Coronado plundered pueblos and searched for riches from the Grand Canyon to Kansas. In 1598 Juan de Oñate proclaimed the royal colony of New Mexico, which barely survived repeated Indian attacks and uprisings.

B. France: Initial Failures and Canadian Success

French attempts at planting permanent colonies in the St. Lawrence Valley in 1541, South Carolina in 1562, and Florida in 1564 all ended in failure. However, the French carried on lucrative fur trading with the Indians from Newfoundland to Maine and along the St. Lawrence. In 1608, Samuel de Champlain founded Quebec, the first permanent French settlement in Canada, and allied it with the Hurons.

C. The Enterprising Dutch

In 1614, Dutch traders erected Fort Nassau, at present-day Albany, and established New Netherlands. In 1626 the Dutch purchased Manhattan Island from local Indians and started the city of New Amsterdam. Most of the settlers lived by the fur trade. They dealt primarily with the Iroquois, the enemies of the French-backed Hurons.

D. Elizabethan England and the Wider World

By the late 1500s, intensifying conflicts with Catholic Spain were leading Protestant England to take interest in the Western Hemisphere. Queen Elizabeth encouraged English "sea dogs" like Francis Drake and John Hawkins to raid Spanish treasure ships and ports in the Western Hemisphere, and she split the rich plunder with them. Also, the English searched for the Northwest Passage and scoured America for gold and colony sites. After an English colony in Newfoundland disbanded, Sir Walter Raleigh sponsored a settlement on Roanoke Island. The English colonists antagonized the initially friendly Indians, wasted time hunting for gold, and failed to plant crops to feed themselves. Their pleas to England for more supplies went unanswered because of the Anglo-Spanish war then raging. England's victory in that struggle, including her 1588 defeat of the Spanish Armada, established the English as a major power in the Atlantic. However, in 1590, when a relief ship did finally land in Roanoke, it found no Englishmen. To this day historians do not know what became of that "lost colony."

E. The Beginnings of English Colonization: Virginia

In May 1607 a party of 105 English people landed in Virginia and began the settlement of Jamestown. The venture was organized and financed by an English joint-stock company, the Virginia Company of London. The only role of the English government was to grant a charter to the company giving it the right to land anywhere from Cape Fear to the Hudson River. Many of the early arrivals were "gentlemen" who refused to farm, hoping instead to find gold and quickly return to England. Because the company had given them inadequate supplies, they were soon starving. During the first years, or "starving time," the majority of the settlers died, and the survivors were on the verge of leaving several times. The discipline and forced work imposed for a while by Captain John Smith helped save the colony. Settler John Rolfe's development of a tobacco palatable to Europeans gave the colony the profitable export that ensured its financial success.

At first the stockholders in England treated the settlers as company employees, denying them any say in the colony's government or ownership of any of its land. To attract additional settlers and capital, the company started awarding land to people who paid their own and other people's passage to Virginia. This "headrights" system enabled planters who imported many indentured servants to acquire large estates. In 1619 the company also granted inhabitants the right to elect delegates to a legislative assembly, thus marking the beginnings of representative government in North America. An Indian attack in 1622 killed many of the English settlers. Charges of company mismanagement led King James I to revoke the charter in 1624, and Virginia became a royal colony.

F. The Origins of New England: Plymouth Plantation

In the winter of 1620, the *Mayflower* landed 102 English men and women at Plymouth Bay, where they founded Plymouth Plantation. The settlement was financed by some London merchants headed by Thomas Weston, who had received a patent from the Virginia Company of London to establish a colony. Weston had entered into an agreement with a group of English Separatists who had been living in Holland to escape Anglican persecution. The Separatists and other non-Puritan Englishmen who joined the expedition promised to send lumber, furs, and fish back to Weston for seven years in return for his investment.

Winter storms, however, blew the *Mayflower* off course, and the colonists landed outside the boundaries of Virginia and the jurisdiction of its government. Therefore, the adult males signed the Mayflower Compact, creating their own civil government and pledging to abide by its laws. Half the Pilgrims, as they came to be called, died during the first winter in Plymouth. Those still alive in the spring of 1621 were greatly helped by two friendly Indians, Squanto and Samoset, who taught them how to plant corn and arranged treaties with neighboring tribes. While Plymouth Plantation never grew wealthy or large, it was the vanguard of a mighty Puritan migration to New England in the 1630s and has shaped our image of the sturdy, freedom-seeking English colonists.

V. Conclusion

By 1630 European settlement of North America was well under way. The Spanish had advanced as far into Florida and New Mexico as they thought necessary to protect their Mexican and Caribbean possessions. The English were planting tobacco in the Chesapeake region of Virginia and farming at Plymouth. Dutch and French colonies engaged in brisk commerce in furs. This European expansion into the Western Hemisphere had taken a tremendous toll, however, in lives lost, native peoples displaced and decimated, and Africans transported and enslaved.

Vocabulary

The following terms are used in Chapter 2. To understand the chapter fully, it is important that you know what each of them means.

monotheistic   pertaining to belief on only one god (as opposed to *polytheistic*, having to do with belief in and worship of many gods)

hierarchy   a system of placing persons or things in a graded order, from lower to higher, in wealth, power, status, and so on

sumptuary laws   laws regulating personal habits that offend the moral or religious conscience of the community

yeomen   free, landowning small farmers, below the gentry in status

capitalism   a system under which the means of production, distribution, and exchange are in large measure privately owned and directed, and in which prices and wages are determined by supply-and-demand market forces

indoctrination   teaching or inculcating a doctrine or set of beliefs

Eucharist   the Christian sacrament of the Lord's Supper; communion; the sacrifice of the Mass; also the consecrated elements of the Lord's Supper, such as the bread

gentry   landowners with substantial amounts of property and without aristocratic titles; considered "gentlemen" and therefore not to do manual labor; played an important role in English government

caravel   a type of small, maneuverable ship developed by the Spanish and Portuguese in the 1400s

astrolabe   an astronomical instrument for taking the altitude of the sun or stars, useful in solving problems in astronomy and navigation

Huguenots   French Protestants

patent   an official document conferring a right (such as the exclusive right to make use of or sell an invention) or a grant of land (such as the charter given to the Virginia Company of London)

Identifications

After reading Chapter 2, you should be able to identify and explain the historical significance of each of the following:

"Crusades" versus jihad

English "Poor Laws"

enclose (enclosure movement)

joint-stock company

indulgences, Martin Luther, and the Protestant Reformation

John Calvin and the doctrine of predestination

Counter-Reformation

Puritans versus Anglicans

conversion experience, "saints," and the "elect"

Prince Henry the Navigator

Vasco da Gama

Vasco Núñez de Balboa

Ferdinand Magellan

Northwest Passage

conquistadores and *encomiendas*

Hernán Cortés

Juan Ponce de León, Cabeza de Vaca, Hernán de Soto, Francis Drake, and Walter Raleigh

Spanish Armada, 1588

lost colony of Roanoke

Elizabeth I and James I

Samuel de Champlain

Virginia Company of London

Captain John Smith

John Rolfe

headrights

Separatists

Thomas Weston, Pilgrims, and Plymouth Plantation

Mayflower Compact

Skill Building: Maps

1. On the map of Africa and southern Europe on the following page, locate each of the following and explain its historical significance :

    Iberian peninsula

    Mediterranean Sea

    Morocco

    Sahara Desert

    Ghana

    Mali

    Songhai

    Timbuktu

    Benin

    Guinea

    Senegambia

    the Equator

    Cape of Good Hope

    Congo

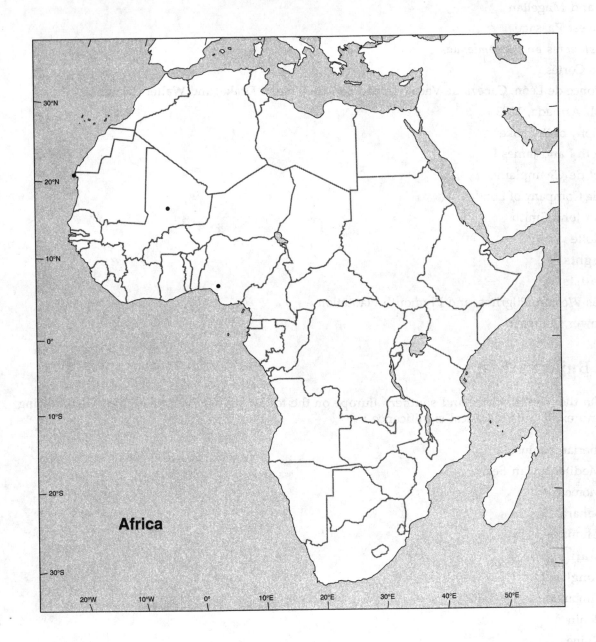

Africa

2. On the map of Central and South America and the Caribbean on the following page, locate each of the following places and explain which European explorer and conqueror is associated with it:

San Salvador and the Bahama Islands

Hispaniola (Haiti and the Dominican Republic)

Isthmus of Panama

Caribbean Sea

Pacific Ocean

Atlantic Ocean

Strait of Magellan

Tenochtitlán (Mexico City)

Puerto Rico

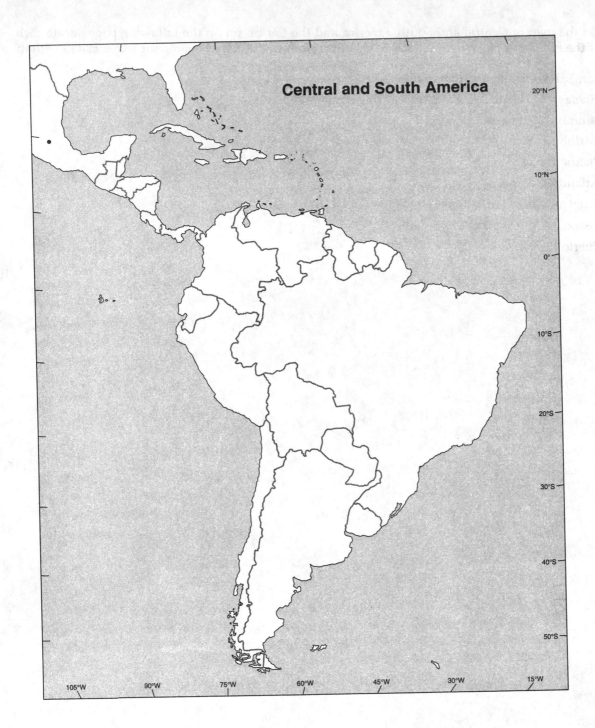

Central and South America

20°N

10°N

0°

10°S

20°S

30°S

40°S

50°S

105°W   90°W   75°W   60°W   45°W   30°W   15°W

2. On the map of North America on the following page, locate each of the following and indicate which European country had claimed and/or settled it by 1625:

   Great Lakes

   Chesapeake Bay

   Mississippi River

   Great Plains

   Newfoundland

   Acadia (Nova Scotia)

   Santa Fe

   St. Lawrence River

   St. Augustine, Florida

   Jamestown, Virginia, and James River

   Bermuda

   Quebec

   Fort Nassau (later Albany, New York)

   New Amsterdam (later New York City)

   Roanoke Island (off the coast of North Carolina)

   Plymouth Plantation

North America

Skill Building: Graphs and Charts

On page 26 in your textbook there is a line graph titled "Decline in Real Wages in England, 1500–1700." This graph shows the index of real wages, using 1500 as the base year. Real wages are not the mount of money a person earns but an estimate of what that amount of money at that time would allow the person to purchase. Economists derive these indexes by looking at the prices of a variety of goods and services offered in a given year and the actual wages earned by workers in the same period. Thus the index of real wages is a better indicator of people's standard of living than just looking at the amount of their earnings. In the graph the real wages, or standard of living, of English workers in 1500 is represented as 100. By following the line on the graph to 1700, one can see at a glance by how much that standard of living declined over the period. The importance of this graph is the light it can throw on historical causation. Based on this graph, how would you answer the following questions?

1. Did English people have strong economic motives for emigrating?

2. During which years would English people have had the greatest economic reasons for leaving home? Do these years correspond to periods of rapid population growth in the New England, Chesapeake, and Caribbean colonies?

3. After 1700 the proportion of non-English immigrants arriving in England's mainland colonies increased and the proportion of English immigrants declined. Does the graph offer any clues as to why this occurred?

Historical Sources

Too often students read a history textbook uncritically. They simply assume that the information in print is correct. Such readers do not ask the important questions: How does the historian learn about the past? How reliable are the sources historians commonly use?

In Chapter 2, for instance, what are the descriptions of West African society and religion based on? How does the historian know about the early years of the Plymouth settlement and the relations of the Pilgrims and the Indians?

Turn to page 31 of the text. There the author quotes Olaudah Equiano on African religious beliefs and practices. Equiano, born in the area around Benin, was sold as a young man in 1756 to a British slaver who brought him to the New World. In 1766 he bought his freedom and settled in England, where he became active in the antislavery movement. The quotation in the text comes from *The Interesting Narrative of the Life of Olaudah Equiano or Gustavus Vasa, the African*, which Equiano published in 1791. This narrative is one of a number that were written by former slaves. Like Equiano's, most of them were published many years after their authors last lived in Africa. Why are the autobiographies of former slaves a useful historical source? Can you see any reasons to question their accuracy?

One of the earliest and best sources that historians have for learning about the Pilgrims and the Plymouth settlement is William Bradford's *Of Plymouth Plantation*. Bradford wrote this detailed history of the colony and its people between 1630 and 1650. A Separatist, he arrived on the *Mayflower* and was elected governor by the settlers over and over again from 1621 to 1656, the year before his death. Can you explain why *Of Plymouth Plantation* is an excellent source for historians but must also be used with caution?

Carefully read "A Place in Time: Lake Champlain, 1609." Whose descriptions of the lake and surroundings, Indian peoples, and the battle does the author use? Who was Samuel de Champlain? Why are his writings a good historical source? Can historians rely on his accuracy and objectivity?

Multiple-Choice Questions

Circle the letter of the item that best completes each statement or answers the question.

1. By the 1500s the nuclear family unit was becoming increasingly important among
   a. Western Europeans.
   b. South American Indians.
   c. North American Indians.
   d. West Africans.

2. The beginnings of representative government in the European settlements in North America can be found in
   a. the Spanish colony at St. Augustine, Florida.
   b. the Dutch New Netherland, where the inhabitants were granted the right to elect their own legislature in the colony's charter.
   c. Virginia, when, in 1619, the company provided for election of an assembly by the inhabitants.
   d. the small Swedish fur-trading colony in the lower Delaware Valley.

3. Which of the following statements about West African society at the time of first contact with Europeans is correct?
   a. Slavery was unknown in Africa.
   b. The majority of West Africans were either Muslims or Christians.
   c. Agriculture had not yet developed. The majority of West Africans were hunters and gatherers.
   d. Kinship groups were the most important unit holding people together.

4. The financing of the Virginia settlement came from
   a. the English government.
   b. a joint-stock company.
   c. the Church of England.
   d. all of the above.

5. In which European settlement was fur trading with the Hurons and other tribes the primary economic activity?
   a. New Mexico
   b. Florida
   c. New France
   d. Virginia

6. The great majority of sixteenth-century Europeans were
   a. nobles.
   b. middle class.
   c. urban craftsmen and artisans.
   d. peasants.

7. The primary aim of the explorations of Balboa, Magellan, Verrazano, and Cartier was to find
   a. a water passage through the Americas and reach Asia.
   b. the fabled fountain of youth.
   c. the Seven Cities of Gold.
   d. favorable places for their respective nations to plant new colonies.

8. All of the following statements about England's Queen Elizabeth I are correct *except*
    a. she eagerly embraced Puritanism and denounced the vestiges of Catholicism in the Church of England.
    b. she helped finance the raids of the English "sea dogs" on Spanish ports and shipping and shared in the plunder.
    c. she secretly aided Protestant revolts in Europe against Spanish domination.
    d. after the pope declared her a heretic, she viewed English Catholics as potential traitors.

9. All of the following statements about English Puritans are correct *except*
    a. they were Calvinists.
    b. they rejected the doctrine of predestination.
    c. the majority of them did not want to separate from the Church of England but to reform it from within.
    d. they rejected magnificent cathedrals and ornate rituals in favor of plain sermons in ordinary churches.

10. Which of the following is *incorrectly* matched with his deeds?
    a. Hernán Cortés—conquered the Aztecs, built Mexico City
    b. Francisco Coronado—found the Grand Canyon, plundered the New Mexico pueblos
    c. Giovanni da Verrazano—founded Quebec, sent *coureurs de bois* to live with the Indians
    d. Jacques Cartier—explored the St. Lawrence, made an early French attempt to colonize in North America

Short-Answer Questions

1. Explain what the Reformation and Counter-Reformation were. how did they lead to religious and political conflict in Europe?

2. Compare and contrast the attitudes of Native Americans, West Africans, and Europeans about land ownership and cultivation.

3. How any why did Elizabethan England challenge Spanish dominance in Europe and the Western Hemisphere?

4. Explain the beliefs of English Puritans. Why did James I and Charles I wish to suppress Puritanism?

5. Explain the various motives of the English for coming to America as settlers.

Essay Questions

1. Compare and contrast the founding and early development of Virginia and Plymouth. Since both were English colonies, how do you account for their differences?

2. Compare and contrast the early-seventeenth-century settlements in North America of the Spanish, French, Dutch, and English.

3. Discuss the religious and political conflicts and the economic conditions in sixteenth- and early seventeenth-century England that made the English interested in exploration and colonization in the Western Hemisphere.

4. "The Atlantic world brought few benefits to West Africans and Native Americans." Illustrate this statement by discussing the African slave trade and its impact and the effects of European settlements in America on the indigenous peoples.

5. Discuss the concept of social reciprocity. How did it operate in Native American, West African, and traditional European societies? In what ways was it breaking down in Western Europe by the sixteenth and seventeenth centuries?

CHAPTER 3

Expansion and Diversity: The Rise of Colonial America

Outline and Summary

I. Introduction

By 1700 more than 250,000 people of European ancestry, mostly English, lived in what would one day be the United States. Also, during the seventeenth century about 300,000 West African slaves were brought to North America and the Caribbean, the majority to the West Indian sugar colonies and the remainder to the mainland. These great migrations from Europe and Africa resulted in the depopulation and uprooting of the native inhabitants.

This chapter attempts to answer four questions: (1) How and why did the four regions of English North America develop in such divergent ways in the seventeenth century? (2) Why did indentured servitude evolve into slavery in the plantation colonies, and why did non–plantation colonies have both fewer indentured servants and fewer slaves? (3) How and why did Indian-European relations take the courses they did in each colonial region? (4) Why had England's North American colonial empire outstripped those of her European rivals by the end of the seventeenth century?

II. The New England Way

A. A City upon a Hill

In 1628 a group of Puritan merchants formed the Massachusetts Bay Company and obtained a charter from the king permitting them to establish a colony in North America. They decided that the company's officers and stockholders would emigrate along with the settlers. Thus, Massachusetts Bay would not be under the control of stockholders or proprietors back in England. In 1630 the company sent over eleven ships carrying seven hundred settlers under Governor John Winthrop. As the ships sailed westward, Winthrop delivered his lay sermon, "A Model of Christian Charity," in which he articulated the Puritans' mission. They would create a godly community, "a city upon a hill" that would serve as an example for sinful England to emulate. Unlike Virginia and the West Indies, Massachusetts was founded primarily for religious, rather than acquisitive, reasons. The Puritans did not object to material gain, but they believed that moral and/or government restraint must limit ruthless exploitation and profiteering.

During the first severe winter in Massachusetts, 30 percent of Winthrop's party died. Nonetheless, within a year the colony was economically self-sufficient, and the population grew because heavy English immigration persisted through the 1630s.

B. The Pequot War

At first Native Americans offered little opposition to Puritan colonization. But as the English pushed into the Connecticut Valley, the Pequots resisted. In 1637 the Puritans waged a bloody war of extermination against them. This cleared the way for Puritan settlement of Connecticut.

C. The Development of a Puritan Orthodoxy

Although claiming still to be part of the Church of England, the Puritans followed congregational practices that were quite different from Anglicanism. They had no church hierarchy. Each congregation was run by its male members and guided by its minister. Only those who could prove that they were saved through their public testimony about their conversion experiences were accepted by the congregations as church members. However, all residents of the colony had to attend services and pay taxes for support of the church. In other words, Massachusetts had a state (or established) church. Because the Puritans felt that everyone must be able to read the Bible to avoid Satan's snares, they required each town of fifty or more households to appoint a teacher for all children. To produce a continuing supply of learned Congregational ministers, they founded Harvard College in 1636. This early establishment of Harvard provided New England with a college-educated elite during the seventeenth century, which no other part of the English colonies possessed.

D. Dissenting Puritans

Despite the efforts of the Puritans to enforce conformity to their religious mission and doctrines, there were dissenters. The first challenge came from Roger Williams, a devout Puritan minister who preached that church and state should be separate and that government must not interfere with private religious beliefs or compel church attendance. Because the Massachusetts civil authorities held that the purpose of government was to protect the true religion and prevent heresy, they banished Williams in 1635 for his subversive opinions. He fled southward, bought land from the Indians, and eventually established the colony of Rhode Island, which was the first to practice religious tolerance and separate church and state. Massachusetts also expelled Anne Hutchinson, who was regarded as a troublemaker for meddling in theology and questioning the clergy's moral authority. She and many of her followers also migrated to Rhode Island, and Massachusetts imposed greater restrictions on women. In the long run the challenge that most undermined the Puritan mission came from merchants who resented community restrictions on their business practices.

E. Power to the Saints

Unlike the board of directors and stockholders of the Virginia Company of London, who stayed back in England, the Massachusetts Bay Company directors settled themselves and their charter in the colony. Male church members were eligible to vote for governor and members of the legislative body, at first called the General Court and after the bicameral Governor's Council and House of Representatives. In 1641 about 55 percent of adult males could vote under that church membership requirement, which was a higher percentage of the male population than was enfranchised in England or Virginia, where the vote was based on land ownership. The basic unit of local government, the town meeting, was generally open to participation by all male taxpayers (including non–church members).

F. Community Life

New Englanders generally lived in tightly clustered villages with everyone within walking distance of the meetinghouse. Each family's land was in fields or strips surrounding the town; people went out daily to farm but returned to town each night. This compact system of settlement promoted community interaction and allowed Puritans to watch each other to enforce godly conduct.

G. Puritan Families

"In a proper Puritan family, the wife, children, and servants dutifully obeyed the household's male head." Unlike Anglicans and Catholics, the Puritans allowed divorce, but it happened rarely. Because the Puritans believed healthy families were vital for the welfare of the community, the courts could and did discipline disobedient children, wives, and servants and irresponsible husbands. Puritans followed English common law in giving the wife no property rights independent of her husband's. Better living conditions resulted in a longer life expectancy in New England than in England. New Englanders also had larger families and therefore a faster rate of population growth. Most depended on the labor of their large families to support themselves modestly by farming. Rocky soil and a short growing season made it unlikely that anyone would become rich from agriculture. New Englanders seeking better opportunities turned to part- or full-time lumbering, fishing, rum distilling, and commerce. As they prospered, they became more worldly and materialistic and less preoccupied with religion.

H. The Demise of the Puritan Errand

The restoration of the Stuart kings in 1660, after the brief Cromwellian era, doomed the Puritan hopes that the Church of England would follow their Congregational example. Their mission in New England also was faltering as the founding fathers failed to pass on their intense religious fervor to the second and third generations. Declining church membership necessitated compromises like the Half-Way Covenant adopted in 1662.

I. Expansion and Native Americans

As European settlers increased and prospered, the Indian population declined. Many Native Americans died from diseases brought by the newcomers, such as diphtheria, measles, and tuberculosis. As Europeans cut down forests and cleared land to farm, they destroyed Indian hunting and gathering areas, reducing their food supply. New England's Indian population fell from 125,000 in 1600 to 10,000 by 1675. Demoralized, some Native Americans turned to alcohol; others agreed to convert to Christianity and live in the "praying towns" that the Puritans established for them. The last-ditch attempt of the Wampanoag chief Metacom (King Philip) to unite the remaining Indians and oust the English, in 1675–1676, ended in disaster. Metacom was killed, and many other Indians were captured and sold into slavery. King Philip's War reduced southern New England's Indian population by nearly 40 percent and ended all overt resistance to white expansion.

J. Economics, Gender and Satan in Salem

Economic resentments, the breakdown of the religious mission and sense of community, and resentment of economically independent and assertive women all may have contributed to the witchcraft hysteria that began in Salem in 1691 and engulfed Massachusetts until the end of 1692. It started with accusations by a group of young girls in Salem against a few residents of low standing. It escalated as more and more people made charges against others, including the wife of the governor. Twenty persons were convicted of witchcraft and executed, and hundreds more were in jail by the time the governor halted the trials and released the imprisoned.

By 1700 the Puritan phase of New England's development was waning. Its mark remained, however, on the emerging self disciplined Yankees of New England.

III. *Chesapeake Society*

A. State and Church in Virginia

In 1619 the Virginia Company of London granted the settlers the right to elect a representative assembly. After Virginia became a royal colony, the settlers repeatedly petitioned the king to continue that right. In 1628 Charles I grudgingly agreed. The assembly eventually became a bicameral legislature composed of a House of Burgesses elected by landowners and an appointed Royal Governor's Council. Local government in Virginia, with most officials appointed rather than elected, was less democratic than in New England. The Anglican church was the established church, and all Virginians were required to pay fixed rates for its support. Religion was less important to Virginians than to New Englanders.

B. Virginia's First Families

From the mid-1600s on, Virginia developed an elite upper class. Most members of that class were from English merchant families and had arrived with capital. They used their money to acquire and develop huge tobacco plantations in Virginia. By 1670 they controlled the Royal Council and, through their public offices, further enriched themselves with additional land grants. These first families, including the Byrds, Lees, and Randolphs, would dominate Virginia politics for two centuries.

C. Maryland

Maryland, the first proprietary colony, was founded by Cecilius Calvert, Lord Baltimore, on a tract of land given to him by Charles I. Lord Baltimore wanted to create a haven for fellow Catholics who could not worship in public, had to pay tithes to the Anglican church, and were bared from holding political office in England. However, Calvert remained in England, trying to govern as an absentee proprietor, and more Protestants than Catholics settled in Maryland. To protect the Catholic minority, Lord Baltimore drafted the Act of Religious Toleration and convinced the Maryland assembly to pass it in 1649. But in 1654 the Protestant majority disfranchised Catholics and repealed the act. Thereafter, the Protestant-controlled legislature battled continuously with the proprietary Calverts and resisted any political role for the Catholic minority.

D. Tobacco Shapes a Way of Life

Life in Virginia and Maryland was shaped by tobacco growing, the main occupation. The population spread out on farms and plantations near rivers. Few commercial centers or towns developed because ships from England came directly to riverfront docks built by the planters. There they sold their goods from Europe and bought the outgoing tobacco, with the planters serving as the middlemen for the surrounding small farmers.

Ninety percent of the English who arrived in Virginia and Maryland between 1630 and 1700 came as indentured servants.

E. Mortality, Gender, and Kinship

In the early decades in Virginia and Maryland, the life expectancy was twenty years shorter than that in New England and deaths exceeded births. Disease and overwork killed off perhaps 40 percent of indentured servants within six years of their arrival, and the shortage of women settlers prevented many men from marrying and starting families. By the late 1600s, however, deaths from epidemics had fallen off, there were almost as many women as men, and the population was growing through natural increase.

F. Tobacco's Troubles

The best chance for upward social mobility in the Chesapeake colonies was before 1660. After that, depressed tobacco prices afflicted Maryland and Virginia. Profits and wages fell. Former indentured servants were unable to earn enough money to buy land and become independent farmers. They formed a frustrated underclass that seemed destined to remain landless.

G. Bacon's Rebellion

Depressed tobacco prices and the resentments of the small farmers and landless toward the wealthy planters probably helped cause Bacon's Rebellion. Economically hard-pressed farmers on the Virginia frontier, under the leadership of Nathaniel Bacon, fought an unauthorized war against the Indians in 1676. When the royal governor tried to restrain them, they marched on Jamestown, burned it, and looted their enemies' plantations. The rebels dispersed, however, after Bacon's death later that year.

H. Slavery

The first Africans arrived in Virginia in 1619 and may have been treated initially as indentured servants. During the period 1640–1660, the status of Africans deteriorated into that of lifelong slavery. After 1660 the Chesapeake colonies recognized the institution of African slavery with laws that defined the condition and rigidly controlled blacks. Still, as late as 1660 fewer than one thousand slaves lived in Virginia and Maryland. Heavy importation of African slaves did not begin until late in the 1600s, and only after 1700 did slaves increasingly replace white indentured servants as plantation laborers. Even so, the population of the Chesapeake, unlike that of the West Indies, always remained predominantly white. As slaves became the predominant work force, whites of all classes closed ranks to cooperate in controlling the growing population of African origin.

IV. *The Spread of Slavery: The Caribbean and Carolina*

A. Introduction

Between 1630 and 1642 almost 60 percent of English migrants headed for the Caribbean, rather than the North American mainland. In the West Indies they developed a plantation-slave economy and passed stringent slave codes to control the majority black populations. Some of these English Colonists later resettled in the Chesapeake and Carolina colonies, bringing their slaves and slave-control practices with them. As a result, by 1710 black slaves comprised the majority of the Carolina inhabitants.

B. Sugar and Slaves

Tobacco was the first export of the British West Indies, and it was raised primarily with the labor of white indentured servants. In the 1640s, however, most planters switched to sugar growing, which required more workers than tobacco did. Therefore, planters imported more and more slaves, until by 1713 blacks outnumbered whites by a margin of four to one.

C. Carolina: The First Restoration Colony

In 1663 King Charles II gave a group of his English supporters a grant of land in America, which they named Carolina in his honor. To attract colonists the proprietors adopted the headright system. Most of the settlers came from other English mainland colonies and Barbados. There were also some French Huguenots (Protestants). The northern Carolinians cultivated tobacco and exported it, along with lumber and pitch. The southern Carolinians raised livestock. They carried on these economic activities primarily with their own family labor, using few black slaves.

By the 1690s southern Carolinians had found a staple crop that would make them rich—rice. Those few who possessed sufficient capital to invest in the costly dams, dikes, and slaves necessary for large-scale rice production became fabulously wealthy, forming the only mainland elite that was as rich as the West Indian sugar planters. As the rice growers imported ever more African slaves, the black population burgeoned to 67 percent of South Carolina's residents, making South Carolina the only British mainland colony with an African majority. Outnumbered and frightened, the white minority adopted a brutal slave code similar to that of Barbados.

The Carolinians met resistance from the Indian tribes on whose lands they were encroaching, culminating in the Tuscarora and Yamasee wars that drove the natives from the area. In the 1700s the crown revoked the proprietary charter and by 1729 turned South Carolina and North Carolina into royal colonies.

V. The Middle Colonies

A. Precursors: New Netherland and New Sweden

The Dutch-founded fur-trading colony of New Netherland became America's first multiethnic society. Its population included Dutch, Germans, Swedes, Africans (free and slave), Protestants, Catholics, Jews, and Muslims. Eighteen different languages were spoken there. In 1638, New Netherland's governor Peter Stuyvesant took over and annexed the Swedish fur-trading settlement in the lower Delaware Valley. By 1664 New Netherland had 9,000 people and a thriving port city of New Amsterdam.

B. English Conquests: New York and the Jerseys

In 1664 Charles II presented the seized Dutch colony, New Netherland, to his brother James, Duke of York, who called it New York. Most of the Dutch settlers were allowed to keep their land and remained in the colony. When James became king in 1685, New York became a royal colony. The British royal governors rewarded their loyal followers with immense land grants, mostly along the Hudson River from New York City to Albany. These patroons, or manor lords, grew almost as wealthy as the South Carolina rice planters on rents they collected from their tenant farmers.

James gave part of former New Netherland, which came to be known as the Jerseys, to two court favorites, Lord Berkeley and Sir Philip Carteret. The settlers, who were a mixture of New England Puritans, Quakers, Anglicans, Scottish Presbyterians, and Swedish Lutherans, quarreled continually with the absentee proprietors and with each other. In 1702 the king took over, and New Jersey became a royal colony.

C. Quaker Pennsylvania

Charles II, to repay a debt he owed the Penn family, gave a huge grant of territory in America to William Penn, a wealthy Englishman who had joined the much-persecuted Quakers. Penn hoped to found a colony based on Quaker principles that would offer a haven to his fellow worshipers, and, like other proprietors, he wanted to make a profit. In 1681 Penn laid out the city of Philadelphia and started the settlement. True to Quaker teachings against forced worship, he imposed no established church and allowed peoples of all faiths to settle. He also drafted a constitution, which created a legislative assembly to give residents a voice in running the colony. Relations with the Indians were favorable, for the most part, because Penn bought land from them on fair terms. The settlers prospered by growing grains on the fertile land and selling them to the West Indies. Indeed the trade made Philadelphia a major port by 1700. Since most of the colonists had come as families, the population quickly expanded through natural increase as well as immigration. Despite all their good fortune, some of the colonists resented the proprietor and his request for rents. The counties on the lower Delaware, inhabited by many Swedes and Dutch, gave Penn the most trouble. In 1704 they gained the right to elect their own legislature and separate from the rest of Pennsylvania, forming the colony of Delaware.

VI. Rivals for North America

A. France Claims a Continent

As the English colonies developed along the Atlantic coast, the French empire spread inland. In the 1660s and 1670s Louis XIV sent some six hundred settlers yearly, and French fur traders and missionaries fanned out over the Ohio Valley and explored the Mississippi from Wisconsin to the Gulf of Mexico. By the early 1700s the French claimed the entire Mississippi basin, called it Louisiana, and had erected forts and started fur-trading centers at Mobile, Alabama and Biloxi, Mississippi. Few Frenchmen lived in this vast empire but many of those who did mingled with the Indians, carrying on the all-important fur trade.

B. The Spanish Borderlands

To protect its hold on Mexico and the region north of it from the French, Spain established the province of Texas (Tejas) in 1691, but permanent settlement there did not begin until 1716. Rather, Spain was preoccupied with New Mexico, where long-standing Spanish attempts to suppress the Pueblo people's way of life resulted in a 1680 uprising led by Popé, an Indian religious figure. The Spanish did not fully regain control of New Mexico until 1700. As late as 1750, only about 3,800 Spaniards lived in the territory, most of them as sheep and cattle ranchers. In Florida, too, Spain faced recurring Indian resistance. In the 1690s, when a new round of European wars commenced, Spain's northern borderlands were in a weakened condition.

VII. Conclusion

By 1715, European nations had staked claims to most of the territory in the present-day United States east of the Mississippi River. Though the Spanish and French North American empires were larger in territory, the more compact English colonies along the Atlantic coast contained by far the most European settlers, about 250,000 in 1700. At the start of the eighteenth century, English America was becoming two distinct regions. The South, dominated by slave-owning planters, contained the great majority of black slaves. The North increasingly concentrated on commerce and developed a dominant merchant class. In both sections, however, most of the white colonists were small farmers.

Vocabulary

The following terms are used in Chapter 3. To understand the chapter fully, it is important that you know what each of them means.

tithes   taxes due for the support of the clergy and church, usually a tenth of one's income

established church   a church that is officially recognized and given legal and financial support by the government

dissent   to object or disagree

theocracy   government by priests or clergy

heresy   an opinion or doctrine at variance with established religious beliefs

subversive   tending to undermine existing or established institutions or doctrines; tending to cause the overthrow of existing governments or other established institutions

bicameral   composed of two houses, chambers, or branches, as in a two-house legislative body

sacrament   any of seven rites that the historical Christian church considered to have been instituted by Jesus to convey divine grace. In Catholicism that includes matrimony, but not in Puritan doctrine

social stratification   the different levels of caste, class, privilege, or status in a society

proprietor   a person who has legal title to something; the owner or owner-manager of a business or other institution

proprietary colony   a settlement organized in territory granted by the crown to a proprietor or proprietors, like Maryland, the Carolinas, and later Pennsylvania and New York

blasphemy   any contemptuous or profane utterance, act, or writing concerning God; any word or deed meant to dishonor God or his works

Identifications

After reading Chapter 3, you should be able to identify and explain the historical significance of each of the following:

conversion relation

John Winthrop and "A Model of Christian Charity"

Roger Williams

Anne Hutchinson and Antinomians

Massachusetts General Court

New England town meeting

indentured servants

Charles I and the English civil war

Oliver Cromwell

Stuart Restoration

Half-Way Covenant

"praying towns," "praying Indians"

King Philip's War

Virginia House of Burgesses and Royal Governor's Council

First Families of Virginia

Bacon's Rebellion

Cecilius Calvert (Lord Baltimore)

Maryland Act of Religious Toleration

Anthony Ashley Cooper and John Locke

Peter Stuyvesant

William Penn and the Quakers

coureurs de bois

Popé and the Pueblo Revolt (1680)

Skill Building: Maps

1. On the map of eastern North America and the Caribbean on the following page, locate each of the following and explain how its climate, soil, and other physical characteristics helped shape the economy and society there.

Massachusetts

Rhode Island

Connecticut

North Carolina

South Carolina

New York

New Jersey

Pennsylvania

Jamaica

the Bahamas

Barbados

Virginia

Maryland

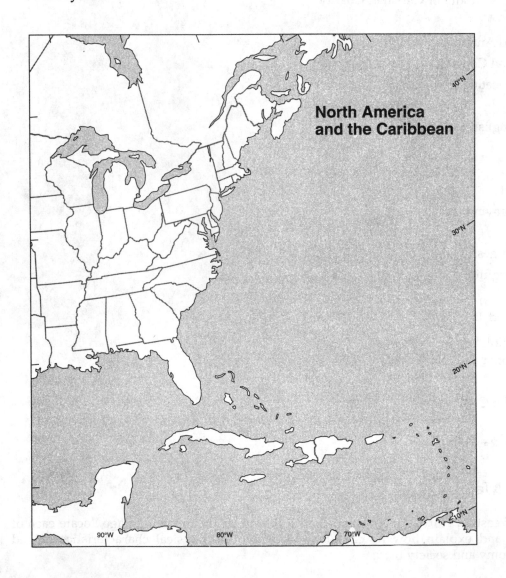

North America and the Caribbean

2. On the map of North America, locate each of the following and explain its significance in seventeenth-century American history:

   lands claimed by France

   Mississippi River

   Ohio River

   Gulf of Mexico

   Biloxi, Mississippi

   Mobile, Alabama

   lands claimed by England

   lands claimed by Spain

   Texas (Tejas)

   Taos

   Santa Fe

   Florida

   Great Lakes

North America

Historical Sources

In Chapter 3 the author tells us much about Puritan hopes, beliefs, religious practices, views on church and state, and family life. How did the historian discover this information? One useful historical source on New England Puritan thinking is the numerous sermons that ministers and lay leaders gave, many of which were carefully written down and preserved for posterity. Look at page 48, where you will see a reference to John Winthrop's lay sermon "A Model of Christian Charity." What does the historian learn about the Puritans' sense of their mission from it? Find other places in Chapter 3 where references are made to sermons. How is the author using the sermon or sermons mentioned in each case?

Another valuable source for gaining insight into past societies is their legal codes. For example, if the historian reads the code known as the Body of Liberties, adopted by the Massachusetts General Court in 1641, he or she finds there the guarantee that every man may participate in the town meeting. There are several sections of the Body of Liberties dealing with rights and duties of husbands, wives, children, and servants. Particularly revealing about the lack of separation of church and state is the part of the code titled "Capitall Laws." Here we see that religious or moral offenses, such as blasphemy, heresy, adultery, witchcraft, and "Carnall Copulation," were crimes for which civil authorities could impose the death penalty. As you review Chapter 3, look for other references to laws and legal codes. Notice particularly the discussions of the slave codes of the British West Indies, the Carolinas, and the Chesapeake colonies. In each case what has the historian found from studying these statutes?

Of course, laws are not always fully enforced and at times do not reflect what is really happening in a society. Therefore, the historian often does research among old records of court cases as well as consulting statutes. For instance, on page 55 of the text we read that divorce was legal in Puritan Massachusetts, but we learn how rarely it happened from looking at court records: "Massachusetts courts allowed just twenty-seven divorces from 1639 to 1692." Similarly, on page 68 the author states that the first laws officially recognizing slavery in Virginia and Maryland were passed after 1660, but there is evidence that Africans were being treated as slaves by the 1640s and 1650s. Some of that evidence comes from court records.

Now look at "A Place in Time: Taos Pueblo, New Mexico, in 1680." Here we learn of an uprising of the Taos and other Indians against Spanish civil and religious authorities. In the account we are told about Spanish officials arresting, executing, whipping, and selling into slavery Indian religious leaders, such as Popé. The historian also quotes Popé's words to his temporarily victorious people. How does the historian know these things? See if you can figure out possible historical sources.

Multiple-Choice Questions

Circle the letter of the item that best completes each statement or answers the question.

1. The area that had the longest life expectancy and the fastest growing population growth through natural increase was
   a. England.
   b. New England.
   c. the Chesapeake colonies.
   d. the British West Indies.

2. The first colony in English America that had separation of church and state and practiced religious tolerance was
   a. Maryland.
   b. Massachusetts.
   c. Rhode Island.
   d. Virginia.

3. Harvard College was chartered in 1636 primarily to
   a. train learned Congregational ministers.
   b. produce an educated governing class.
   c. educate lawyers who could defend the rights of the colonists.
   d. teach Puritans how to farm the rocky New England soil.

4. A man's right to vote for governor and members of the General Court in seventeenth-century Massachusetts was based on
   a. land ownership.
   b. wealth.
   c. length of residence in America.
   d. church membership.

5. The greatest extremes of inequality in land ownership in the seventeenth century were found in
   a. New England.
   b. Maryland.
   c. the West Indies.
   d. Virginia.

6. The Half-Way Covenant was adopted because
   a. too few second- and third-generation Puritans were willing to testify publicly about their conversion experiences.
   b. Puritans believed that Indians were not capable of becoming fully Christian.
   c. Puritans wanted to justify enslavement of converted Indians and Africans.
   d. Puritans wanted to show Anglicans that they were willing to meet them halfway on resolving differences over religious doctrine.

7. Which colonies had the most ethnically, religiously, and racially diverse population in North America?
   a. Virginia and Maryland
   b. Massachusetts and Connecticut
   c. North and South Carolina
   d. New Netherland-New York

8. Which of the following statements about Maryland is correct?
   a. It was founded by a joint-stock company.
   b. Although it was intended as a haven for Catholics, they were often more persecuted there than were Catholics back in England.
   c. The dominant crop that shaped its economy and society was sugar cane.
   d. Unlike neighboring Virginia, Maryland never adopted the institution of African slavery.

9. The great majority of those arriving in Virginia between 1630 and 1700 were
   a. Africans.
   b. British gentry.
   c. non-English middle- and working-class people.
   d. British indentured servants.

10. Which of the following statements about Virginia is correct?
    a. Unlike Massachusetts, it had no established church.
    b. It was governed by an appointed royal governor and governor's council and a House of Burgesses elected by landowners.
    c. By 1640 the great majority of its plantation laborers were African slaves.
    d. The indentured servants' chances of upward social mobility improved in the second half of the 1600s.

Short-Answer Questions

1. In what ways was New England Congregationalism different from Anglicanism? How did these differences affect life in Massachusetts?

2. Why did Massachusetts expel Roger Williams and Anne Hutchinson?

3. Discuss what happened to New England's Indian population between 1600 and 1700. Why did it happen?

4. Explain the impact of sugar growing on British West Indian society and rice growing on South Carolina's evolution.

5. How did New Netherland turn into New York and New Jersey?

6. Who was William Penn, and what were his motives for founding Pennsylvania?

7. Describe the extent of the British, French, and Spanish North American empires in 1700 and how they differed from each other in settlement and economic patterns.

Essay Questions

1. "In the course of the seventeenth century, New England evolved from a highly religious, community-oriented society to a region characterized by rising worldliness, individualism, and competitiveness." Discuss how and why this evolution took place.

2. Compare and contrast the economies, social structures, and racial and ethnic composition of New England, the Chesapeake colonies, the Carolinas, and the Middle colonies in the seventeenth century.

3. Discuss the evolution and spread of slavery in the Chesapeake colonies in the seventeenth century. Why did African slavery develop there? How did the gradual shift from a plantation labor force of indentured servants to one of African slaves affect life in Virginia and Maryland?

4. Chapter 3 concludes that while the majority of white colonists everywhere in English North America lived on small family farms, by 1700 two distinct regional economies and ways of life were emerging: northern and southern. Discuss this regional development and how it evolved.

5. Discuss the Salem witchcraft trials, telling first the known facts about what happened and then reviewing and evaluating the interpretation of the causes of the witchcraft accusations and hysteria offered in Chapter 3.

CHAPTER 4
The Bonds of Empire, 1660–1750

Outline and Summary

I. Introduction

Chapter 4 attempts to answer the following questions: (1) Why was Britain more successful in building a mainland North American empire between 1660 and 1750 than were France and Spain? (2) In what ways did British mercantilism help and/or harm the English mainland colonies? (3) How and why did the racial and ethnic makeup of the mainland British colonies change? (4) What were the Enlightenment and the Great Awakening, and in which features were they similar, in which, different?

II. Rebellion and War

A. Introduction

Until the restoration of the Stuart kings in 1660, England made little effort to rule its overseas territories. However, with the accession of Charles II (ruled 1660–1685), the mother country sought to expand its empire and trade, impose royal authority on the colonies, and regulate their economic activities so as to benefit English commercial interests.

B. Royal Centralization

The Restoration Stuart kings dreamed of becoming absolute monarchs like France's Louis XIV. They rarely called parliament into session and ignored the colonial legislatures. In 1684 Charles II revoked Massachusetts's charter. Between 1686 and 1688 his successor, James II, consolidated all the New England colonies, New York, and New Jersey into a Dominion of New England, abolished their assemblies, and placed full power into the hands of his arbitrary and dictatorial royal governor, Sir Edmond Andros. The colonists bitterly resented this denial of their rights. Tensions ran particularly high in Massachusetts and New York.

C. The Glorious Revolution in England and America

In 1688–1689 James II's high-handed, pro-Catholic actions led to the Glorious Revolution in England. He was forced into exile. The throne went to William and Mary, who agreed to a limited monarchy and promised to summon Parliament annually and respect the civil liberties of English people. When news of the Glorious Revolution reached America in 1689, New Englanders also rebelled. The Boston militia arrested Andros and his councilors, and Massachusetts and other colonies appealed to William and Mary for return of their charters. The new monarchs dissolved the dominion of New

England and issued charters granting each colony the right to have a representative assembly. However, Massachusetts's new charter did not give it as much independence as it had formerly enjoyed. Its governors would be appointed by the crown, not elected, and it would have to tolerate and share power in the colony with Anglicans. Leisler's Rebellion in New York and John Coode's uprising in Maryland also were inspired by the Glorious Revolution.

D. A Generation of War

Between 1689 and 1713, the British and French fought against each other in two wars. The conflicts spread to North America, where the British colonists called them King William's and Queen Anne's wars. When peace returned in 1713, France still controlled the North American interior, and the English colonists felt a heightened sense of British identity and dependence on their mother country's protection from their powerful neighbor.

III. Colonial Economies and Societies

A. Mercantilist Empires in America

The policies followed by Britain, France, and Spain toward their colonies in America were guided by the political-economic doctrine of mercantilism, which held that, to increase the nation's wealth in gold and silver, the country should produce within its own empire as much of what it needed as possible: its exports to foreign competitors should exceed its imports. To achieve these goals, the British Parliament passed a series of laws known as the Navigation Acts between 1651 and 1733. The laws required all trade to be conducted on British-owned ships; barred Americans from selling certain products, such as tobacco, rice, furs, indigo, and naval stores, to foreign countries unless they first passed through England; placed high taxes on products that Americans bought from outside the empire, like molasses from the French Caribbean; and forbade colonials from competing with British cloth and iron manufacturers. Although Parliament intended these laws to benefit only England, the acts in practice did not unduly hamper the colonists. Although the laws cut into the profits of rice and tobacco planters and raised the price of foreign imports in America, the Navigation Acts also were beneficial. Colonials were considered English subjects, so the requirement that shipping be done on British vessels stimulated the growth of America's merchant marine, shipbuilding, and ports. The bounties paid to producers of hemp, lumber, and other items under the Navigation Acts encouraged the development of those industries in the colonies. The restrictions on large-scale manufacturing did little harm, since only home production and small workshops were economically feasible in America.

The French and Spanish colonies in North America did not develop nearly as robust economies as the British. New France's main export was furs, but by the eighteenth century these did not bring in much profit. In fact, the French government underwrote this money-losing trade with the Indians in order to keep on good terms with their Native American allies. Spain, which did little manufacturing but insisted her colonists buy finished goods only from her, simply drove her colonists into widespread smuggling of British and French products. Though all three mother countries followed mercantilist theories, those principles did not work well for France and Spain because they did not have the large merchant class with liquid assets to invest in the colonies and other commercial ventures that the British had.

B. A Burgeoning, Diversifying Population

The French and Spanish colonies in North America lagged behind the British in population growth as well as economic development. By 1750 British North America had 1,170,000 non-Indian inhabitants as compared to 60,000 in New France, and 19,000 in Spanish North America. While the British opened their colonies to all Europeans of whatever religion, the French and Spanish barred non-Catholics and made no effort to attract settlers from countries other than their own.

After 1700 British North America grew rapidly from both natural increase and the arrival of newcomers. The eighteenth-century immigrants came less from England and more from other places: 140,000 Africans brought on slave ships under horrible conditions; 100,000 Irish and Scots-Irish; and 65,000 Germans. Consequently, the English colonies became more racially and ethnically diverse, a change sometimes resented by those of English extraction. Since most of the eighteenth-century white immigrants were too poor to buy land in the already developed coastal areas, they tended to push into the piedmont region, which stretched along the eastern slope of the Appalachians. By 1750 one-third of the colonial population resided there.

From 1713 to 1754, the importation of slaves to the mainland was greatly increased, with the result that the black colonial population rose from 11 percent to 20 percent. Most slaves lived in the South, but 15 percent were in the colonies north of Maryland. The African-American population also multiplied through natural increase.

C. Rural Men and Women

Most rural families worked small farms and depended on the labor of their sons and the supplemental production of clothing, vegetables, and poultry of their wives and daughters. Few inherited much land from their parents since holdings were modest and families were large. Therefore, most young couples starting out had to work for others for a time and borrow money to buy their own farms.

D. Colonial Farmers and the Environment

Colonial farmers rapidly cut down the forests to bring more land under cultivation. They used the timber for fences, fuel, and buildings. Farmers and planters also sold wood to townspeople. The resulting deforestation drove away large game and caused greater extremes in temperature and less dependable water levels in streams, which drastically reduced the amount of fish. As the farmers grew tobacco and other soil-depleting plants without fertilizer and without beneficial methods, such as crop rotation or letting fields lie fallow some years, the land lost its fertility and yields seriously diminished.

E. The Urban Paradox

By 1740 about 4 percent of the colonists lived in cities. The four largest were Philadelphia, New York, Boston, and Charles Town (now Charleston). All were thriving ports that shipped the livestock, grain, and lumber that enriched the countryside, but each also had escalating problems of urban poverty, crowding, poor sanitation, and periodic epidemics of contagious diseases.

F. Slavery's Wages

Slaves worked harder and longer and had lower standards of living than whites. Masters generally spent 60 percent more to maintain their white indentured servants than their black slaves. As the number of slaves residing in cities mounted—they were 20 percent of New York's inhabitants and the majority in Charles Town and Savannah—urban racial tensions ran high, leading to incidents such as the 1739 Stono Rebellion in South Carolina and the 1712 and 1741 slave conspiracies in New York. All were brutally suppressed by frightened whites.

G. The Rise of the Colonial Elites

In the eighteenth century class differences were becoming more apparent in America. Wealthy rural gentry and urban commercial elites attempted to imitate the fashions and lifestyles of the European upper crust.

H. Elites and Colonial Politics

The elites also dominated politics. They were elected to the colonial assemblies and appointed to the governors' councils. Women, blacks, and Indians could not vote, and property qualifications probably excluded about 40 percent of white males from doing so. Still, the proportion of men who did have the vote was much higher than in England and Ireland of the same period.

The most significant political development after 1700 was the shift in power away from royal governors and appointed officials to the colonial assemblies. The legislatures exercised influence over the governors by controlling their salaries. The assemblies authorized spending and imposed taxes. The British Board of Trade, which could disallow laws passed by these legislatures, rarely interfered because of its own inefficiency. Thus America, or at least its upper classes, became more and more self-governing, except for trade regulations, restrictions on printing money, and declaring war.

Overall, most Americans prospered and some grew rich in the eighteenth century, but class distinctions were never as extreme as in Europe. While in the French and Spanish colonies the mother countries' hereditary nobility, state church, and military hierarchy exercised much control, in British America they did not. Rather, power rested in the hands of the local colonial elite.

IV. Competing for a Continent

A. France and Native Americans

After making peace in 1713 with its rivals, Britain and Spain, France resumed building its empire in North America. In 1718, the French founded New Orleans and made it the capital of their province of Louisiana. There settlers survived by a combination of farming, hunting, fishing, and above all trading with the Indians. The French managed to forge an alliance with the Choctaws in Louisiana and tried to win over Native American trading partners in the Ohio Valley and on the Great Plains. While generally more successful in getting along with the Indians than the British, the French also crushed tribes that stood in their way, such as the Natchez.

B. Native Americans and British Expansion

British colonies, too, were expanding at the expense of Native Americans. Pennsylvania coerced the Delaware Indians into ceding their lands and moving into territory adjacent to that of the Iroquois. Other eastern tribes also were pushed westward, where they were used by the Iroquois as a buffer between themselves and the aggressive English.

C. British Settlement in the South: Georgia

Georgia was the last of the original thirteen colonies to be established on the North American mainland and the only one to receive some financial support from the British government. James Oglethorpe, its founder and early guiding spirit, wanted it to be both a haven for English debtors who could rehabilitate themselves there and an outpost protecting the Carolinas from the Spanish empire to the south. Oglethorpe laid out the port city of Savannah in 1733, and by 1740 about 2,800 settlers had arrived. Most, however, were not English debtors. Nearly half were not even English, but German, Swiss, Scottish, and Jewish. To promote a society of industrious small farmers able to defend their homes from attack, Georgia banned African slavery and limited the size of landholdings. But once the settlers realized that their best chance of making their fortunes lay in rice cultivation, they chafed at these restrictions, which were dropped by 1750. In 1770 Georgia had 23,000 inhabitants, 45 percent of whom were black slaves.

D. Spain's Struggles

While trying to fend off the Indians, French, and British, Spain spread its empire throughout the Southwest and part of the Southeast. European population in New Mexico grew very slowly, but at least Navajo and Apache raids ceased. Instead, these tribes made an alliance with the Spanish against the Utes and Comanches, whom they all feared. In Texas the Spanish established outposts and missions, including the one later known as the Alamo. However, the Indians in Texas seemed more interested in trading with the French than in farming for the Spanish. Periodic raids on the province by the French and Comanches discouraged Hispanic settlement in Texas: as late as 1760, only 1,200 Spaniards lived there. The Spanish attempted to weaken the British Carolinas and Georgia by offering freedom to English-owned slaves who fled to their colony of Florida.

V. Enlightenment and Awakening

A. Introduction

New England had the highest literacy rates in America because its Puritan religion encouraged primary education to ensure that all could read the Bible. Among white males elsewhere in the colonies, literacy ranged from 35 to 50 percent, but this was still considerably higher than in England.

B. The Enlightenment in America

American intellectuals, like Benjamin Franklin, were much influenced by the ideals of the eighteenth-century Enlightenment. Enlightenment thinkers emphasized reason, progress, science, and the capacity for human improvement. Some Enlightenment figures were Deists—that is, they believed in a god who created the universe and set it in motion according to natural laws discoverable by human intellect but did not intervene thereafter with miracles. Deists such as Franklin and Thomas Jefferson, while formally considering themselves Christians and attending church, disliked zealots who persecuted others in the name of religion.

C. The Great Awakening

Enlightened intellectuals took a dim view of the emotional excesses of the 1740s Great Awakening, "an outpouring of passionate Christian revivalism" that swept through the thirteen colonies. Overcome by the fiery preaching of Jonathan Edwards, William Tennent, Theodore Frelinghuysen, and above all George Whitefield, thousands of colonists repented and flocked to churches and prayer meetings seeking salvation. This reawakened interest in religion caused unprecedented splintering of American Protestantism into ever more denominations. The many denominations began another round of college founding to educate ministers for their faiths: the New Light Presbyterians' Princeton, the Anglicans' King's College (Columbia), the Baptists' Brown, and the Congregationalists' Dartmouth. The Great Awakening may also have had unintended political effects through its insistence on the equality of all born-again Christians in God's eyes and the corruption of "unsaved" upper-class leaders.

VI. Conclusion

By the 1750s British colonial society had matured. The colonies' population and wealth had swelled mightily. Their standard of living equaled that of England. Their number of institutions of higher learning exceeded those of the mother country. Further, Anglo-America was much more firmly planted in what would one day be the United States than were either the French or Spanish settlements. However, despite all of British America's successes, it harbored within it deep tensions generated by economic inequality, black slavery, and Anglo-Indian conflicts, and religious and social divisions fostered by the Great Awakening. In the 1750s and 1760s, the British would expel the French entirely from North America and seriously weaken the Spanish, but in doing so England would open irreconcilable conflicts with its own colonies. These new clashes would fuse with the long-simmering inner tensions to produce revolution.

Vocabulary

The following terms are used in Chapter 4. To understand the chapter fully, it is important that you know what each of them means.

provincialism displaying a narrow or localized outlook or lifestyle; displaying a countrified or rustic outlook or lifestyle

dissemination spreading abroad; diffusion; promulgation

manumission releasing an individual from slavery or servitude

antithesis opposition; contrast, the direct opposite

urbanization the growth of cities

autonomous self-governing; independent; subject to one's own will, choice, or law

dowry the money, goods, or estate that a woman brings to her husband at marriage

artisans persons skilled in industrial arts or crafts—for example, silversmiths, blacksmiths, cobblers, and printers

journeyman person who has learned a skilled trade and works at it for another person

oral culture a way of life in which people normally obtain most of their information and communicate by word of mouth

print culture a way of life in which people rely on books, newspapers, and other printed sources for much of their information

Identifications

After reading Chapter 4, you should be able to identify and explain the historical significance of each of the following:

Sir Edmond Andros and the Dominion of New England

the Glorious Revolution

Leisler's Rebellion

John Coode

King William's War and Queen Anne's War

mercantilism and the Navigation Acts

Adam Smith, *The Wealth of Nations*

redemptioners

James Oglethorpe

Francisco Menéndez

Stono Rebellion

Board of Trade

Enlightenment

Benjamin Franklin

American Philosophical Society

Royal Society

Deists

Great Awakening

Jonathan Edwards

George Whitefield

New Lights versus Old Lights

Skill Building: Graphs

Look at the pie graph titled "Distribution of Non-Indian Nationalities Within the British Mainland Colonies, 1700–1755" on page 91 of the text. It visually presents important demographic data about the British mainland colonies. Was the population of the British mainland colonies more ethnically and racially diverse in the seventeenth or the eighteenth century? How might these demographic shifts affect Britain's relationship with its mainland colonies? By 1755 which group made up roughly one-fifth of the population? How do you account for the growth of that group between 1700 and 1755? For comparison, find out what portion of today's total U.S. population that group makes up.

Historical Sources

In Chapter 4 the author has gathered information from many sources, including travelers' accounts of life in America. In the eighteenth century a number of Europeans took extended trips through the colonies and then published books about their experiences. A fairly typical one was Andrew Burnaby's *Travels Through the Middle Settlements in North America in the Years 1759 and 1760* (London, 1798). Burnaby, an Anglican clergyman, filled his book with detailed observations about the dress; housing; religion; money; and ethnic, racial, and class composition of the colonies. Although Burnaby and other travelers give us wonderful eyewitness accounts, the historian has to be wary of the "facts" found in their books. Why?

Benjamin Franklin's autobiography, *Poor Richard's Almanack*, and other writings have long been a gold mine for historians of colonial America. In Chapter 4 look for the many references to Franklin, his observations, and his opinions. For what purposes has the author used these writings? Although Franklin was an astute observer of his world, he had his biases, as we all do. Can you tell what some of them were from the quotations from his writings that appear in Chapter 4?

In "A Place in Time: Mose, Florida, in 1740" the historian has used a number of sources to discover the story of the black community of former slaves who lived there. These include written documents: letters, treaties, and government papers. In addition, the historian has drawn on findings from archaeological excavations. What did these "digs" show?

Multiple-Choice Questions

Circle the letter of the item that best completes each statement or answers the question.

1. Which of the following statements about the Anglo-American colonies in 1750 is correct?
   a. Colonists living in the port cities were much more prosperous than those in the countryside.
   b. Black slaves made up a greater proportion of the population than they had in 1700.
   c. More immigrants to the colonies were from England and fewer came from other parts of Europe than in the 1600s.
   d. The overall standard of living had risen little since 1700.

2. James Oglethorpe
   a. led the Stono Rebellion.
   b. encouraged the importation of African slaves to Georgia in order to promote profitable rice cultivation there.
   c. hoped Georgia would be a place for the rehabilitation of English debtors and a barrier to Spanish expansion northward.
   d. did all of the above.

3. Which of the following statements concerning colonial government between 1700 and 1763 is correct?
   a. The royal governors and the Board of Trade frequently vetoed or disallowed laws passed by the colonial legislatures.
   b. All white men had the right to vote and hold office.
   c. The lower house of a colonial legislature was generally dominated by representatives of the lower and middle classes, whereas the upper house was dominated by the wealthy.
   d. The colonial legislatures became a powerful force in American government, controlling taxes, the budget, and executive salaries.

4. Which of the thirteen colonies was the last to be settled and the only one to receive some financial assistance from the British government?
   a. Georgia
   b. the Carolinas
   c. Pennsylvania
   d. Delaware

5. Which of the following statements about women in eighteenth-century America is correct?
   a. Women could not inherit their parents' land. Only sons could legally inherit family estates.
   b. Women could not choose their own husbands. The choice was made by their parents.
   c. Women in rural and urban families played an important part in helping to support their households.
   d. Women had legal control over their dowries and other property that they brought with them to marriage.

6. The Glorious Revolution in England touched off rebellions in all of the following colonies *except*
   a. Massachusetts.
   b. New York.
   c. Maryland.
   d. South Carolina.

7. Which of the following resulted from King William's and Queen Anne's wars?
   a. The French were driven from the North American continent.
   b. The Stuart kings were driven from power.
   c. The wars heightened Anglo-Americans' sense of their British identity and made them feel dependent on the mother country for protection.
   d. The British captured New Orleans and started to settle Louisiana.

8. The Dominion of New England was
   a. created by James II to consolidate his hold on the northern colonies and eliminate their colonial assemblies.
   b. welcomed by most New Englanders because it broke the dictatorial rule of the Massachusetts Puritans over the region.
   c. continued by William and Mary because the administrative consolidation made it easier to enforce the Navigation Acts.
   d. created as part of the reforms instituted after the Glorious Revolution.

9. The Navigation Acts
   a. embodied the economic doctrines preached by Adam Smith's *The Wealth of Nations.*
   (b) required British-American colonists to ship their tobacco, rice, and naval stores to England.
   c. encouraged the development of iron and cloth manufacturing in the American colonies.
   d. crippled the economic growth of British America in the 1700s.

10. All of the following institutions of higher learning were originally founded by religious denominations *except*
    (a.) the University of Pennsylvania.
    b. Princeton.
    c. Rutgers. – New Jrisy
    d. Columbia.

Short-Answer Questions

1. What actions of the Restoration Stuart kings led to the Glorious Revolution in England and America?

2. What was the Dominion of New England? What happened to it in 1689?

3. What was Leisler's Rebellion? How did the British royal governor deal with it?

4. What impact did the practices of colonial farmers in the eighteenth century have on the environment of the Atlantic seaboard settlements?

5. Explain why the Spanish and French had more trouble attracting European settlers to their North American colonies than did the British.

6. What were the ideals of the eighteenth-century Enlightenment?

7. What was Deism? Name some American Deists.

Essay Questions

1. How much equality, liberty, and self-government existed in the American colonies in the period 1700–1750? Back up your assessment with as many specific facts as possible.

2. What was the Great Awakening? Who was attracted to it? Who was repelled by it? What impact did it have on religious, social, educational, and political developments in eighteenth-century America?

3. Discuss the racial and ethnic makeup and the social class structure of mid-eighteenth-century America.

4. Historians have long debated the impact of Britain's mercantilist economic policy on the colonies. Explain the mercantilist economic theory and show how Parliament incorporated it into the navigation system. According to Chapter 4, in what ways did that system hurt and benefit America? Does the author believe the harm outweighed the benefits?

5. "In the second quarter of the eighteenth century, no American more fully embodied the Enlightenment spirit than [Benjamin] Franklin." Discuss Franklin's life, beliefs, career, and achievements, and explain how they embodied the Enlightenment spirit.

CHAPTER 5

Roads to Revolution, 1744–1776

Outline and Summary

I. Introduction

Chapter 5 addresses these questions: (1) How and why did the Seven Years' (French and Indian) War sow the seeds for the American Revolution? (2) What were the differences between the mother country and the Americans concerning the role and status of the colonies in the British Empire? (3) In what ways did the protests against Britain affect social and political relations within the colonies? (4) How did the American protest leaders manage to unite thirteen diverse colonies?

II. Imperial Warfare

A. King George's War

King George's War, the third Anglo-French imperial conflict, proved indecisive. Although Americans seized the French stronghold at Louisbourg, in the peace treaty the British returned it in exchange for an outpost the French had taken in India.

B. A Fragile Peace

Since neither power gained dominance in North America, the skirmishing in the Ohio Valley continued. In 1753 the French Canadians began building a series of forts between the Ohio River and Louisiana. An expedition led by George Washington to block them misfired, leaving the Anglo-American frontier in danger. The attempt of seven colonies north of Virginia to forge an effective defensive union with the Albany Plan failed because the colonial legislatures refused to relinquish any of their authority over taxation.

C. The Seven Years' War in America

After the Anglo-French clash at Fort Necessity in 1754, war broke out in America. Then in 1756, full-scale hostilities between Britain and France resumed in the Seven Years' War. At first British colonists fared poorly as France's Indian allies raided western settlements and the French seized key forts and threatened central New York and western New England. Unable to spare large British armies from the other military theaters where they were fighting the French, Prime Minister William Pitt offered British financial support to the colonials if they would do most of the fighting in America. Encouraged by the promise, colonials flocked to the struggle and drove the French from New York and much of the western frontier. Their success was aided by the decision of the Iroquois and other Ohio tribes to stop helping the French. After the fall of Quebec and Montreal, French resistance crumbled, and in the treaty of 1763 France ceded to Great Britain all of its territories in North America.

III. Imperial Reorganization

A. Introduction

After the Seven Years' War, Britain tried to tighten control over its now much-expanded colonial empire and to finance its administration by imposing new taxes on Englishmen at home and overseas. These efforts aroused opposition on both economic and constitutional grounds. At about the same time (1760), George III became king. He was determined to govern more actively than his predecessors, but his shifting policies and frequent ministerial changes further upset British-American relations.

B. Friction Among Allies

British supremacy in eastern North America opened the door to conflict between the mother country and the colonists. The war left the British people staggering under a huge debt and heavy taxes. The British resented repaying the Americans for defending themselves in the French and Indian hostilities and were equally upset that they now had to expend more money and military effort to put down Indian uprisings caused by the western surge of colonists beyond the Appalachians. Hoping to pacify Chief Pontiac and his followers, the British issued the Proclamation of 1763, forbidding whites to settle beyond the crest of the mountains until the crown had negotiated treaties with the Indians under which they agreed to cede their lands. The colonists were angered by this interference with their western land claims. Since continuing to protect the frontier and consolidate control over the newly acquired territories would cost around 6 percent of the peacetime budget, British government officials saw no reason that the colonials should not be taxed to help defray the expense.

C. The Writs of Assistance

To crack down on smuggling, British customs officers began to employ writs of assistance, or blanket search warrants that permitted officials to enter any ship or building to search for smuggled goods and seize them. Colonists protested that the writs violated traditional English guarantees against unreasonable search and seizure and that Parliament could not abridge their rights as Englishmen.

D. The Sugar Act

In 1764 Parliament adopted the Sugar Act, imposing import duties on sugar and other items to raise money for the British treasury. These taxes and a host of new regulations and restrictions burdened Massachusetts, New York, and Pennsylvania merchants particularly, but they also violated the long-standing guarantee of a fair trial. Accused smugglers were to be tried in vice-admiralty courts, without juries, by judges who had a financial stake in finding the defendants guilty.

E. The Stamp Act

Prime Minister George Grenville saw only that the Sugar Act brought in too little revenue to ease Britain's financial woes. He therefore proposed the Stamp Act and in 1765 convinced Parliament to pass it. It required colonists to purchase from government revenue agents special stamped paper for periodicals, customs documents, licenses, diplomas, deeds, and other legal forms. It also provided that violators would be tried in vice-admiralty courts. Since it was an internal tax, it touched many more colonials than the Sugar Act, which affected mainly merchants engaged in importing and exporting.

Colonists objected to Parliament's ability to impose upon them internal or external taxes designed to raise revenue because they elected no representatives to that body. Their own colonial legislatures had sole authority to tax them. Colonists conceded that parliament might regulate trade within the empire, but there could be "no taxation without representation."

F. Resisting the Stamp Act

The Virginia House of Burgesses passed resolutions, proposed by Patrick Henry, denying Parliament's right to tax the colonies. Eight other provincial assemblies followed suit. In Boston a group of artisans, shopkeepers, and businessmen founded the Loyal Nine to fight the act. Similar organizations, usually called the Sons of Liberty, cropped up in other cities. The Loyal Nine and the Sons of Liberty directed outraged mobs in attacks on the homes and property of stamp distributors, causing all of them to resign their posts. In October 1765 representatives from nine colonies convened in the Stamp Act Congress in New York, where they reiterated the principle of no taxation without representation and no parliamentary denial of trial by jury and other English liberties. Most persuasive to the British, however, was the boycott of all English imports undertaken by American merchants. The decrease in their sales led British businessmen to plead for repeal of the Stamp Act. In March 1766 Parliament did revoke the law, but at the same time it adopted the Declaratory Act, restating its right to tax and legislate for the colonies "in all cases whatsoever." The colonists ignored the latter, rejoiced at the repeal, disbanded the Sons of Liberty, and concluded that the mother country would return to its earlier "salutary neglect."

G. Ideology, Religion, and Resistance

Resistance to the Stamp Act had revealed a deep split in thinking between England and its colonists. Influenced by John Locke, the oppositionists, the eighteenth-century English radicals, and the classical philosophers, educated colonists saw in Parliament's actions a conspiracy of a corrupt government to deny them their natural rights and liberties. It was their duty as a free people to resist. Protestant clergymen, with the exception of the Anglicans and many pacifist Quakers, preached sermons to all classes of colonists backing these views. They declared that "solidarity against British tyranny and 'corruption' meant rejecting sin and obeying God."

IV. The Deepening Crisis

A. The Quartering Act

In 1767 George III's new chancellor of the exchequer, Charles Townshend, like Grenville before him, looked to the colonies for much-needed revenue. That same year, Parliament's angry reaction to New York's refusal to comply with the Quartering Act indicated that it was ready to crack down on colonial self-government.

B. The Townshend Duties

Townshend pushed through Parliament the revenue Act of 1767 (the Townshend duties), which imposed taxes on glass, paint, lead, paper, and tea imported into the colonies. Townshend intended to set aside part of the tax money to pay the salaries of royal governors so that they would no longer be subject to pressure from the colonial assemblies that had been compensating them.

C. The Colonists' Reaction

John Dickinson's *Letters from a Farmer* expressed the American majority view that Parliament could use duties to keep trade within the empire but not to raise revenue, as the Townshend duties did. The Massachusetts legislature sent Samuel Adams's "circular letter" making the same point to the other colonial assemblies. In August 1768 Boston merchants adopted a nonimportation agreement that spread to other cities.

D. "Wilkes and Liberty"

Although the boycott probably reduced imports only about 40 percent, this hurt many British merchants and artisans enough to make them again implore Parliament to rescind its taxes. Their appeal became part of a larger British protest movement against the domestic and foreign policies of George III and a Parliament dominated by a tiny elite of wealthy landowners. London journalist John Wilkes led the unrest. For this the government arrested him and denied him the seat in the House of Commons to which he had been elected. The government's actions prompted dissident Englishmen and American colonists to further question the authority of an unrepresentative Parliament.

E. Women and Colonial Resistance

Women bolstered the boycott by refusing to serve taxed tea and by organizing spinning bees to produce homespun apparel rather than buying British-made clothing.

F. Customs Racketeering

Meanwhile the high-handedness and corruption of customs officials, who seized ships and cargoes for technical violations of the Navigation and Sugar acts and broke open sailors' chests to search for small amounts of undeclared merchandise, contributed to Americans' growing alienation from the mother country. Violent attacks by seamen and others on customs inspectors, like the *Liberty* incident in Boston, happened more frequently. The way in which British officials enforced Parliament's trade regulations made more and more colonials broaden their cry from "no taxation without representation" to "no legislation at all without representation."

G. The Boston Massacre

To protect its officials, the British government stationed more troops in Boston. Tension between the seventeen hundred redcoats and the civilian population smoldered, ready to flare up. Then, on March 5, 1770, a group of British soldiers at a guardpost in front of the customs office fired into a disorderly crowd that was hurling dares, insults, and flying objects at them. Five civilians were killed and six more wounded in this so-called Boston Massacre. To defuse the situation, Massachusetts governor Thomas Hutchinson promised to try the soldiers, and the British removed their troops to a fortified island in Boston harbor. With John Adams as their lawyer, all but two of the redcoats were acquitted.

H. Lord North's Partial Retreat

In April 1770 Parliament again bowed to pressure and repealed all of the Townshend duties except the one on tea—to underscore its position that it had the right to tax the colonists. Americans responded by continuing to boycott tea, thus limiting its sale and the customs revenue from it so severely that there was not enough money to pay the salaries of the royal governors as Townshend had intended.

I. The Committees of Correspondence

In 1772 Lord North revived trouble when he prepared to implement Townshend's plan to pay royal governors' salaries out of customs revenue. Sam Adams and others responded by organizing committees of correspondence in each New England town to exchange information and coordinate activities in defense of colonial rights. In March 1773, Virginians also set up a committee of correspondence. Within a year every colony but Pennsylvania had such committees that linked Americans together in a communications web.

J. Frontier Tensions

Meanwhile, tensions in America among Indians, frontier settlers, and colonial authorities increased because of the relentless push of land-hungry whites westward. Colonial speculators and settlers ignored the Proclamation of 1763 and trespassed on Native Americans' lands. New Hampshire's Green Mountain Boys settled in Vermont, rejected New York's ownership of the area, and created a separate government and later new state. In North Carolina the frontier regulator movement rebelled against the eastern-dominated colonial legislature and was suppressed. These and others incidents demonstrated the readiness of the westerners to defy all established authority violently.

V. Toward Independence

A. The Tea Act

The British East India Tea Company was on the verge of bankruptcy in 1773 because Americans were buying so little taxed tea. Parliament tried to save it with the Tea Act, which allowed the company to sell its tea directly to American consumers, cutting out all middle-men's profits. As a result, the company would be able to sell its product, even with the import duty still on it, at a lower price than Americans paid for smuggled tea. The committees of correspondence denounced the act because they saw it as an attempt to seduce colonists into paying a parliamentary-imposed tax and they knew Lord North planned to compensate the royal governors with the customs receipts. That would surely endanger colonial representative government. At most ports, when the company's ships arrived, no one accepted the cargo and the captains turned around and left. But the governor of Massachusetts insisted on Bostonians' receiving and paying the duties on the shipment that arrived there. On the night of December 16, 1773, Sam Adams convened a protest meeting, at the end of which a band of colonials disguised as Indians boarded the East India Company's vessel and dumped its tea into the harbor.

B. The Coercive Acts

Infuriated by the Boston Tea Party, the British retaliated with a series of punitive laws, the Coercive Acts, which Americans dubbed the Intolerable Acts. These closed the Boston harbor, causing serious economic distress in Massachusetts; revoked the colony's charter and restructured its government to make it less democratic; banned the holding of more than one town meeting a year; provided for the housing of British troops in privately owned buildings; and permitted soldiers and other officials charged with killing colonials to be tried in England. General Thomas Gage, military commander in North America, took over as governor of Massachusetts. These measures and the unrelated Quebec Act, which provided no elected legislature for that province, convinced people in all the colonies that the British were out to destroy representative government and civil liberties in America.

C. The First Continental Congress

To resist the Intolerable Acts, all the colonies except Georgia sent representatives to a Continental Congress that convened in Philadelphia in September 1774. The Congress approved the Suffolk Resolves, which, among other things, advised colonials to begin arming themselves against attacks by royal troops. The Congress also created the Continental Association to enforce a total cutoff of trade with England and the British West Indies and sent a Declaration of Rights to George III, begging him to dismiss the ministers responsible for the Coercive Acts.

D. The Fighting Begins

Committees of the Continental Association coerced wavering colonists into cooperating with the trade ban. Loyalists, or Tories, were intimidated. Volunteer militias, often calling themselves minutemen, drilled, and extralegal congresses met and tried to supplant the existing colonial assemblies headed by royal governors. On April 19, 1775, general Gage dispatched seven hundred soldiers to Lexington and Concord to seize the minutemen's weapons stockpiles and arrest key patriotic leaders. Forewarned by William Dawes and Paul Revere, the residents of Lexington and Concord challenged the redcoats arriving from Boston, and the first fighting of the Revolution broke out. As news of the battles at Lexington and Concord spread, twenty thousand New Englanders rushed to besiege Boston and oust the English. The British defeated the colonials at Breed's and Bunker hills but suffered heavy casualties in doing so.

Soon after Lexington and Concord the Second Continental Congress convened in Philadelphia. The majority of the delegates still hoped for reconciliation with England and sent the Olive Branch Petition to George III, pleading for a cease-fire at Boston, repeal of the Coercive Acts, and negotiations to establish American rights. The British ignored the plea and, in December 1775, declared the colonists in rebellion.

E. The Failure of Reconciliation

Immediately after it met, the Second Continental Congress established an American continental army and appointed George Washington to command it, although it was not yet ready to declare independence. Loyalty to the king and hopes that he would restrain irritated ministers and members of Parliament lingered on through the summer and fall of 1775. Publication of Thomas Paine's pamphlet *Common Sense* in January 1776 did much to kill any remaining affection for monarchs.

F. Declaring Independence

On June 7, 1776, Virginia delegate Richard Henry Lee proposed that Congress declare independence. The members first appointed a committee, including Thomas Jefferson, John Adams, and Benjamin Franklin, to draft a statement justifying the colonies' separation from England. Most of the writing was done by Thomas Jefferson. Much influenced by the Enlightenment natural rights philosophy, Jefferson's Declaration of Independence emphasized equality of all men and their universal right to justice, liberty, and self-fulfillment. On July 2 Congress formally adopted Lee's independence resolution and created the United States of America. On the third it reviewed and revised Jefferson's Declaration, approving and signing it on July 4. While the equal rights for all championed by the Declaration of Independence did not exist in America in 1776, the document's ideals inspired the revolutionary generation and many who followed to bring the realities of American life closer to the Declaration's bold proclamation.

VI. *Conclusion*

Triumphant over France in the Seven Years' War, Britain in 1763 was the world's leading power. However, her subsequent attempts to centralize imperial power and tax her colonies aroused American resistance. In the years between 1763 and 1776, the colonists strove to reestablish the empire as it had existed earlier when British supervision was minimal and colonial assemblies controlled taxes and internal legislation. Different classes acted out of different motives: colonial elites resented erosion of their autonomy, merchants and middle class colonists protested new economic restrictions, and the urban and rural poor questioned all authority—British and domestic elite as well. Unable to reconcile the mother country's and colonial's viewpoints, the Americans finally severed their ties with England and then had to fight for their independence on the battlefield. America also had to decide to what degree it would implement the idealistic statements in the Declaration of Independence.

Vocabulary

The following terms are used in Chapter 5. To understand the chapter fully, it is important that you know what each of them means.

ceded   yielded or formally surrendered to another; given over, as by treaty

federation   a government body formed by a number of states, societies, or other units, each retaining control of its own internal affairs

boycott   an organized refusal to buy or use products or trade for the purpose of persuading, intimidating, or coercing

chancellor of the exchequer   the minister of finance in the British government, similar to the U.S. secretary of the treasury

rhetorical   pertaining to the art of influencing the thought and conduct of one's hearers

allusions   passing references to something either directly or by implication

lobby   to try to influence legislators

despotism   government exercising absolute power or control; tyranny

allegiance   faithfulness or loyalty to any person or thing; obligation or duty of a citizen to the government

beleaguered   surrounded by an army, troubles, or other adverse conditions

requisition   act of requiring or demanding; authorities taking or demanding something for military or public needs

Tories   the name given during the Revolution to Americans who remained loyal to England

vigilantes   members of groups using extralegal means to control or intimidate

Identifications

After reading Chapter 5, you should be able to identify and explain the historical significance of each of the following:

King George's War

Albany Plan of Union

Acadians, Cajuns

Seven Years' War (French and Indian War)

Neolin, Pontiac's uprising, and the Proclamation of 1763

King George III

writs of assistance and James Otis

Sugar Act and vice-admiralty courts

George Grenville

Stamp Act and Stamp Act Congress

virtual representation

Patrick Henry

Loyal Nine and Sons of Liberty

Declaratory Act

Charles Townshend and the Townshend duties (Revenue Act of 1767)

John Wilkes

American Board of Customs Commissioners, customs racketeering

Samuel Adams

John Adams

spinning bees

Lord North

John Hancock

Crispus Attucks and the Boston Massacre

committees of correspondence

Tea Act and the Boston Tea Party

Coercive or Intolerable Acts and Quebec Act

Suffolk Resolves and Continental Association

minutemen, Paul Revere, and Lexington and Concord

Olive Branch Petition

Thomas Paine, *Common Sense*

Second Continental Congress and Declaration of Independence

Skill Building: Maps

On the map of eastern North America on the next page, locate each of the following and explain its importance in the imperial wars between Britain and France or at the beginning of the American Revolution:

Nova Scotia

Louisbourg

Ohio River and Ohio Valley

Lake Champlain

Albany, New York

Fort Duquesne

Fort Necessity

Pittsburgh

Acadia

Quebec

Montreal

British North America under the terms of the Treaty of Paris, 1763

Detroit

Halifax, Nova Scotia

Fort Ticonderoga

Boston

Lexington, Massachusetts

Concord, Massachusetts

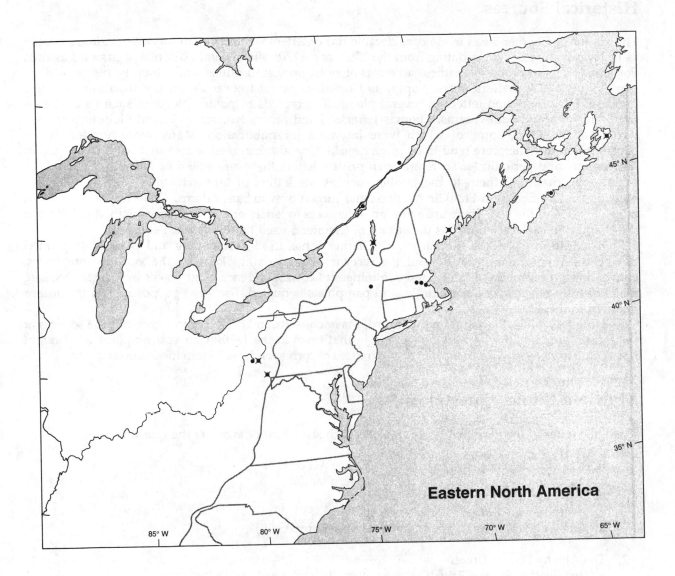

Eastern North America

Historical Sources

The author of Chapter 5 has made considerable use of letters written by famous and ordinary people as historical sources. Letters dating from the 1760s and 1770s often contain colonial arguments against Parliament's actions and eyewitness accounts of riots, protest meetings, and other events, as well as expressions of the writers' fears, hopes, and opinions about the revolutionary situation that was brewing. Historians find letters in several places. The records of political leaders such as Benjamin Franklin, John and Sam Adams, Thomas Jefferson, and others frequently include letters that they wrote and received, some of which were intended for publication. Many were not for public consumption and therefore tend to be more candid. One also can read letters that were published in newspapers and periodicals. There are even private letters that were stolen or fell into the hands of others who disclosed them to the public, such as the letters of Massachusetts governor Thomas Hutchinson that Benjamin Franklin obtained and turned over to Sam Adams. These are referred to on pages 135–136 of the text. There are abundant references to letters or information contained in letters in the chapter. In each case how has the author of Chapter 5 used these historical sources?

In addition to letters, the author of Chapter 5 has used newspapers and pamphlets printed during the revolutionary period and the records of proceedings kept by the various congresses, conventions, committees of safety, and committees of correspondence. Find places in Chapter 5 where material from newspapers, periodicals, and pamphlets is quoted. For what purposes does the author quote from these historical sources?

Now look at "A Place in Time: Concord, Massachusetts, in 1775." Try to figure out the sources of the information about what was happening in that town in the 1770s. Can you pinpoint what might have come from letters? From records of committees of correspondence? From local newspapers?

Multiple-Choice Questions

Circle the letter of the item that best completes each statement or answers the question.

1. Both the Proclamation of 1763 and the Quebec Act of 1774
   a. interfered with colonial claims to western lands.
   b. extended religious freedom to Catholics.
   c. were repealed after colonial protests.
   d. imposed new taxes on goods imported from Europe.

2. The Albany Plan of Union
   a. was vetoed by the British because it challenged royal authority.
   b. united Anglo-Americans in a loose confederation during the Seven Years' War that fell apart after the French defeat.
   c. was not implemented because of opposition by colonial legislatures, but it set a precedent for future plans to unite the British mainland colonies.
   d. represented the earliest British attempt to suppress the colonial assemblies and exercise more imperial control.

3. Which of the following helped convince the delegates to the Second Continental Congress to vote for independence?
   a. the unexpected success of the colonists in clearing British troops out of New England
   b. Tom Paine's *Common Sense*
   c. the Boston Massacre
   d. John Dickinson's *Letters from a Farmer*

4. In the Declaratory Act, Parliament stated that
   a. it had the right to legislate for the colonies in all matters, including taxes.
   b. the colonists were in rebellion and therefore subject to martial law.
   c. it would repeal all the Townshend duties except the one on tea.
   d. it would take over payment of the salaries of the royal governors and other colonial officials.

5. Which of these events occurred last?
   a. the Battle of Bunker Hill
   b. fighting at Lexington and Concord
   c. adoption of the Declaration of Independence
   d. the Boston Massacre

6. How did the French and Indian War differ from King William's, Queen Anne's, and King George's wars?
   a. In the French and Indian War, France rather than Spain was England's chief enemy.
   b. Americans participated only in the French and Indian War.
   c. The French and Indian War was the only one in which the Indians sided with the French rather than the British.
   d. As a result of the French and Indian War, France lost her empire in North America.

7. The chief reason for the repeal of the Stamp Act and the Townshend duties by Parliament was the
   a. conviction that the colonists were on the verge of revolution.
   b. pleas of Burke and Pitt to conciliate the colonists by recognizing their right to tax themselves.
   c. harmful effects of colonial boycotts and nonimportation agreements on British business.
   d. expectation that the colonial assemblies would voluntarily vote for higher taxes.

8. Americans objected to the Tea Act because
   a. it would raise the price they had to pay for tea.
   b. there was still a tax on tea and the customs duties collected on it would be used to pay the salaries of royal governors.
   c. it forced them to drink tea when they preferred coffee.
   d. it forced them to buy from the British East India Company, which sold low-quality, overpriced tea.

9. The Declaration of Independence was primarily written by
   a. John Adams.
   b. Patrick Henry.
   c. John Hancock.
   d. Thomas Jefferson.

10. John Adams, a key figure in the Revolution,
    a. drafted a "circular letter" to colonial legislatures condemning the Townshend duties.
    b. started committees of correspondence.
    c. served as the lawyer for the soldiers tried for shooting civilians in the Boston Massacre.
    d. convened the protest meeting at Old South Church that preceded the Boston Tea Party.

Short-Answer Questions

1. Explain why the colonists objected to writs of assistance and vice-admiralty courts.

2. Explain what the British meant by virtual representation and why the American colonists rejected the concept.

3. Why did the British pass the Coercive (Intolerable) Acts? What did the colonists think the laws showed about British intentions?

4. Where and when did the First Continental Congress meet? What actions did it take?

5. Why did General Gage send British troops to Lexington and Concord in 1775, and what happened as a result?

6. Why did the Second Continental Congress reverse itself on the question of independence between 1775 and 1776?

Essay Questions

1. Between 1689 and 1763 Britain and France and their respective allies fought four wars for supremacy in Europe and control of India and North America. Discuss the impact of those wars on America and relations between Britain and her thirteen colonies.

2. In 1763 a French statesman predicted that England would rue the day she expelled France from North America. Did events prove the Frenchman right? How are the French and Indian War and its outcome related to the American Revolution? Discuss.

3. One historian has written, "The British ruled the colonies for one hundred and fifty years and lost them in twelve." Do you agree with this statement? Why or why not? Use as many specific facts in your answer as possible.

4. Another historian claims, "A salient feature of our Revolution was that its animating purpose was deeply conservative. The colonials revolted against British rule in order to keep things the way they were, not to initiate a new era." Do you agree? Use as many facts in your answer as possible.

5. Discuss the role of each of the following groups in the events that led to America's break with England: colonial merchants, Virginia planters, workers, sailors, artisans, frontier dwellers, and women.

CHAPTER 6

Securing Independence, Defining Nationhood, 1776–1788

Outline and Summary

I. Introduction

Chapter 6 answers these questions: (1) How were the Americans able to win the Revolutionary War? (2) What impact did the Revolution have on the ideals of liberty and equality? (3) Why did it take Americans twelve years to create a workable form of federal government?

II. America's First Civil War

A. Introduction

The Revolution was both a war of the American people against the British and a civil war between American patriots, or Whigs (supporters of independence), and American loyalists, or Tories (who were opposed to breaking with the mother country).

B. Loyalists and Other British Sympathizers

About 20 percent of all whites became loyalists. The proportion of loyalists was greatest in New York and New Jersey, where the leading families had split between the two sides. Recent British immigrants and French Canadians tended to be loyalists. Twenty thousand slaves escaped to the royal army, and most Indian tribes sided with the British against westward-moving, land-hungry Americans.

C. The Opposing Sides

The British entered the war with major advantages: they outnumbered the Americans 11 million to 2.5 million, and they possessed the world's largest navy and one of the best professional armies. But they also had disadvantages. Because of their difficulty in recruiting soldiers, they had to employ twenty-one thousand loyalists and thirty thousand Hessian mercenaries. Supplying armies across three thousand miles of ocean was a formidable task. They managed to reach and hold coastal cities, but penetrating the interior with its poor roads proved especially trying. Further, as the financial strain of the conflict mounted, English domestic support for it waned. The Americans mobilized their smaller population behind the war more effectively, but they also were beset with problems: one-fifth of the free population was opposed to the Revolution, the state militias did well in guerrilla raids but lacked training for pitched battles, and there were few experienced officers to command the raw recruits of the Continental Army. Fortunately, the Americans did not have to conquer the redcoats; the rebels just had to keep resisting until the British public tired of the struggle.

D. George Washington

Washington, a Virginia tobacco planter who had sat in the House of Burgesses and the Continental Congress, was chosen commander of the army because of his military experience in the imperial wars with France. For much of the revolution, America's fate depended on his ability to inspire his men to continue fighting despite numerous defeats.

E. War in Earnest

The British evacuated Boston in March 1776 and moved into New York, where they almost overwhelmed Washington's army on Long Island. In subsequent battles in and around the city, the British killed or captured a quarter of Washington's soldiers and forced him to make a hasty retreat across New Jersey. During the winter of 1776–1777, Washington struck back at Trenton and Princeton. The redcoats pulled back to New York, and in New Jersey the Whigs forced loyalists remaining in the state to pledge loyalty to the Continental Congress.

F. The Turning Point

The Americans realized that their best hope for victory lay in French diplomatic recognition and military alliance, but Louis XVI held back until he became convinced that the Americans had a chance of winning. When forces under General Horatio Gates foiled a major British offensive, surrounded General John Burgoyne's outnumbered army, and compelled the surrender of 5,800 British troops in October 1777 near Saratoga, New York, the French were impressed. By February 1778 France recognized the United States, and four months later she declared war on England. Subsequently the Spanish and the Dutch Republic also declared war on Britain. French and Spanish blows to British naval power and the diversion of English troops from America to fight in other theaters greatly aided the United States.

G. The Continentals Mature

In the fall of 1777, the British inflicted defeats on Washington's army at Brandywine Creek and Germantown, Pennsylvania, and occupied Philadelphia, compelling the Continental Congress to flee. While the royal army enjoyed the comforts of Philadelphia for the winter of 1778, Washington's men froze and drilled in nearby Valley Forge. In June the Continentals caught up with the British marching back to New York at the battle of Monmouth Court House, New Jersey. Badly mauled, the redcoats escaped to New York, where they sat under the protection of the British Navy, and Washington hovered across the Hudson keeping an eye on them.

H. Frontier Campaigns

Although the number of people involved in the frontier battles was small, the skirmishes were deadly, as the British, the new country, and the Indians realized what was at stake—namely, who would control the area west of the Appalachians. The battles commenced in the South, where the Cherokees attacked from Virginia to Georgia. By 1777 the frontiersmen had crushed the Cherokees and forced them to cede much of their land in the Carolinas and Tennessee. Expeditions led by George Rogers Clark, John Bowman, and Daniel Brodhead inflicted heavy losses on hostile Ohio Indian tribes, who nonetheless kept up the struggle into the 1780s. Joseph Brant led the Iroquois on deadly raids against the western New York and Pennsylvania settlers until he was stopped at a battle near Elmira, New York. By the war's end the Iroquois population had dropped by a third.

I. Victory in the South

After 1778 the British shifted their attention to the South. They took Charles Town, South Carolina, in 1780, and General Charles Cornwallis led English forces into the Carolina backcountry. There he fought three major battles against American militiamen commanded by Nathaniel Greene. The British won all three encounters but suffered such heavy casualties that Cornwallis decided to leave the Carolina backcountry and head to Virginia. Cornwallis established a new base on Virginia's Yorktown Peninsula, where he was later cut off and surrounded by American and French armies and a French fleet. On October 19, 1781, Cornwallis surrendered, and the fight in the Revolutionary War ended.

J. The Peace of Paris

John Adams, John Jay, and Benjamin Franklin represented America at the Paris peace negotiations that began in June 1782. Under the terms of the treaties signed in 1783, the British recognized American independence and promised to remove all troops from American soil. The Mississippi River became the western boundary of the new nation, but New Orleans and the outlet of the river to the Gulf of Mexico, as well as East and West Florida, went to Spain. Although the confederation agreed to compensate loyalists for their property losses and repay British creditors, several states later refused to comply. American victory had been costly: at least 5 percent of free white males between sixteen and forty-five years of age died in the war. Many Loyalists and former slaves fled to Canada, Britain, and the West Indies.

III. Revolutionary Society

A. Egalitarianism

Although there was no significant redistribution of wealth in America during the Revolution, the Declaration of Independence's bold assertion that all men are created equal did promote more egalitarian attitudes. The upper classes found it prudent to simplify their standard of living and treat common people with respect. Ordinary folks were less likely to defer to their "betters" or automatically leave governing to them. Americans began to feel that political leaders should come from the "natural aristocracy"—that is, men who demonstrated virtue, accomplishments, and dedication to the public good.

B. A Revolution for Black Americans

In 1776 blacks accounted for 20 percent of the U.S. population, and almost all of them were enslaved. Five thousand blacks served in the Continental Army. The Declaration of Independence's words about equality made Whigs uneasy about slavery. The Quakers had taken the lead in attacking slavery. Then, between 1777 and 1810, all the northern states instituted gradual emancipation. No southern states, however, where the majority of blacks lived, outlawed bondage. Several did make the voluntary freeing of slaves easier, and by 1790 about 5 percent of Virginia and Maryland blacks had been freed. Most free blacks remained poor laborers or tenant farmers. They relied on each other for help and began to build their own institutions, such as the African Methodist Episcopal church. Although most states granted freedmen certain civil rights, blacks continued in other respects to be treated as second-class citizens.

C. White Women in the New Republic

The Revolution brought little change in the status of women. In the 1780s, as earlier, the great majority of people believed a woman's duty was to take care of her household and raise her children. The revolutionary emphasis on liberty and equality did, however, bring some improvements in female schooling. These were justified by the argument that women had to be educated so that they could inculcate republican virtues in their sons and daughters. But, the organized fight for women's rights did not begin until the nineteenth century.

D. Native Americans and the Revolution

The newly independent nation posed a serious threat to the Indian's future. For many whites the republic's promise of equal opportunity meant moving west to obtain their own land, thus impinging on Indian territory. The tribes of the Ohio Valley were especially vulnerable because between 1754 and 1783 war and uprooting had reduced the Native American population east of the Mississippi by nearly 50 percent. Those Indians still living east of the river adapted some features of white culture, combined it with their old ways, and carried on trade with whites, but they insisted on their right to control their own communities and lives.

E. The Revolution and Social Change

The overall distribution of wealth in the nation did not change as a result of the Revolution. Property taken from rich loyalists tended to end up in the hands of equally well-to-do Whigs. Slavery persisted in the South. Racial injustice and the subordination of women continued. But the Revolution did start the extinction of slavery in the North and increase the numbers of free blacks and the rights they had. The Revolution also gave rise to the earliest questioning of relations between the sexes.

IV. Forging New Governments

A. Tradition and Change

Certain beliefs inherited from the colonial era stood in the way of a thorough democratization of politics. Most Whigs believed that voting and office holding must be tied to property ownership. They frowned on political parties as strife-causing factions and did not see the need for apportioning seats in a legislature on the basis of population. Their revolutionary experience did, however, make them wary of unchecked executive authority, inclined to augment the role of elected legislatures, and interested in framing governmental institutions that would balance the interests of different classes to prevent any one group from gaining absolute power.

B. From Colonies to States

The first state constitutions reflected both the radical and traditional features of Whig thought. Except for Pennsylvania's, they did not provide for election districts that were equal in population. Nine of the thirteen states reduced property qualifications for voting, but none abolished them entirely. By 1784 all state constitutions included bills of rights. They provided for frequent elections and stripped the governors of most of their powers. In the 1780s, however, many states revised their constitutions to strengthen the executive branch and increase the political power of wealthy elites. Most of the states also enacted social reforms. In Virginia, for example, Thomas Jefferson framed legislation abolishing primogeniture, entails, and the established church, as well as guaranteeing religious freedom.

C. The Articles of Confederation

In 1777 the Continental Congress drafted a constitution called the Articles of Confederation and sent it to the states for ratification, which was finally achieved in 1781. The Articles created a weak central government. There was a unicameral congress in which each state had one vote, but there was no national court system or executive. Financial, diplomatic, and military affairs were managed by congressional committees. The congress could request funds from the states but could not tax the people directly. The Articles reserved to each state full sovereignty, freedom, and independence, leaving the national government "severely limited in important respects."

D. Finance, Trade, and the Economy

The confederation proved too weak to meet its greatest challenge, putting the country's finances on a sound basis. Unable to tax the people or force the states to contribute funds, the congress could not pay off its Revolutionary War debt or meet its operating expenses. Its paper currency, the Continental, depreciated by 98 percent. Nor could the government under the Articles win diplomatic concessions from the British, who badly hurt New England shippers and merchants by shutting them out of the West Indian trade and imposing steep customs fees on goods entering England. Declining exports depressed the economies of both New England and the South.

E. The Confederation and the West

The confederation also had to decide on the future of the trans-Appalachian west. The confederation was caught between speculators and settlers resolved to acquire these lands immediately and Native Americans determined to keep their homes. It responded by forcing Indian leaders to sign treaties ceding western lands, which the tribes then repudiated. In addition, the congress passed the Ordinance of 1785 and the Northwest Ordinance of 1787. These laws set a successful pattern for surveying, selling, and administering western lands, as well as providing the way for territories to become states with the same powers and privileges as the original thirteen states. Equally important, the Northwest Ordinance for the first time banned slavery from a territory.

Meanwhile the British and Spanish governments made life difficult for western settlers. The British refused to evacuate seven forts in the Ohio Valley and supplied Indians in the region with arms and ammunition. The Spanish, too, sided with the Indians against American frontier families and closed off New Orleans to western farmers who wanted to ship their produce down the Mississippi and out to eastern cities and Europe through that port. The ineffectual confederation failed to persuade Britain and Spain to stop these practices.

F. Shays's Rebellion

Shays's Rebellion, in 1786 in Massachusetts, led some Americans to fear that the government was unable to protect even domestic law and order. Further, producers wanted a stronger government to regulate interstate and foreign commerce. Merchants and shippers desired a government that could secure foreign trade opportunities for them. Westerners hoped for better protection from the Indians. A 1786 Annapolis, Maryland meeting to promote interstate commerce instead called for a general convention of all the states to amend the Articles and thereby create a more effective national government.

G. The Philadelphia Convention

Fifty-five delegates from every state but Rhode Island gathered during the spring and summer of 1787 in Philadelphia. The majority of them were wealthy, had legal training, and shared a nationalist rather than a local perspective. In sessions closed to the press and the public, they decided to abandon the Articles and write a new constitution. The convention worked from a draft written by delegate James Madison. His Virginia Plan proposed a national government with broad powers to tax, legislate, and use military force against states. There would be a two-house congress, with representation in both chambers based on population. The small states, worried that they would always be outvoted, objected and countered with William Patterson's New Jersey Plan. It called for a unicameral congress in which each state, regardless of population, had an equal voice. The convention finally agreed to the Connecticut Compromise, with a two-chamber legislature: representation in the

House based on population and representation in the Senate based on the principle of equality for each state.

The Constitution finished in September 1787, vested in the federal government the power to levy and collect taxes, conduct diplomacy, and protect domestic order. It also granted to the national government (and denied to the states) authority to coin money and regulate interstate and foreign commerce. The Constitution carefully balanced state and federal power, the interests of one social group against another, and the authority of one branch of the national government versus another with its systems of federalism, separation of powers, and checks and balances. Many features of the Constitution were not democratic. It recognized and in some ways protected slavery and allowed direct election only of members of the House of Representatives. On the other hand, it acknowledged the people as the "ultimate source of political legitimacy" and, through the amendment process, opened the door for democratization of the government in the years ahead. Finally, the delegates provided for ratification of the Constitution by special state conventions composed of delegates elected by the people. As soon as nine conventions had approved the document, the new government would commence.

H. The Struggle over Ratification

During 1787 and 1788 the country divided into proratification Federalists and opposing Antifederalists. Antifederalists feared that the Constitution concentrated too much centralized power in the hands of a national elite and that individuals' freedoms would be trampled because the document contained no bill of rights. Leading Antifederalists included Virginia's Patrick Henry, George Mason, and James Monroe, New England's Mercy Otis Warren, and New York governor George Clinton. The Federalists ultimately prevailed, because of their vigorous leadership and promise that they would amend the Constitution to provide a bill of rights once the new government was under way. In an effort to win New Yorkers over to the Constitution, John Jay, Alexander Hamilton, and James Madison published a series of articles, later collected in a book called *The Federalist* papers. These articles still afford us a valuable commentary on the Constitution and insight into the political philosophy of the Founding Fathers.

V. Conclusion

The final triumph of the nationalism born of the War for Independence came in late 1789 and early 1790, when the last two reluctant states, North Carolina and Rhode Island, ratified the Constitution and joined the new union. The Constitution did not create a democratic government for the United States, but it did establish the "legal and institutional framework within which Americans could struggle to attain democracy."

Vocabulary

The following terms are used in Chapter 6. To understand the chapter fully, it is important that you know what each of them means.

mercenaries   hired soldiers serving in an army

egalitarian   asserting the equality of all people

confiscate   to seize for public use; to take away property as a penalty

emancipation   freedom from slavery

peers   persons of the same civil rank or standing; equals before the law

sovereignty   supreme or independent power or authority in government

republic   a government in which the supreme power rests in the body of citizens entitled to vote and is exercised by representatives chosen directly or indirectly by them. Also, the head of government is nominated and/or elected rather than inheriting the position as a king.

ideology   the body of doctrine, myth, and symbols of a social movement, institution, social class, or large group

agrarian   relating to farming, agricultural economy, or a rural way of life

connotations   secondary, implied, or associated meanings of a word or term rather than its dictionary definition

compact   an agreement between parties; a contract; a treaty

prorogue   to dismiss a legislature or discontinue its session

entails   legal requirements that prevent an heir and all his descendants from selling or dividing an estate

primogeniture   legal requirement that, in the absence of a will, only the eldest son inherits all a family's property

confederation   a league or alliance; a body of sovereign states more or less united for common purposes

interstate commerce   business carried on in more than one state; transactions across state lines (as opposed to business done entirely within one state, or *intrastate* commerce)

anarchy   a state of society without government or law; political and social disorder due to absence of government control

ratification   the act of confirming by expressing formal consent or approval

Identifications

After reading Chapter 6, you should be able to identify and explain the historical significance of each of the following:

Henry Knox

loyalists (Tories) versus patriots (Whigs)

Hessians

Marquis de Lafayette

General John Burgoyne, General Horatio Gates, and Saratoga

Frederick von Steuben

George Rogers Clark

Joseph Brant

Daniel Boone

Yorktown

John Adams, John Jay, Benjamin Franklin, and the Peace of Paris

"natural aristocracy"

Benjamin Banneker

African Methodist Episcopal church

Abigail Adams

"republican motherhood"

Virginia Statute for Religious Freedom

the Articles of Confederation

Ordinance of 1785 and Northwest Ordinance of 1787

Continentals

Shays's Rebellion

Virginia Plan, New Jersey Plan, and Connecticut Compromise

checks and balances, functional separation of powers, and federalism

Federalists versus Antifederalists

John Jay, Alexander Hamilton, James Madison, and *The Federalist* papers

Skill Building: Maps

1. On the map of eastern North America on the following page, locate each of the following and explain its importance in the Revolutionary War.

   Fort Ticonderoga

   Boston

   New York City

   Long Island

   Delaware River

   Trenton, New Jersey

   Princeton, New Jersey

   Albany

   Philadelphia

   Saratoga, New York

   Brandywine Creek and Germantown, Pennsylvania

   Valley Forge, Pennsylvania

   Monmouth, New Jersey

   Appalachians

   Tennessee

   Illinois

   Vincennes, Indiana

   Detroit, Michigan

   Ohio River

   Elmira, New York

   Savannah, Georgia

   Charles Town, South Carolina

   Yorktown, Virginia

**Eastern
North America**

2. Draw on the map the boundaries of the United States as set by the Peace of Paris in 1783. Also draw the boundaries of the Northwest Territory created by the Ordinances of 1785 and 1787.

Historical Sources

On page 172 the author tells us that the sessions of the Constitutional Convention were closed to the press and the public and that the delegates kept no official journal of their proceedings. How, then, do historians know what went on at the convention? How does the author of Chapter 6 know who said this or that about the Virginia Plan or the New Jersey Plan? How does he know about the "grand committee," or that Madison and the Virginians continued to fight against the Connecticut Compromise until they were overruled by the July 17, 1787 vote? Much of our information comes from detailed notes that James Madison took on the debates as he attended and participated in the sessions. He did not make these notes public during his lifetime, but after his death in 1836, Congress purchased Madison's papers that contained the notes. They were first published in 1840. While Madison's notes have proved a most valuable source of information, can you see why it is wise for historians also to look at any memoirs, letters, and comments they can find by other convention participants?

A way that historians have learned much about the thinking of Federalists and Antifederalists is by reading the articles and letters that they published in the press during the fight over ratification. John Jay, Alexander Hamilton, and James Madison wrote many essays, which appeared in such New York newspapers as the *Daily Advertiser* in 1787, arguing in support of the Constitution. New York governor Clinton, a leading Antifederalist, countered with letters attacking the proposed Constitution in the *New York Journal*. In addition to these newspaper pieces, historians can turn to the records of the speeches given for both sides at the state ratifying conventions.

As well as finding their sources, historians also have to decide which past events they will focus on. Traditionally, historians of the Revolutionary War concentrated on battles that Washington and the Continental Army fought or dramatic turning points in the struggle, such as Saratoga. In more recent decades historians, like the author of Chapter 6, have tried to offer a broader, or more balanced view of revolutionary fighting that includes the bitter clashes between white frontier settlers and Native Americans for control of the trans-Appalachian west. Look at "A Place in Time: Boonesborough, Kentucky in 1778." What light does it throw on the complex relations between whites and Indians and what motivated each side in the siege of Boonesborough?

Multiple-Choice Questions

Circle the letter of the item that best completes each statement or answers the question.

1. Which of the following statements about the Revolutionary War is correct?
   a. The fighting ended with Cornwallis's surrender at Yorktown.
   b. Help from most Indian tribes enabled the Americans to win their independence from Britain.
   c. Most of the men who fought in the Continental Army were drafted and therefore had no choice but to serve.
   d. American victory at Boonesborough, Kentucky turned the tide in the war in favor of the new nation.

2. Which statement about the men who wrote the U.S. Constitution is correct?
   a. Most of them doubted that a republic could effectively govern so large a nation as the United States.
   b. Most were wealthy men who were convinced that unless the national government was strengthened, the country would fall victim to foreign aggression or simply disintegrate.
   c. Most were men in their fifties and sixties who distrusted the younger revolutionaries.
   d. They wanted to get on with creating a democratic government that would enforce their belief that all men are created equal.

3. The Northwest Ordinance did all of the following *except*
   a. forbid slavery in the Northwest Territory.
   b. permit the citizens of a territory to elect a legislature and make their own laws.
   c. permit the citizens of a territory to write a state constitution and apply to Congress for admission as a new state.
   d. remove Native Americans and guarantee white settlers the right to buy land in the territory.

4. The British justified their refusal to evacuate their military forts in the Ohio Valley after the Revolution by pointing to America's failure to
   a. stop Indian attacks against Canada.
   b. pay for damage done to British shipping during the war.
   c. return or pay for loyalists' property and pay British creditors.
   d. allow British goods to enter the United States duty free.

5. Which of the following represented the most serious difficulty facing American commercial interests at the end of the Revolution?
   a. loss of the protection of the British Navy
   b. British restrictions on trade with the West Indies
   c. decreased demand for American goods in Europe
   d. France's refusal to sign a commercial treaty

6. Shays's Rebellion was provoked by
   a. retention of the northwest posts by Britain.
   b. the failure of the government to protect frontier settlements from Indian attacks.
   c. an excise tax imposed by Congress on whiskey.
   d. the heavy burden of taxes on the farmers of western Massachusetts.

7. Which of the following men was both an author of the U.S. Constitution and an outspoken supporter of its ratification?
   a. Thomas Jefferson
   b. Patrick Henry
   c. James Madison
   d. George Clinton

8. The greatest achievement of the Antifederalists was to
   a. force the Federalists to agree to add a bill of rights to the Constitution.
   b. convince New York and Virginia to turn over their western lands to the new national government.
   c. delay ratification of the Constitution until a section guaranteeing all white men the right to vote and hold office was added.
   d. force the Federalists to bestow citizenship under the new government to free blacks.

9. Who was the author of Virginia's Statute for Religious Freedom and bills abolishing entails and primogeniture?
   a. George Washington
   b. Richard Henry Lee
   c. Thomas Jefferson
   d. Patrick Henry

10. All of the following were true of the state constitutions adopted during the Revolution *except*
    a. they concentrated power in the popularly elected legislatures.
    b. they all contained bills of rights.
    c. they provided for weak executives and frequent elections.
    d. they abolished property and tax-paying qualifications for voting.

Short-Answer Questions

1. Which groups of people tended to be loyalists, or British sympathizers, during the American Revolution?

2. Why is the Battle of Saratoga considered a turning point in the American Revolution?

3. In the Peace of Paris ending the Revolutionary War, what were the terms affecting America?

4. What was the relationship between Shays's Rebellion and the calling of the Constitutional convention?

5. Explain the differences between the Virginia plan and the New Jersey plan for the Constitution. In what ways was the Connecticut proposal a compromise between them?

6. What was the three-fifths controversy at the Constitutional convention? In what other ways did the Constitution recognize and deal with slavery?

7. Briefly describe the checks and balances and separation of powers in the U.S. Constitution. Give examples to illustrate.

8. Who were the Antifederalists, and what were their objections to the U.S. Constitution?

Essay Questions

1. Besides being a war for independence from Britain, the American Revolution was also a civil war of American against American and a war of Native Americans to defend their homelands. Discuss and illustrate this statement with as many facts as possible.

2. Discuss the advantages and disadvantages the British and the Americans each had in fighting the Revolutionary War. What do you think accounts for the Americans' ultimate victory?

3. Discuss the social, economic, and political changes within the thirteen states produced by the American Revolution. Be sure to consider things such as slavery, status of women, property distribution, voting rights, and religion.

4. Discuss the domestic and foreign difficulties the United States experienced under the Articles of Confederation. What were the accomplishments of the government under the Articles?

5. Discuss the backgrounds and political beliefs of the men who wrote the U.S. Constitution. What did they hope to accomplish by establishing this Constitution?

CHAPTER 7

Launching the New Republic, 1789–1800

Outline and Summary

I. Introduction

Chapter 7 concentrates on these questions: (1) How and why did a two-party system develop by 1796? (2) What caused conflicts in the 1790s between the United States and each of the following nations: Spain, Britain, and France? (3) Over what issues did Federalists and Republicans divide in the election of 1800? (4) How and why did the position of American nonwhites decline in the 1790s?

II. Constitutional government Takes Shape

A. Introduction

The men elected to Congress under the new Constitution began assembling in New York City, the first national capital, in March 1789. George Washington arrived on April 23 and was sworn in as president on April 30. The lawmakers immediately devoted their attention to filling in the details in areas left vague in the Constitution: the president's cabinet, the national court system, and rights of the individual.

B. Defining the Presidency

The Constitution mentions executive departments only in passing. Through legislation Congress established the first cabinet. It consisted of four departments headed by secretaries of state, treasury, and war and an attorney general.

C. National Justice and the Bill of Rights

The Constitution authorized Congress simply to provide the federal courts below the level of the Supreme Court. This the lawmakers did by passing the Judiciary Act of 1789. It created a three-tier system of federal district courts, circuit courts of appeals, and the Supreme Court.

James Madison, who had been elected to the House of Representatives, led the way in drafting the first ten amendments, which became known as the Bill of Rights when they were ratified by the states in December 1791. The first eight protected individual rights, including freedom of speech, press, assembly and religion, and procedures for a fair trial and punishment. The Ninth and Tenth amendments reserved to the people and the states powers not specifically granted to the federal government by the Constitution.

III. National Economic Policy and Its Consequences

A. Hamilton and His Objectives

Washington's secretary of the treasury, Alexander Hamilton, soon emerged as the leading figure in the administration. He wanted to promote national economic self-sufficiency through industrialization and a strong merchant marine. He also believed that the federal government's success depended on gaining the support of the politically influential commercial classes by benefiting them economically.

B. Report on the Public Credit

Hamilton's Report on the Public Credit, sent to Congress in January 1790, outlined a plan to establish the country's credit while at the same time wedding the upper classes to government. He proposed that the federal government quickly pay off the outstanding foreign debt. Domestic holders of Revolutionary War bonds issued by the Continental Congress and the states could exchange them at full face value for new U.S. government bonds carrying 4 percent interest. Further, Hamilton urged Congress to maintain a perpetual debt, issuing new interest-bearing bonds as the old ones were retired. Hamilton hoped with these arrangements to provide former state creditors and other bond holders with a safe, attractive investment opportunity that would in turn give them a stake in the continued survival and economic health of the U.S. government.

Repayment of foreign creditors aroused no opposition, but Hamilton's other proposals provoked bitter controversy. Most of the domestic Revolutionary War bond holders had long since sold their certificates to speculators for a fraction of their value. Now these speculators, mostly well-to-do northeasterners, stood to reap a fortune. The states that had already paid back their creditors also objected to the federal government's assuming the burden for states that had lagged in discharging their financial obligations, most of which were northern states, except South Carolina. James Madison led the southern congressional opposition to both proposals but was unable to defeat them. Hamilton garnered just enough southern votes to put through his assumption of state debt scheme by making a deal to round up northern votes for placing the nation's permanent capital on the Potomac, where the Virginians wanted it. Hamilton's measures dramatically improved America's credit rating but alienated many southerners.

C. Reports on the Bank and Manufactures

Next Hamilton asked Congress to charter a national bank. The government would own one portion of its stock, and private individuals the rest. This bank would serve as a depository for federal tax receipts, make low-interest loans to the government, issue notes that would circulate as a national currency, regulate practices of state-chartered banks, and provide credit to expand the country's economy. The bank would, of course, further Hamilton's objective of tying rich businessmen to the federal government by affording them still another profitable investment. The secretary of the treasury also proposed to encourage manufacturing and other industries by enactment of protective tariffs and subsidies.

D. Challenge to Limited Government

Some government leaders began to see in Hamilton's bank and other proposals a disturbing pattern of favoring the interests of, and giving undue influence to, an elite group of investors. Led by Secretary of State Thomas Jefferson and Representative James Madison, opponents of the bank charter argued that it endangered the republic and was unconstitutional. When Congress passed the bill by a slim margin, a troubled President Washington asked Hamilton and Jefferson to advise him on the measure's constitutionality. The opinion each wrote presented the first clear-cut statements of the strict versus loose interpretations of the Constitution. Washington, more impressed with Hamilton's loose interpretation than Jefferson's strict reading of the Constitution, signed the bank bill into law. But Hamilton was not able to convince Congress to enact a high protective tariff, although it did aid shipping and fishing in other ways.

E. Hamilton's Legacy

Beneficiaries of Hamilton's policies, including speculators, merchants, and other monied men of the port cities, rallied behind the administration in a budding political party calling itself Federalist. The Federalists had their strongest support in New England, New Jersey, and South Carolina. They also had many adherents in Pennsylvania and New York. But the agricultural interests of the South, West, and Middle Atlantic states saw no gains for themselves in Hamilton's programs. They began to coalesce in opposition to the administration and in favor of the "true principles" of republicanism.

F. The Whiskey Rebellion

To fund the assumption of state debts, Congress in March 1791 imposed a federal excise tax on domestically produced whiskey. Western Pennsylvania farmers who earned a little cash income by turning their surplus grain (which was too bulky to ship) into compact corn liquor for sale viewed the excise tax as an unfair levy. In July 1794 a mob of frontier farmers attacked U.S. marshals who had come west to serve summonses on sixty persons for non-payment of the tax. Washington and Hamilton decided to crush this Whiskey Rebellion forcefully to demonstrate that citizens must obey federal law. Almost thirteen thousand militiamen marched west and rounded up rebellious farmers. Twenty were sent to Philadelphia for trial, and two received death sentences, but Washington later pardoned them.

IV. *The United States on the World Stage*

A. Introduction

After 1793 the political polarization created by Hamilton's financial policies became even more pronounced as Americans argued over foreign policy.

B. Spanish Power in the Far West

In the late eighteenth century Spanish ambitions to dominate much of North America revived. Spain strengthened its hold on its colonies of New Mexico and Texas by improving relations with Native Americans. It also spread its settlements from Mexico up the coast of California. By doing so, Spain hoped to control trade with Asia and possess the Pacific Northwest, both of which were being challenged by the Russians, British, and Americans.

C. The Trans-Appalachian Frontier

The greatest dangers to the United States in the trans-Appalachian west lay in British and Spanish assistance to Native Americans resisting settlers moving in and in the attempts of those foreign powers to detach the region from the rest of the United States. To counter this peril, the federal government, between 1791 and 1796, admitted Vermont, Kentucky, and Tennessee as new states. Both whites and Native Americans rejected Washington's efforts to "civilize" and integrate the eastern tribes into white society. The government instead continued to pressure the Indians to cede their lands and move farther west.

D. France and Factional Politics

In 1789 the French Revolution began. Almost all Americans were initially sympathetic, but when the revolution became more radical and France went to war with Britain, Spain, and other European monarchies, opinion in this country divided. Most southerners and westerners remained pro-French. Western settlers and southern land speculators hoped a French victory would leave Britain and Spain too weak to keep stirring up Indians on America's frontier. However, northeastern merchants, shippers, and seamen were dependent on trade with England and feared a pro-French foreign policy would lead to British retaliation against U.S. commerce. Meanwhile, the French ambassador, Edmond Genet, was actively recruiting Americans to fight for France. Instead of abiding by the 1778 treaty of alliance, however, Washington, in 1793, proclaimed U.S. neutrality.

E. The British Crisis

To discourage the pro-French activities of some Americans, the British began seizing U.S. merchant ships and impressing seamen, as well as stepping up their incitement of the Indians in the Ohio Valley. The Spanish also increased their incursion on American western lands. To halt the drift into war, Washington dispatched John Jay to England and Thomas Pinckney to Spain. Jay's Treaty with England won few concessions except a British promise to evacuate their western forts, which owed much to Anthony Wayne's victory at the Battle of Fallen Timbers. Most southerners and westerners denounced Jay's Treaty, but a Federalist-dominated Senate ratified it to avoid war. Pinckney's Treaty with Spain was more satisfactory, especially because it opened full use of the port of New Orleans to western farmers. Disagreements about foreign policy, especially ratification of Jay's Treaty, furthered the partisan split.

V. Battling for the Nation's Soul

A. Ideological Confrontation

Horrified by the intensifying radicalism of the French revolution, the Federalists grew more suspicious of the common people and of unchecked democracy. But the Jeffersonian Republicans retained their sympathy for revolutionary France and did not fear popular participation in politics. Jefferson and Madison sought the support of ordinary citizens against Federalist policies by encouraging the publication of anti-administration newspapers like the *National Gazette*. They also approved of the Democratic societies that were springing up in various locations.

B. The Republican Party

By 1793 President Washington was clearly identified with the Federalists and Jefferson had resigned from his cabinet to lead the opposition. Federalist and Republican newspapers were engaged in a press war of exaggerated charges and countercharges. Stung by partisan criticism, Washington decided to retire after 1796. In his farewell address, he warned Americans to avoid political parties and entangling alliances with European countries. His decision not to run, however, opened the presidential election of 1796 to the first partisan contest.

C. The Election of 1796

The Republicans ran Thomas Jefferson; the Federalists, John Adams. The Federalists won control of Congress and the presidency by a narrow margin. Jefferson, who lost, became vice president, however, because the Constitution (written without providing for an organized opposition and political parties) had provided that the runner-up should have the number-two spot.

D. The French Crisis

The French, angered by America's signing of Jay's Treaty with the British, began to seize U.S. merchant ships. Hoping to avoid war with France, President Adams sent a peace commission to Paris to negotiate. There, in what became known as the XYZ Affair, agents of the French government demanded a bribe as the price for negotiations. The affair outraged Americans and provoked an anti-French and anti-Republican backlash. Republican candidates were defeated in the 1798 congressional elections, and an undeclared naval war broke out with France.

E. The Alien and Sedition Acts

The Federalist-dominated Congress took advantage of the anti-French hysteria to push through a series of repressive measures known as the Alien and Sedition Acts, which aimed at silencing the opposition press and in other ways weakening the Republican party. One measure attempted to rob the Republicans of the votes of their Irish- and French-immigrant supporters by imposing a fourteen-year wait for citizenship. Under the Sedition Act, which made it a crime to speak, write, or print anything unfavorable about the government or the president that would bring him "into contempt or disrepute," the Federalists prosecuted and jailed a number of Republican journalists and political candidates. Madison and Jefferson fought back with the Virginia and Kentucky resolutions. Passed by the legislatures of those two states, the resolutions claimed that state governments could interpose themselves between their residents and the enforcement of unconstitutional federal laws such as the Alien and Sedition Acts. The resolutions set a precedent for the later states' rights position that states were the proper judges of federal actions and could nullify unconstitutional statues.

F. The Election of 1800

The election took place in an atmosphere of tense and bitter partisanship. The Republicans nominated Jefferson and Aaron Burr for president and vice president. President Adams, running for a second term, greatly disappointed the "High Federalists" and hurt his own election prospects by reopening negotiations with France and thus quieting the war scare on which Federalist fortunes had thrived. The negotiations eventually patched things up with France and spared this nation an unnecessary war. The Republicans won the election, but Jefferson and Burr ended up tied for president because, under the Constitution as originally written, electors did not vote separately for president and vice president. The tie threw the election into the House of Representatives, which took thirty-six votes to name Jefferson president. The nation soon added the Twelfth Amendment to the Constitution to prevent such muddled elections in the future.

VI. Economic and Social Change

A. Introduction

In part the clashes between political parties, classes, regions, and races grew out of the economic and social changes occurring in America after independence. These changes included a shift away from small-scale subsistence farming in the Northeast, a migration westward of both whites and enslaved blacks, and an economic revival of slavery.

B. The Household Economy

In colonial America the vast majority of whites lived and produced on small family-owned farms. Husbands, wives, children, and sometimes hired hands and/or servants grew and consumed their own food and made almost everything else they needed. Whatever little surplus the farm family accumulated, they traded with neighbors or merchants for items they could not fashion. By the 1780s, however, New England farms, with their thin, rocky soil, were insufficient to support burgeoning families. Grown sons and young couples moved west. Remaining daughters, wives, and sometimes husbands began supplementing their income by home manufacturing, for example, weaving cloth, sewing garments and shoes, and making nails. Merchants traveling into the countryside supplied them with the raw materials and later collected their output, paying them by the piece. This putting out system was the forerunner of the industrial revolution. The merchants behind these innovations were also, in the 1780s and 1790s, opening the first banks and stock exchanges, preaching the need for the United States to industrialize, and supporting Hamilton's economic policies, which they saw as good for business.

C. Indians in the New Republic

By 1800 eastern Indians had suffered devastating losses of land and population, and Indian culture was buckling under the strain of continual frontier warfare. The broken survivors sank into alcoholism and clung to their traditional ways. Reformers, such as the Seneca prophet Handsome Lake, attempted to combat liquor and convince Iroquois men to become farmers. However, many Native Americans resisted further social change.

D. Redefining the Color Line

As the revolutionary idealism that had eased out slavery in the North and won some rights for free blacks ebbed in the 1790s, the position of African-Americans deteriorated. In the late 1790s and early 1800s, states such as Delaware, Maryland, Kentucky, and New Jersey, which had earlier given freedmen the vote, rescinded it. Congress protected southern masters with the 1793 Fugitive Slave Law. White fears generated by the slave uprising in Saint Domingue and the 1800 Gabriel's Rebellion in Virginia further eroded any sentiment for abolition and racial equality. The demand of the British textile industry for cotton and Eli Whitney's invention of the cotton gin in 1793 also revived southern plantation slavery, making the institution too profitable to question.

VII. *Conclusion*

By 1801 the dangers of civil war and national disintegration had declined, if not disappeared. Two rival political parties had developed, but with the election of 1800 the nation managed a peaceful transfer of power from Federalists to Republicans. Slavery and racism, after some abatement, were again on the rise.

Vocabulary

The following terms are used in Chapter 7. To understand the chapter fully, it is important that you know what each of them means.

speculator   a person trading in land, commodities, or stocks and bonds in the hope of profiting from changes in the market price; one who engages in business transactions involving considerable risk but offering large gains

default   to fail to meet financial obligations; to fail to perform a legally required act or obligation

secession   formal withdrawal from an association, as in states withdrawing from the union

entrepreneurs   persons who develop and carry out new economic enterprises

mechanic   an artisan who practices a trade using his home as a workshop and employing family members, apprentices, journeymen, and servants

journeyman   a person who has served an apprenticeship in a trade and who works at it for another

tariff   a tax imposed on products imported from abroad

excise tax   a tax levied on goods and services manufactured, sold, or offered within the country

ex post facto law   a law criminalizing previously legal actions and punishing those who have been engaging in such actions

bill of attainder   a legislative act proclaiming a person's guilt and stipulating punishment without a judicial trial

bounties or subsidies   rewards or payments given (usually by governments) to encourage certain actions or economic activities

privateer   a privately owned and manned armed vessel commissioned by a government in time of war to fight the enemy, especially its commercial shipping

impress   to force into service, as with a seaman; to seize or take for public use or service

constituents   the voters and residents of a district, state, or country whom an elected official represents

abomination   an object greatly disliked or hated; a horror

demagoguery   using the methods or practices of a demagogue—that is, a leader who uses the passions or prejudices of the people for his or her own interests; using the methods or practices of an unprincipled popular orator or agitator

partisan   a support of a political party or cause; actions motivated by support of a political party or cause

cabal   a small group of secret plotters

libelous   writing that contains damaging or malicious misrepresentation

emoluments   profits or rewards arising from office, such as government service

apostate   one who forsakes his church, cause, or party

electorate   the body of persons entitled to vote in an election

sedition   incitement of discontent or rebellion against the government; action or language promoting such discontent or rebellion

Identifications

After reading Chapter 7, you should be able to identify and explain the historical significance of each of the following:

Samuel Slater

Judiciary Act of 1789

Bill of Rights

Hamilton's Report on the Public Credit, 1790

James Madison

Hamilton's Report on a National Bank

Hamilton's Report on Manufactures

strict versus loose interpretation and the "necessary and proper" clause of the Constitution

Federalists versus Republicans

Whiskey Rebellion

citizen Edmond Genet

Jay's Treaty

Treaty of San Lorenzo (Pinckney's Treaty)

Washington's farewell address

XYZ Affair

Quasi-War with France

Alien and Sedition Acts, 1798

Virginia and Kentucky resolutions, 1798

interposition and nullification

election of 1800

Jefferson-Burr tie and the Twelfth Amendment

Handsome Lake

Fugitive Slave Law, 1793

Saint Domingue (Haiti) slave uprising

Gabriel Prosser and Gabriel's Rebellion, 1800

Eli Whitney and the cotton gin

Skill Building: Charts and Graphs

Look at the chart titled "Number and Percentage of Free Blacks, by State, 1800" on page 207 of the textbook. By studying that bar graph, you should be able to answer the following questions:

1. Had the revolutionary ideology of the Declaration of Independence resulted in the freeing of most African-Americans?

2. Had slavery been totally eliminated in any state by 1800?

3. Which northern states had made the least progress in eliminating slavery by 1800?

4. Which southern or border states had made the most progress in eliminating slavery by 1800? Which had made the least?

5. In which four states did the bulk of free blacks live in 1800?

Historical Sources

In Chapter 7 the author discusses the birth and development of opposing political parties. One source for historians writing on this topic is the newspapers that aligned themselves with either the Federalist or Republican party, like the *Gazette of the United States* and the *National Gazette*. Early in the Washington administration, Alexander Hamilton helped set up John Fenno's *Gazette of the United States* to build public opinion behind the treasury secretary's financial program. James Madison countered in the 1790s by encouraging his friend Philip Freneau to establish the *National Gazette* to arouse the people against Federalist policies. On page 198 there is a reference to the contents of these newspapers. How is the author of Chapter 7 using these historical sources? Can the historian rely on these newspapers for accurate, unbiased reporting of events in the 1790s? If not, why is the press of the 1790s still a valuable historical source?

On page 208 Gabriel's Rebellion of 1800 is discussed and a statement of one of the rebels is quoted. Where do historians gain this information? Gabriel Prosser and thirty-five of his followers were tried. James Monroe, then governor of Virginia, questioned Prosser about the uprising. Prosser would say little, but some of his codefendants did testify about their plans, motives, and intentions. These records are preserved in Documents Relating to the Trial and Execution of Gabriel in the Virginia State Historical Library. Such state historical archives afford historians much of the material they use to learn about the past.

Now look at "A Place in Time: Philadelphia in the 1790s." What illustrations of economic, social, and political developments of the 1790s can one find in this short urban history? Note the brief references to the position of black Philadelphians and to the yellow-fever epidemic in 1793. A pertinent historical source on these two subjects is a pamphlet written by two black Philadelphia clergymen, Absalom Jones and Richard Allen, *A Narrative of the Proceedings of the Black People, During the Late Awful Calamity in Philadelphia . . . 1793 . . .*, published in 1794. Today historians can look at a copy of the pamphlet in the Library of Congress, which houses a treasure trove of publications and documents pertaining to American history.

Multiple-Choice Questions

Circle the letter of the item that best completes each statement or answers the question.

1. The main purpose of the Alien and Sedition Acts was to
   a. publicize the activities of French revolutionaries in the United States.
   b. strengthen the policy of neutrality.
   c. strengthen the Republican party.
   d. suppress the Republican opposition to Federalist policies.

2. Hamilton wanted the federal government to take over in full the Revolutionary War debt of the Continental Congress and the states because he believed that
   a. this would cause a heavy loss to speculators in certificates.
   b. the payment of all such obligations was guaranteed in the Constitution.
   c. this would cause well-to-do creditors to favor the new federal government and the extension of its powers.
   d. the states unanimously favored such a policy.

3. Hamilton's financial program was designed to do all of the following *except*
   a. gain the support of the commercial classes for the new national government.
   b. encourage the rapid industrialization of the United States.
   c. pay off the national debt as quickly as possible.
   d. establish the credit of the United States at home and abroad.

4. Hamilton's national bank
   a. provoked the first clear-cut argument over the strict versus loose interpretation of the Constitution.
   b. was a fully government-owned-and-operated institution.
   c. helped the United States retire its old revolutionary debt as quickly as possible.
   d. did or was all of the above.

5. The XYZ Affair
   a. arose out of the French government's demand for a bribe as the price of negotiating.
   b. increased the popularity of the Republican party and hurt the fortunes of the Federalists.
   c. was provoked by Hamilton to increase the popularity of the Washington administration.
   d. arose out of the Whiskey Rebellion.

6. The Virginia and Kentucky resolutions
   a. attacked the Alien and Sedition Acts.
   b. were written by Madison and Jefferson.
   c. claimed the right of a state to protect its people from unconstitutional federal laws.
   d. all of the above.

7. Speculators were able to take advantage of which of these Federalist measures?
   a. the excise tax
   b. the refunding of the national debt by paying full face value of Revolutionary War bonds
   c. the tariff
   d. placing the federal capital on land donated by Virginia and Maryland

8. Which action of President John Adams angered the "High Federalists"?
   a. his handling of the XYZ Affair
   b. his signing of the Alien and Sedition Acts
   c. his decision to improve relations with France in 1799–1800
   d. his request for a larger army

9. Which of these people would probably *not* be a supporter of Jefferson's Republican party?
   a. a Virginia planter
   b. a Boston merchant
   c. a western Pennsylvania farmer
   d. a recent Irish immigrant

10. Which of the following people scored a victory over the Indians that opened Ohio to white settlement and won a promise by the British to evacuate forts in the Northwest Territory?
    a. Gabriel Prosser
    b. Anthony Wayne
    c. Stephen Girard
    d. Matthew Lyon

Short-Answer Questions

1. What problems in the West faced the new federal government in 1789?

2. Briefly describe the drafting, content, and ratification of the Bill of Rights.

3. Explain Hamilton's reasoning in support of a loose interpretation of the U.S. Constitution and Jefferson's in defense of a strict interpretation.

4. Why did farmers in western Pennsylvania object to the excise tax on whiskey? How did the Washington administration deal with their rebellion? Why?

5. Why did President Washington make his Farewell Address? What advice did it offer his fellow citizens?

6. What happened to eastern Indians in the 1790s and early 1800s, and why?

7. Explain the reasons for heightened racism and declining abolitionist sentiment in the 1790s and early 1800s.

Essay Questions

1. Discuss the rise of political parties in the United States. Did the Constitution provide for political parties? If not, when and why did the first two parties develop? Who led and supported each party?

2. Discuss the economic and financial programs of Secretary of the Treasury Alexander Hamilton. What did they include? What was Hamilton trying to accomplish? How and why did his programs politically divide Americans?

3. Discuss the deteriorating positions of African-Americans and Native Americans in the post–Revolutionary War period. How do you account for the deterioration? What were the major changes or events that marked the declining status of each group?

4. Explain how differences over foreign policy in the period 1789–1800 encouraged the development of political parties and partisanship.

5. Discuss the dangers the nation faced during the Federalist era (1789–1800) and how it overcame or survived them. In your answer be sure to include conflict among social, economic, and sectional interest groups; challenges from foreign nations; and threats to individual liberties and the Bill of Rights.

CHAPTER 8

Jeffersonianism and the Era of Good Feelings

Outline and Summary

I. Introduction

On March 4, 1801, Thomas Jefferson, without fanfare, walked to the Capitol and took the oath of office as president. His actions reflected his belief that the "pomp and circumstance" in which Washington and Adams had engaged ill-fitted republican government. Despite the partisan bitterness of the election of 1800, Jefferson, in his inaugural address, attempted to conciliate Federalists by emphasizing the principles on which most Americans agreed—federalism and republicanism.

The period 1801 to 1823 would see major changes, if not the reconciliation Jefferson hoped for. The Federalist party would slowly die out, and the Republicans would be rent by factionalism. Renewed war in Europe would again endanger America and open opportunities. Taking advantage of these, the United States would acquire new territory that doubled its size. However, sectional strife over statehood for Missouri would nearly tear that expanded nation apart.

Chapter 8 addresses these questions: (1) How did Jefferson's philosophy of government affect his administrations? (2) Why did Jefferson's Republican party split into warring factions? (3) Why did Jefferson's successor, James Madison, ask Congress to declare war on Great Britain? (4) How did war in Europe both endanger and benefit the United States.

II. The Age of Jefferson

A. Introduction

Thomas Jefferson, a complex, contradictory, and gifted individual, championed equality but owned over two hundred slaves. He distrusted power concentrated in the federal government as a danger to republican liberty, preferring the state governments, which he saw as closer and more responsive to the people. Republican liberty could best be retained by a virtuous and vigilant citizenry that put the public good ahead of selfish private interests. To Jefferson, the group that displayed those qualities were small farmers. Cities and their landless inhabitants, on the other hand, were a potential menace to the republic. Jefferson as president, whatever his philosophy, showed himself to be flexible and practical.

B. Jefferson's "Revolution"

Jefferson attempted to repeal Federalist measures that he felt were a danger to the simple republic, such as parts of Alexander Hamilton's economic program and the Alien and Sedition Acts. He reduced taxes and the national debt, primarily by slashing expenditures for the army and for the diplomatic establishment. In these ways he felt he was lifting an economic burden from hardworking farmers.

90

C. Jefferson and the Judiciary

Although Jefferson was willing to cooperate with the moderate Federalists in many ways, he attacked the underhanded Federalist move to retain control of the judiciary. Jefferson demanded that Congress repeal the Federalist-sponsored Judiciary Act of 1801 and remove the partisan Federalist judges that outgoing President Adams had just appointed. Jefferson had little success with impeachment of Federalist judges, however, gaining only one conviction and removal from the bench. The reason was that the majority in Congress apparently viewed the impeachment process as an inappropriate way to solve the problem of partisan judges. Jefferson's drive to keep additional Federalists out of the judiciary led to the landmark Supreme Court case of *Marbury* v. *Madison*. Chief Justice John Marshall used the case to claim that federal courts had the right to review laws passed by Congress—the right of judicial review. For the first time, the Supreme Court declared a portion of a law passed by Congress unconstitutional. Jefferson did not oppose the concept of judicial review, but he believed that judges should not use it for partisan purposes.

D. The Louisiana Purchase

Napoleon Bonaparte forced Spain to cede the Louisiana Territory to France. The French action alarmed Jefferson because it placed a major European power on the U.S. border and blocked the gradual expansion of the United States. The problem became especially pressing in 1802, when Spanish authorities, just before the territory's transfer to France, denied western farmers use of the port of New Orleans. Jefferson sent James Monroe and Robert R. Livingston to France with a request to buy the city. Napoleon countered with an offer to sell the entire Louisiana Territory for $15 million. Since the Constitution did not explicitly give the federal government the power to acquire new territories, and since Jefferson was wedded to strict interpretation, he briefly thought of first seeking an enabling amendment to the Constitution. His practicality won out, however, and he submitted the purchase treaty to the Senate, where it was quickly ratified.

E. The Lewis and Clark Expedition

Jefferson requested funding from Congress for an expedition across the continent to explore the new Louisiana Purchase. The party, led by Meriwether Lewis and William Clark, left St. Louis in 1804; followed the Missouri, Snake, and Columbia rivers; crossed the Rockies; and reached the Pacific. It returned with a wealth of scientific information (and some misinformation), descriptions, and maps that stimulated interest in the West.

F. The Election of 1804

Republicans in Congress renominated Jefferson for president and dropped Aaron Burr in favor of George Clinton for vice president. The Federalists chose Charles C. Pinckney and Rufus King. The successes of Jefferson's first term—doubling the size of the United States, maintaining peace, and reducing taxes and the national debt—won over many former Federalist voters, resulting in an overwhelming Republican victory.

III. *The Gathering Storm*

A. Introduction

Jefferson's second term as president was beset by problems caused by the breakdown of Republican party unity and the renewal of the Napoleonic Wars.

B. Jefferson's Coalition Fragments

Aaron Burr, Jefferson's first-term vice president, stirred up factionalism within the Republican party. Jefferson believed that Burr was the chief plotter in a conspiracy to separate the western states from the Union. The president had Burr arrested and tried for treason. At the trial, over which John Marshall presided, the jury found the charges "not proved."

C. Jefferson and the Quids

Jefferson also was attacked by another faction of Republicans known as the Quids, led by John Randolph. They criticized the president's handling of the Yazoo land scandal and other actions that they saw as compromising Republican simplicity.

D. The Suppression of American Trade

The British and French, at war with each other, forbade American ships from entering each other's ports and trading with the other side. Both powers seized U.S. ships, but the actions of the British caused greater harm because they had the larger navy and their warships often hovered just off the U.S. coast.

E. Impressment

Also, the British removed sailors on American ships and forced (pressed) them into service in the Royal Navy. When the British warship HMS *Leopard* attacked the American frigate USS *Chesapeake* near the Virginia coast and impressed four of its crewman, the country was outraged, but Jefferson still sought to avoid war.

F. The Embargo Act

Jefferson persuaded Congress to pass an embargo as a means of "peaceable coercion. " He hoped that U.S. refusal to export any goods or to buy any products from abroad would put sufficient economic pressure on Britain and France to make them respect U.S. neutral rights. Unfortunately, the cutoff of trade did not hurt them enough to change their actions, but it proved disastrous to the U.S. economy. Seamen were unemployed; merchants and farmers who depended on foreign sales were ruined. The impact was hardest on New England. An unintended consequence of the embargo was to encourage transfer of capital into domestic manufacturing, a development Jefferson had initially opposed.

G. The Election of 1808

The unpopularity of the embargo, especially in New England, revived the Federalist party. In 1808 it nominated Charles C. Pinckney to run against Republican James Madison. Although the Federalists carried much of New England, Madison won because of continued Republican strength in other sections.

H. The Failure of Peaceable Coercion

Just before Jefferson left office, Congress repealed the embargo and replaced it with the weaker Non-Intercourse Act. This law worked no better than the previous one. For the next year and a half, President Madison tried variations on the theme of peaceable coercion, such as Macon's Bill No. 2, but all failed to change British and French behavior.

By 1810 Madison faced increasing pressure from Republican congressmen from the South and West who demanded a more aggressive policy toward Britain and France. These "war hawks" resented the insults to American honor and blamed the interference in trade for the economic recession hitting their home states.

I. Tecumseh and the Prophet

The war hawks wanted the British to get out of Canada, partly because they believed the British were arming and inciting the Indians on the American frontier. Tecumseh and his brother the Prophet were two Shawnees attempting to unite the tribes of Ohio and Indiana against white settlers. They initially had no connection with the British, but after William Henry Harrison attacked the Prophet's town and won the battle at Tippecanoe, Tecumseh did join forces with England.

J. Congress Votes for War

Madison, on June 1, 1812, asked Congress to declare war on England. The vote reflected party and sectional splits. Most of the no votes came from New England Federalists, while the majority of Republicans passed the declaration.

K. The Causes of the War

The United States declared war in 1812 because of Britain's incitement of the Indians, the belief that continuing British restrictions on U.S. shipping were causing the recession in the South and West, and Madison's view that England intended to ruin America as a commercial rival.

IV. The War of 1812

A. On to Canada

In 1812 American attempts to conquer Canada failed. The British took Detroit and were routed only by Oliver H. Perry's victory on Lake Erie and William Henry Harrison's success in 1813 at the Battle of the Thames.

B. The British Offensive

In 1814 the British landed on the shores of Chesapeake Bay and marched to Washington, which they captured and burned. After they failed to take Baltimore, they broke off the campaign.

C. The Treaty of Ghent

U.S. and British commissioners met at Ghent, in Belgium, to make peace. At first the British, based on their superior military position, demanded territory from the United States. When the Americans refused, the British, anxious for peace now that they had defeated Napoleon, backed down. In December 1814 they signed a treaty with the United States that restored the prewar status quo. The United States' victory at the Battle of New Orleans, fought two weeks after the treaty was concluded, had no bearing on its terms.

D. The Hartford Convention

The unpopularity of the war in the Northeast contributed to the revival of the Federalists. In the election of 1812, antiwar Republicans and Federalists supported De Witt Clinton for president against Madison. Although Madison won reelection, Clinton carried most of the Northeast. American military losses intensified Federalist discontent to the point that, in the fall of 1814, a group of party members from New England convened at Hartford, Connecticut, and passed resolutions aimed at strengthening their region's power within the Union. The return of peace and public disapproval of the Hartford Convention led to the rapid demise of the Federalist party. In the election of 1816, the Republican presidential nominee, James Monroe, scored an easy victory over his Federalist opponent. In 1820 Monroe won reelection with every electoral vote but one.

V. The Awakening of American Nationalism

A. Madison's Nationalism and the Era of Good Feelings

The postwar period, characterized by a heightened spirit of nationalism and a new political consensus, has been called the Era of Good Feelings. As the Federalist party disappeared, the Republicans, to make the nation more economically self-sufficient, enacted many of the measures that the Federalists had earlier supported. Among these were the chartering of a new national bank and help for domestic manufacturing with a protective tariff. The sectional harmony started to break down almost immediately, however, because of the issue of slavery and its spread westward.

B. John Marshall and the Supreme Court

During the Era of Good Feelings, Chief Justice John Marshall wrote opinions that strengthened the power of the federal government at the expense of state sovereignty. Among these were *Dartmouth College* v. *Woodward*, which forbade state interference with contracts, and *McCulloch* v. *Maryland*, which favored the Hamiltonian broad interpretation of the Constitution and prohibited states from interfering with the exercise of federal powers.

C. The Missouri Compromise

National harmony crumbled in the 1819 controversy over Missouri's application for statehood. For the first time, bitter sectional debate took place over the issue of the spread of slavery because the institution had become embroiled in political and economic issues dividing North and South, Republicans and Federalists. Admitting Missouri as a slave state would upset the balance of eleven free and eleven slave states that existed in 1819 and would give the South a political advantage. The issue was settled for the time being when Congress in 1820 approved the Missouri Compromise: (1) Missouri entered the Union as a slave state; (2) Maine entered as a free state; (3) in the remainder of the Louisiana Territory slavery would be permitted only south of 36 degrees, 30 minutes latitude, the southern boundary of Missouri.

D. Foreign Policy Under Monroe

Under the leadership of president James Monroe and his able secretary of state, John Quincy Adams, the United States achieved several foreign-policy successes. Good relations with the British were cemented by the Rush-Bagot Treaty and the British-American Convention. In the 1819 Adams-Onís Treaty, Spain ceded East Florida to the United States and renounced its claims to West Florida.

E. The Monroe Doctrine

In December 1823 President Monroe proclaimed a policy later known as the Monroe Doctrine. Its purpose was to discourage European powers from helping Spain regain her lost colonies in the Americas while, at the same time, reserving the right of the United States to expand further in the Western Hemisphere. The Monroe Doctrine stated that (1) the United States would not become involved in strictly European affairs, (2) the American continents were not available for further European colonization, and (3) the United States would look upon any attempt by European countries to regain lost colonies or to interfere in the Americas as an "unfriendly act."

VI. Conclusion

In the election of 1800 the Republicans gained control of the federal government. President Jefferson in his first term cut government spending and taxes, protested Federalist stacking of the judiciary, and purchased Louisiana. His second term was beset by factionalism within his party and foreign difficulties as Britain and France, again at war, both violated U.S. neutral rights. When the policy of "peaceable coercion," initiated by Jefferson and followed by Madison, failed, Congress declared war on Britain. The War of 1812 caused sectional divisions. Federalist denunciation of the war at the Hartford Convention hastened the demise of the party. The remaining Republicans, anxious to make America economically self-sufficient, passed many of the nationalist measures once advocated by Hamiltonian Federalists: a new national bank, federally supported internal improvements, and protective tariffs. Even U.S. foreign policy, especially the Monroe Doctrine, reflected assertive nationalism. However, national harmony shattered as Congress battled over the spread of slavery and Missouri's admission as a slave state.

Vocabulary

The following terms are used in Chapter 8. To understand the chapter fully, it is important that you know what each of them means.

infidel   an unbeliever; one who does not accept a particular religion, such as Christianity

writ   legal order in writing

judicial review   right of the federal courts to declare legislative acts unconstitutional

impeach   to charge a public official, such as a judge or president, with misconduct in office; an impeachment is equivalent to an indictment, not to a conviction

caucus   a meeting of political party members to nominate candidates and/or decide on other party actions

coalition   a combination or alliance among different groups, parties, or states in support of a particular cause, individual, or purpose

internal improvements   roads, canals, and other projects to improve transportation and communication

consensus   general agreement

Identifications

After reading Chapter 8, you should be able to identify and explain the historical significance of each of the following:

Tripolitan (Barbary) pirates

Judiciary Act of 1801

midnight judges

Marbury v. *Madison*

John Marshall

Lewis and Clark Expedition

Sacajawea

Aaron Burr conspiracy

British Orders in Council and Napoleon's Continental System

impressment

Chesapeake-Leopard Affair

Embargo and Non-Intercourse acts

war hawks

John C. Calhoun

Henry Clay and the American System

Tecumseh and the Prophet

William Henry Harrison and the Battles of Tippecanoe and the Thames

Oliver H. Perry and the Battle of Lake Erie

Treaty of Ghent and the *status quo ante*

Battle of New Orleans

Hartford Convention

Era of Good Feelings

Dartmouth College v. *Woodward*

McCulloch v. *Maryland*

Missouri Compromise

John Quincy Adams

Rush-Bagot Treaty and British-American Convention, 1818

Adams-Onís, or Transcontinental, Treaty

Monroe Doctrine

Skill Building: Maps

On the map of the United States on the following page, locate each of the places listed below. How is each connected with one or more of the following historical events: U.S. treaties with Spain and France, Lewis and Clark expedition, War of 1812, sectional conflict and compromise?

East and West Florida

New Orleans

Louisiana Territory

Appalachian Mountains

Mississippi River

Missouri River

Snake River

Columbia River

St. Louis

Ohio River

Indiana Territory

Lake Erie and Lake Champlain

Chesapeake Bay

36°30 latitude

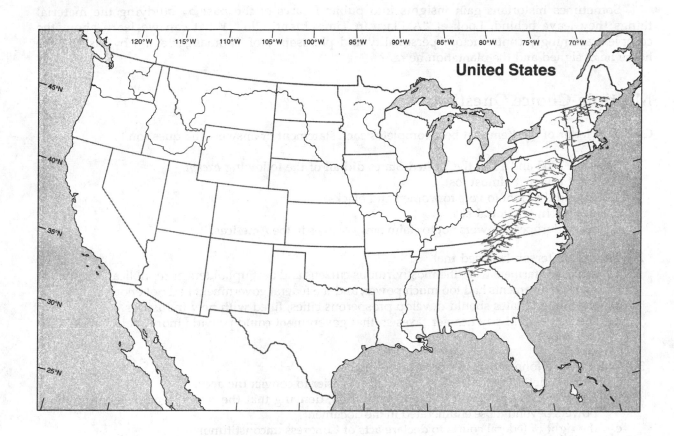

Historical Sources

Pages 218–219 of Chapter 8 give an account of the Lewis and Clark expedition. How did the author find out about the adventures of the party, the role of Sacajawea, and the mass of scientific information and some tall tales that Lewis and Clark brought back with them? Much of what we know about the expedition and its findings comes from the journals kept by Meriwether Lewis and William Clark, first published in 1814. Probably the definitive edition of the record of Lewis's and Clark's trip is the eight-volume *Original Journals of the Lewis and Clark Expedition, 1804–1806,* edited by Reuben Gold Thwaites and published in 1904–1905. A single-volume, abridged version, *The Journals of Lewis and Clark,* edited by Bernard De Voto, is available for the general reader who would like to taste the flavor of this valuable historical source.

The author of Chapter 8 also discusses the reasons for America's declaration of war on England and the sectional controversies over that war. How does the historian know which congressmen from which states voted for war? How does the author know that John C. Calhoun and other southern and western congressmen believed that British policy was damaging America's economy, or that President Madison attributed British actions to their desire to monopolize trade? The historian can read the speeches of senators and representatives and find the record of their votes in the *Debates and Proceedings in the Congress of the United States,* often cited as *Annals of Congress,* printed by the U.S. government. Madison's statement about British motives was part of his war message to Congress. Like all public communications of American presidents, it is published in the multivolume *A Compilation of the Messages and Papers of the Presidents.*

Sometimes historians gain insights into public figures of the past by studying the material things they leave behind. Look at "A Place in Time: Monticello." What can we learn about the complex, seemingly contradictory personality and philosophy of Thomas Jefferson by visiting the home he designed and the plantation he ran?

Multiple-Choice Questions

Circle the letter of the item that best completes each statement or answers the question.

1. Between 1800 and 1823, the United States did all of the following *except*
   a. fight a war it almost lost.
   b. extend the right to vote to women and blacks.
   c. double in territorial size.
   d. warn European powers not to claim new colonies in the Americas.

2. Thomas Jefferson believed that
   a. educated farmers were the most virtuous citizens and best upholders of republican liberty.
   b. state governments had too much power, and the federal government had not enough.
   c. the United States should develop prosperous cities, filled with new industries.
   d. the rich should pay heavier taxes so that government could provide more social services for the poor.

3. Chief Justice John Marshall's opinions backed
   a. a broad definition of treason that made it easier to convict the accused.
   b. a narrow interpretation of the Constitution, denying that the federal government had any powers beyond those enumerated in the document.
   c. the right of federal courts to declare acts of Congress unconstitutional.
   d. the doctrine that states could nullify illegal actions of the federal government.

4. The Embargo Act
   a. badly damaged the British economy.
   b. stimulated the growth of manufacturing in the United States.
   c. convinced the French to drop their trade restrictions against the United States.
   d. was favored by New England but resisted in the South.

5. By the terms of the Treaty of Ghent, ending the War of 1812,
   a. the United States gained Florida and some territory from Canada.
   b. the British agreed to stop impressment and other violations of U.S. neutral rights.
   c. neither the United States nor Britain gained territory or made concessions.
   d. the British agreed to evacuate New Orleans and compensate the United States for burning Washington.

6. The war hawks were
   a. mostly from New England.
   b. eager for war against Napoleon to gain the Louisiana Territory.
   c. supporters of Jefferson's and Madison's policy of economic coercion.
   d. Republicans from the West and South who wanted to take Canada from Britain and Florida from Spain.

7. Which of the following occurred during Madison's presidency?
   a. The United States sent a naval squadron against the Barbary pirates of North Africa.
   b. Congress chartered a second national bank.
   c. The United States bought Florida from Spain.
   d. Congress passed the embargo.

8. Secretary of State John Quincy Adams is associated with which of the following foreign-policy initiatives?
   a. purchasing Texas from Mexico
   b. purchasing Louisiana
   c. formulating the Monroe Doctrine and purchasing Florida
   d. British sale of the Oregon Territory to the United States for $15 million

9. During the Era of Good Feelings
   a. the Federalist party disappeared but the Republican party adopted some of its policies.
   b. the United States won a war against England.
   c. sectional and partisan conflicts became more acute.
   d. President Monroe signed new treaties of alliance and friendship with Britain and France.

10. During the War of 1812
    a. the United States successfully occupied Canada.
    b. the British captured Baltimore, Maryland.
    c. Tecumseh, the Prophet, and their Indian followers proved valuable allies to the Americans against the British.
    d. the northeastern states became increasingly unhappy about the war.

Short-Answer Questions

1. Explain what the Federalists were trying to accomplish with passage of the Judiciary Act of 1801 and appointment of the midnight judges.

2. Explain why Napoleon first forced Spain to cede Louisiana to France, and then turned around and offered to sell the territory to the United States.

3. Why did President Jefferson want to buy Louisiana from France? Why did the purchase pose a dilemma for him? How did he justify the purchase?

4. What happened at the Hartford Convention in 1814? What impact did it have on the Federalist party? Why?

5. Why did Missouri's request for statehood touch off a sectional crisis? How was the crisis resolved, at least, in the short run?

Essay Questions

1. Compare and contrast the political and economic views of the Hamiltonian Federalists and the Jeffersonian Republicans. When, why, and how did the differences between the two parties blur?

2. Thomas Jefferson's first term as president was so successful that he overwhelmingly won reelection in 1804. His second term, in contrast, was marked by frustration and failure. Discuss the achievements of Jefferson's first term and the problems that beset his second.

3. Discuss the foreign-policy achievements of President James Monroe and his secretary of state, John Quincy Adams. How do those achievements still affect the United States and its foreign policy today?

4. Why did the United States engage in a nearly disastrous war against the British from 1812 to 1814? What, if anything, did the United States gain from that war?

5. Jefferson once wrote, "What is practicable must often control pure theory." In light of that statement assess Jefferson's actions as president. How much of his policies can be explained by his philosophy of government? How much by compromise with what was practicable?

CHAPTER 9

The Transformation of American Society, 1815–1840

Outline and Summary

I. Introduction

Chapter 9 discusses the economic and social changes that took place in the United States between 1815 and 1840. Some of the questions it attempts to answer are (1) Why did westward migration accelerate after the War of 1812? (2) What caused the growth of banking during this period? (3) What brought about the transportation and industrial revolutions that occurred and how did these affect the lives of Americans? (4) Who benefited and who was hurt by the rapid economic and social transformations?

A. The Sweep West

The sweep of population westward had by 1821 added the states of Vermont, Kentucky, Tennessee, Ohio, Louisiana, Indiana, Mississippi, Illinois, Alabama, Maine, and Missouri to the Union. Although New York merchant John Jacob Astor established a fur-trading post in the Oregon territory and hardy "mountain men" like Jedidiah Smith roamed and trapped on the Great Plains and beyond, most westerners prior to 1840 settled in the region between the Appalachians and the Mississippi River.

B. Western Society and Customs

Pioneers usually migrated west with families rather than alone. Between 1790 and 1820, they clustered near the navigable rivers; only after the coming of canals and railroads in the 1820s and 1830s could they afford to fan out a bit. Westerners also tended to settle near others who had come from the same region back east. Before 1830 life in the West was crude and difficult. Easterners often looked down on westerners' lack of refinement, and westerners in turn resented eastern pretentions to gentility.

C. The Federal Government and the West

Midwestern settlement was encouraged by the Ordinance of 1785; the Northwest Ordinance; the Louisiana Purchase; the Transcontinental Treaty of 1819; the land warrants given to War of 1812 veterans; the extension of the National Road into Illinois by 1838; and the declining strength of the Indians, who by 1820 no longer received Spanish and British aid.

D. The Removal of the Indians

By the 1820s the Cherokees, Creeks, Choctaws, and Seminoles of the South were under heavy pressure to cede their lands to whites. In 1830 Andrew Jackson pushed through Congress the Indian Removal Act, which granted the president the power to move all Native Americans, by force if necessary, west of the Mississippi River. The Creeks in Georgia and Alabama had already started to migrate by that point, and in 1836 the remainder were forced out. The Choctaws and Chickasaws suffered a similar fate. After losing a war of resistance that lasted from 1835 to 1842, most Seminoles also were expelled from Florida. The Cherokees, the most assimilated of the Indians, appealed to the U.S. Supreme Court for protection. Although Chief Justice John Marshall ruled in their favor, President Jackson ignored the court and compelled the tribe to cede its land and travel the "Trail of Tears" westward. After putting up some futile resistance in the Black Hawk War, the Sac, Fox, and other Northeast Indians also had to move west of the Mississippi.

E. The Agricultural Boom

The removal of the Indians and the high prices and escalating demand for wheat and corn drew more whites than ever into the old Northwest. Eli Whitney's invention of the cotton gin in 1793 and the boundless need of the British textile industry for raw cotton had similar results in the old Southwest. After the War of 1812, southeasterners poured into Alabama and Mississippi, driving land prices skyward and tripling the nation's cotton production. By 1836 cotton accounted for two-thirds of America's foreign exports.

F. The Rise of the Market Economy

High crop prices after the War of 1812 tempted many western farmers to switch from subsistence to commercial agriculture and to borrow money to buy additional land and tools. This left them vulnerable, however, to the fluctuations of distant markets over which they had no control.

G. Federal Land Policy

Jeffersonian Republicans introduced land policies aimed at a speedy transfer of the public domain to small farmers. Between 1800 and 1820, the government cut the minimum price per acre and the minimum number of acres that could be purchased. However, most government land was sold at auction, and speculators, believing it would soon shoot up in value, often bid the price up far above the minimum. The easy availability of credit encouraged this speculation.

H. The Speculator and the Squatter

Many poor settlers who did not have the money to buy at auction simply squatted on government land. They exerted mounting pressure on Congress to grant them preemption rights over speculators and finally won their demand in 1841. Squatters, wanting to accumulate the cash to buy their farms, quickly turned to commercial agriculture. Many western farmers, after exhausting the soil's fertility growing cash crops, simply moved on to new land.

I. The Panic of 1819

Crop and western land prices plummeted and many speculators were ruined in the panic and depression of 1819. The National Bank tightened credit and called in the notes of the overextended western banks, many of which failed. The hard times experienced by agriculture and industry had long-term political effects. Many westerners hated the National Bank, blaming it for the crisis. Manufacturers redoubled their cries for high protective tariffs, and western farmers intensified their search for internal improvements that would cut transportation expenses for shipping their product to market.

J. The Transportation Revolution: Steamboats, Canals, and Railroads

Before 1820 available transportation facilities were unsatisfactory. The National Road and privately constructed turnpikes were adequate for transporting people, but moving bulky loads over them by horse-drawn wagons was slow and costly. Midwestern farmers who floated their produce downriver on flatboats to New Orleans had to travel home by foot or horseback, which took months. Robert Fulton's invention of the steamboat and the institution of regular ferry service on all of the major rivers greatly improved the transportation picture. However, rivers did not always exist where they were most needed for trade. Therefore, Americans in the 1820s began to build canals. Between 1817 and 1825, the State of New York constructed the 363-mile Erie Canal connecting Albany on the Hudson River with Buffalo on Lake Erie. The canal lowered freight rates to a fraction of what they had been and made New York City a leading outlet for midwestern produce. The Erie Canal's success encouraged dozens of other projects. The canal-building boom deflated with the depression of the late 1830s, but by 1840 some three thousand miles of railroad track had been laid and trains were beginning to supplement and compete with canal shipping.

K. The Growth of the Cities

This transportation revolution stimulated the rapid development of towns and cities. First the coming of the steamboat to western waterways caused the growth of such river port cities as Pittsburgh, Cincinnati, Louisville, St. Louis, and New Orleans. Then the Erie Canal made the fortunes of lake port cities like Buffalo, Cleveland, Detroit, Chicago, and Milwaukee, while diminishing the importance of the riverport cities. The rise of manufacturing also heightened urbanization between 1815 and 1840.

III. *The Rise of Manufacturing*

A. Causes of Industrialization

Industrialization was brought about by the Embargo Act of 1807, which induced merchants barred from foreign trade to divert their capital to founding factories. After the War of 1812 fledgling industries received protection from high tariffs, especially in the 1820s. Transportation improvements opened to manufacturers distant markets where customers quickly showed their preference for factory over homemade items. The 5 million immigrants arriving between 1790 and 1860 also stimulated industrialization by bringing technological know-how with them, such as Samuel Slater, and by providing factories with labor and customers. Relatively high wages paid to American workers also made employers eager to adopt labor-saving techniques like Eli Whitney's interchangeable parts.

B. The Faces of Industrialization

New England was the first region to industrialize because its merchants were particularly hard hit by foreign trade disruptions and it had swift-flowing rivers for waterpower and excess female farm population for labor. Textile manufacturing became its leading industry. In 1790 Samuel Slater opened the first American cotton spinning mill in Rhode Island, but the weaving was still given to women working in their homes. The Waltham and Lowell, Massachusetts mills, started by the Boston Associates, were the first to concentrate total cloth production within the factory. Originally 80 percent of the mill operatives were unmarried young women, who lived in company housing under the strict supervision of management. During the 1830s these Lowell women staged two of the largest strikes in American history to that date.

In New York City and Philadelphia manufacturing of products such as shoes, saddles, tools, rope, hats, and ready-made clothing was done in small shops as well as factories. Much of the work was still done by hand rather than machine, but increasingly production was subdivided into small, specialized tasks performed by low-paid, semiskilled or unskilled laborers, including widows and immigrants. This resulted in a declining importance for skilled artisans, who, in protest in the late 1820s, formed trade unions and "workingmen's" political parties.

IV. Equality and Inequality

A. Growing Inequality: The Rich and the Poor

The gap between the rich and the poor grew during the first half of the nineteenth century. The extremes were especially obvious in the cities, where the mansions of the wealthy lined the fashionable avenues while the poor crowded into noxious slums like New York's Five Points district. Contrary to the self-made man, rags-to-riches myth, 90 percent of the very wealthy had started out with considerable means. At the other end of the scale, cities were developing a pauperized class consisting of the aged and infirm; widows; and, in the 1840s and 1850s, destitute Irish immigrants fleeing starvation in their homeland.

B. Free Blacks in the North

Overwhelming discrimination kept most free blacks in poverty. They were generally denied the vote; educated in inferior segregated schools, if at all; forced to use separate and unequal facilities; and kept out of all but the lowest paying, least skilled occupations.

C. The "Middling Classes"

The majority of white Americans were neither rich nor poor but belonged to what was then called the middling classes. For most people in that group the standard of living rose between 1800 and 1860, although members of the middle class experienced a lot of insecurity. And like other Americans, they also exhibited a high degree of transiency, moving from neighborhood to neighborhood, city to city, and region to region.

V. The Revolution in Social Relationships

A. The Attack on the Professions

One sign that economic changes were disrupting traditional relationships and forms of authority could be seen in the intense criticism of professionals such as lawyers, doctors, and ministers between 1820 and 1850. The denial that professionals had any special expertise was particularly prevalent on the frontier.

B. The Challenge to Family Authority

Children became more inclined to question parental authority. Young men left home at an earlier age and struck out on their own. Young women increasingly made their own choice of whom to marry or even whether to marry.

C. Wives, Husbands

Relations between spouses also were evolving. Wives continued to be legally subordinate to their husbands, but under the doctrine of separate spheres, middle-class women were demanding and winning greater voice in those areas where they were deemed to be particularly competent: exerting moral influence on the family and creating within the home a calm refuge from the harsh, competitive world outside. As middle-class women gained more control over the frequency of their pregnancies, the size of white middle-class families declined markedly. However, the birthrate remained high among black and immigrant women.

D. Horizontal Allegiances and the Rise of Voluntary Associations

While the authority of fathers, husbands, professionals, and other social "superiors" waned, new relationships among persons in similar positions were forged through the proliferation of voluntary associations. Temperance and moral-reform societies of white middle-class women, union and workingmen's parties, and black fraternal and other clubs encouraged sociability among members and were attempts to enhance their influence on outside groups.

VI. *Conclusion*

After 1815 white Americans' westward movement speeded up due to heightened European demand for agricultural products, especially cotton. Federal government policies, such as removal of eastern Indians to the west of the Mississippi River and sale of land on more generous terms, also hastened western settlement. Improved transportation—introduction of the steamboat and building of canals and railroads—facilitated the shipment of western farmers' produce to eastern and European markets. This transportation revolution, in turn, encouraged the growth of cities, commerce, manufacturing, and industrialization. The economic transformations made some Americans wealthy and impoverished others and affected social relations within the family and society.

Vocabulary

The following terms are used in Chapter 9. To understand the chapter fully, it is important that you know what each of them means.

mulatto   the offspring of one white and one black parent; a person of mixed black and white ancestry

public domain   the land owned by the government

injunction   a court order to a person or persons to do or not to do a particular thing

annuities   specified payments made at intervals for a period of time, often for life

subsistence agriculture   growing crops to feed and satisfy the needs of the farmer and his family, not cash crops for sale on the market

commercial agriculture   growing crops for sale on the market; farming as a business, big or small

squatter   one who settles on land, especially public or new land, without title or right

preemption   the act or right of purchasing before others or in preference to others

specie   gold, silver, or coined money (as opposed to paper)

capital   wealth (money) used or capable of being used in the production of more wealth

technology   the industrial arts; technical advances in production methods

antebellum   before the war; pre–Civil War

myth   a collective belief that is built up in response to the wishes of the group rather than having a base in fact

pauperism   the condition of being without means of support and living on public or private charity

transiency   moving frequently from place to place (as opposed to establishing permanent residency over long periods)

Identifications

After reading Chapter 9, you should be able to identify and explain the historical significance of each of the following:

transportation revolution

John Jacob Astor

"mountain men": Kit Carson, Jedidiah Smith, and Jim Beckwourth

Five Civilized Tribes

Indian Removal Act, 1830

Cherokee Nation v. *Georgia* and *Worchester* v. *Georgia*

Trail of Tears

Black Hawk War

Eli Whitney, the cotton gin, and interchangeable parts

Panic of 1819

Robert Fulton, the *Clermont,* and the Livingston-Fulton monopoly

Gibbons v. *Ogden*

Erie Canal

Samuel Slater

the putting out system and cottage industry

Boston Associates, Waltham and Lowell mills

Alexis de Tocqueville, *Democracy in America*

New York's Five Points district

middling classes

individualism

doctrine of separate spheres

Andrew Jackson Downing

Skill Building: Maps

On the map of the United States on the following page:

1. Indicate the states that entered the Union between 1790 and 1821.

2. Indicate the main area of western settlement between 1815 and 1840.

3. Locate each of the following rivers or lakes and explain its economic importance to white Americans between 1815 and 1840:

   Columbia

   Missouri

   Mississippi

   Hudson

   Ohio

   Great Lakes

4. Locate each of the following internal improvements and explain its economic and political impact on American life between 1815 and 1840:

   National Road

   Erie Canal

   Baltimore and Ohio Railroad

   Boston and Worcester Railroad

   Massachusetts Western Railroad

5. Indicate the areas from which the Five Civilized Tribes were removed and the areas in which they were resettled between 1820 and 1840.

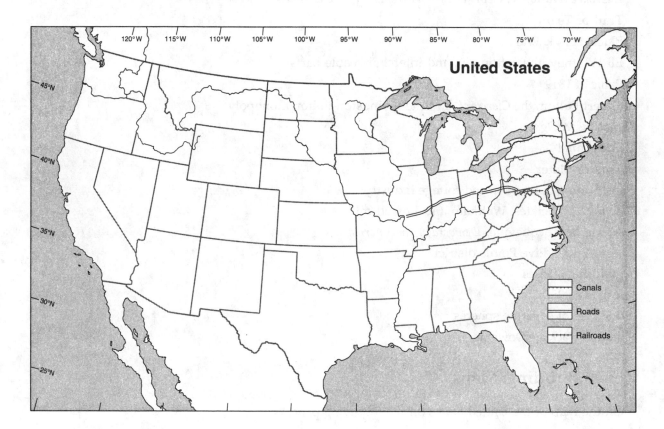

Historical Sources

The workers and working conditions in the Waltham and Lowell textile mills are described on pages 252–253 of Chapter 9. Where did the author find this information? There are numerous historical sources on Lowell and other New England mills, but they do not all paint the same picture. Lowell employees produced their own periodicals: *Operatives' Magazine* (1841–1842), *Lowell Offerings* (1840–1845), and *New England Offerings* (1848–1850). The articles appearing in these publications give quite a favorable view of conditions in Lowell. This makes it difficult to account for the walkout of eight hundred women in 1834 and fifteen hundred in 1836. A group of dissident workers denounced the *Lowell Offerings* as "a mouthpiece of the corporations," which had to approve all items that appeared in it. These unhappy laborers started rival publications, *Factory Tracts* and the *Voice of*

Industry, that stressed the oppressiveness of life in the mills. In 1845 a Massachusetts legislative committee held public hearings on labor conditions in the textile mills. Female workers testified that the overly long workdays and insufficient pay had damaged their health. Management officials, on the other hand, spoke of the contented farm girls who worked a few years in the mills, saved hundreds of dollars from their pay, and then returned home to marry with this nest egg. In addition, European visitors and a Lowell Unitarian minister published accounts of life in the town and mills, which were mostly laudatory. But two thousand textile workers signed petitions sent to the Massachusetts House of Representatives pleading for a ten-hour-day law and other factory reforms. Obviously, such conflicting sources do not make the historian's task easy. In writing about the past, the historian, inevitably influenced by his or her own beliefs and predilections, weighs and evaluates evidence and chooses among available sources.

Just as there are conflicting sources concerning Lowell, Massachusetts, so there are about the forced removal of the Cherokee from Georgia to Oklahoma. Look at "A Place in Time: The Trail of Tears." Who gave the removal the name "trail of tears"? Why? How do the accounts of the journey by the Cherokee compare and contrast with those of an army officer who participated and of President Martin Van Buren?

Multiple-Choice Questions

Circle the letter of the item that best completes each statement or answers the question.

1. Andrew Jackson's remark, "John Marshall has made his decision; now let him enforce it," refers to the president's intention to
    a. destroy the National Bank despite the Supreme Court ruling upholding its constitutionality.
    b. use force, if necessary, to make South Carolina obey federal laws that it thought unconstitutional.
    c. move the Cherokees west of the Mississippi River, regardless of Supreme Court rulings.
    d. disregard Chief Justice Marshall's ruling in *Gibbons* v. *Ogden*.

2. By 1840 about what portion of Americans lived between the Appalachian Mountains and the Mississippi River?
    a. one-quarter
    b. one-third
    c. one-half
    d. two-thirds

3. Which of the following was most responsible for the spread of cotton growing into the old Southwest?
    a. the discovery of methods for getting sea-island cotton to flourish in the interior uplands
    b. the removal of the Five Civilized Tribes
    c. the adoption of a homestead law making the available land free to qualified settlers
    d. Eli Whitney's invention of the cotton gin

4. Which of the following statements about the Erie Canal is correct?
    a. It linked New York City through inland waterways to Ohio and made the city a major outlet for midwestern produce.
    b. It and the National Road were the only major internal improvements financed by the federal government before the Civil War.
    c. It contributed to the growing importance of Mississippi River cities such as New Orleans.
    d. It had little impact on shipping costs.

5. As a result of the Panic of 1819,
   a. western farmers returned to subsistence farming.
   b. many westerners hated the National Bank.
   c. westerners became reluctant to see federal tax monies spent on expensive internal improvements.
   d. industrialists denounced high U.S. tariffs for ruining their sales abroad.

6. In the 1820s and 1830s the majority of the workers in the Lowell and Waltham textile mills were
   a. children from poor immigrant families.
   b. Irish and French-Canadian immigrants.
   c. displaced artisans and skilled workers.
   d. young women from New England farms.

7. Which of the following statements about the professions in the late 1840s is correct?
   a. Lawyers, doctors, and clergymen were highly paid and respected.
   b. Women were entering the professions in significant numbers.
   c. No state required a person to have medical education or a license to be a doctor.
   d. Increasing numbers of doctors, lawyers, and ministers moved to the West because they were most needed and valued there.

8. By the mid-1830s which of the following accounted for two-thirds of America's foreign exports?
   a. wheat and corn
   b. textiles
   c. cotton
   d. farm machinery

9. The transportation revolution in the years after the War of 1812 contributed to the growth of all of the following *except*
   a. industry in the Deep South.
   b. towns and cities in the North and West.
   c. new markets for northeastern manufacturers.
   d. commercial agriculture in the West.

10. The majority of the immigrants who arrived in the United States in the 1840s and 1850s were from
    a. England and Scotland.
    b. Italy and Eastern Europe.
    c. Ireland and Germany.
    d. Asia and Latin America.

Short-Answer Questions

1. Explain the developments between 1815 and 1840 that encouraged white settlement in the Midwest.
2. What stimulated northeastern manufacturing in the years after the War of 1812?
3. Explain why New England led the way in industrialization.
4. Compare and contrast manufacturing in New England with that in New York and Philadelphia.
5. In the period 1815–1840, how much truth was there to the rags-to-riches idea?
6. What changes occurred in the economic and social status of artisans and skilled workers in the period 1815–1840?

Essay Questions

1. Discuss the transportation revolution of the period 1815–1840. What changes took place? What was the impact of those changes on the country economically, politically, and socially?

2. Discuss the doctrine of separate spheres for women. What changes, if any, did the doctrine produce in the lives of white middle-class, white working-class, and black and immigrant women?

3. Alexis de Tocqueville in his *Democracy in America* was impressed by the "general equality of condition among the people." Writing about the same period, New York merchant Philip Hone stated "the two extremes of costly luxury in living, expensive establishments, and improvident waste are presented in daily and hourly contrast with squalid misery and hopeless destitution." How do you account for these very different assessments? Which man came closer to the truth? Why?

4. Discuss federal government policy toward Native Americans during the period 1815–1840.

5. Chapter 9 states that "the pre–Civil War period witnessed the widespread substitution of horizontal allegiances for vertical allegiances." What does this mean, and what evidence is offered in the chapter to support the claim?

CHAPTER 10

Politics, Religion, and Reform in the Age of Jackson

Outline and Summary

I. Introduction

After reading Chapter 10, you should be able to answer the following questions: (1) How were American politics democratized between 1800 and 1840? (2) Why was Andrew Jackson so popular with voters? (3) How and why did the Democratic and Whig parties emerge? (4) What new assumptions about human nature did religious and reform leaders of the 1830s make?

II. The Transformation of American Politics, 1824–1832

In 1824 only one political party existed, the Republican, but it was fragmenting because of pressures produced by the industrialization of the Northeast, the spread of cotton growing in the South, and westward expansion. Out of this fragmentation grew two new political parties. On the whole, those who retained Jefferson's distrust of strong federal government and preferred states' rights became Democrats, while those who favored an active federal government that encouraged economic development became Whigs. Both Democratic and Whig politicians had to adapt to the democratic idea of politics as the expression of the will of the common man rather than "an activity that gentlemen conducted for the people."

B. Democratic Ferment

Politics became more democratic as property qualifications for voting were eliminated, written ballots replaced voting aloud, appointive offices became elective, and presidential electors were chosen by the people. This broadening of suffrage was often brought about by competition between Republicans and Federalists in the 1790s and early 1800s. "Wherever one party was in a minority, it sought to increase the number of eligible voters in order to turn itself into the majority party."

C. The Election of 1824

The fragmenting Republican party could not agree on a single nominee for president. Instead, four Republicans ran. Andrew Jackson received the most popular and electoral votes, but not a majority. Therefore, as the Constitution requires, the House of Representatives had to choose among the three top contenders—Jackson, John Quincy Adams, and William Crawford. Henry Clay, who came in fourth, used his considerable influence with Congress to gain the selection of John Quincy Adams. President Adams in turn appointed Clay his secretary of state. Jackson supporters charged that a "corrupt bargain" had been made, and that charge hung like a cloud over the Adams administration.

D. John Quincy Adams as President

President Adams tried to encourage economic growth, but he was a poor politician with little interest in playing the role of party leader in a democratic age.

E. The Rise of Andrew Jackson

Andrew Jackson's victory over the British in the Battle of New Orleans in 1815 made him a popular hero. At a time of "vague but widespread discontent" with Washington, Jackson's position as political outsider also endeared him to the public. Jackson supporters like Martin Van Buren began to build a strong political organization that increasingly called itself the Democratic party. The Democrats in 1828 nominated Jackson for president. Those who remained loyal to Adams called themselves National Republicans and renominated him in 1828.

F. The Election of 1828

Although Jackson was a wealthy planter when he ran for president, the Democrats portrayed him as a man of the people opposing Adams the aristocrat. Jackson won the election with this common-man appeal. His victory also showed a clear sectional split, with the South and Southwest going heavily for Jackson and New England going mostly for Adams.

G. Jackson in Office

Jackson did not initiate the spoils system, but he defended and practiced it on the grounds that frequent rotation in office gave more people a chance to serve. He also opposed federal support for internal improvements, as demonstrated in his Maysville Road veto. While southerners liked that stand, they resented his lack of action against the 1828 "Tariff of Abominations," which protected northern manufacturers and western farmers from foreign competition but raised the price that southerners had to pay for finished products.

H. Nullification

The tariff issue prepared the way for a break between Jackson and his vice president, John C. Calhoun, who was becoming the chief spokesman for the southern planter class. Calhoun wrote and circulated the *South Carolina Exposition and Protest* in opposition to the Tariff of 1828. In it he argued that protective tariffs were unconstitutional and that states had the right to nullify federal laws that violated the U.S. Constitution.

I. Jackson Versus Calhoun

In November 1832 South Carolina, acting on Calhoun's doctrine, nullified the Tariff of 1828 and the slightly less protectionist Tariff of 1832 and forbade collection of customs duties at its ports. Jackson denounced the state's defiance and threatened to use the army and navy to enforce federal laws. A clash of arms was avoided only by the Compromise of 1833, proposed by Henry Clay. South Carolina rescinded its nullification, and Congress passed a new tariff law that gradually lowered duties over the next nine years.

J. The Bank Veto

Jackson disliked all banks and the issuance of paper money, and he particularly hated the Second Bank of the United States. He regarded it as a privileged monopoly. This national bank, which controlled the nation's credit and was the depository for federal government monies, was run by its private stockholders, "Monied Capitalists," with little control from the federal government. In 1832

Nicholas Biddle, president of the Second Bank, applied for its recharter. The recharter bill passed Congress, but Jackson vetoed it, denouncing the bank for making "the rich richer and the potent more powerful."

K. The Election of 1832

In 1832, the Democrats named Jackson and Martin Van Buren for president and vice president, respectively, while the National Republicans ran Henry Clay. Clay opposed Jackson's record and advocated instead his American System of protective tariffs, rechartering of the national bank, and federally supported internal improvements. Jackson won easily and was ready to complete his destruction of the Second Bank.

III. *The Bank Controversy and the Second Party System*

A. The War on the Bank

Jackson quickly tried to bankrupt the Second Bank by removing federal government deposits and distributing them to accounts in state-chartered banks. The "pet banks" that received the deposits, now having no restraint on them from the defunct national bank, extended much more credit and issued many more bank notes (paper money). This loosening of credit touched off a period of headlong economic expansion, reckless speculation, and rapid inflation. These results dismayed Jackson and other Democrats who opposed use of paper money and bank credit.

B. The Rise of Whig Opposition

During Jackson's second term, the National Republicans changed their name to Whigs. They began to attract broader support, including southerners angry over Jackson's denunciation of nullification; temperance and public-school reformers; anti-immigrant and anti-Catholic Protestants; followers of the Anti-Masonry movement, and the commercial community of merchants, manufacturers, and bankers.

C. The Election of 1836

The Democrats ran Martin Van Buren for president in 1836; the Whigs, unable to agree on a single nominee, ran four candidates. The Democrats claimed the Whigs did this so that no man would receive a majority of the electoral votes, putting the choice into the House of Representatives, where one of their nominees might win. Democratic fears were not borne out because Van Buren won a clear majority.

D. The Panic of 1837

Just as Van Buren was inaugurated, the country's economy went into a severe depression. Its causes were both international and national. Jackson's bank policies had produced a wave of speculation and inflation that so alarmed him that in July 1836 he issued the Specie Circular, a proclamation that barred the purchase of government-owned land with anything but gold. This move burst the speculative bubble and contributed to the panic and depression that followed.

E. The Search for Solutions

President Van Buren, reflecting the antibank, hard-money stand, dealt with the depression by divorcing the federal government from banking. In 1840 he signed the Independent Treasury bill, which provided that federal government money would be kept in its own treasury instead of being deposited in banks.

F. The Election of 1840

The Democrats renominated Van Buren in 1840. The Whigs chose the hero of Tippecanoe, William Henry Harrison, for president and John Tyler of Virginia for vice president. The Whigs adopted the popular appeal-to-the-common-man campaign techniques pioneered by the Democrats in the previous decade. These campaign tactics, along with Van Buren's unpopularity caused by the depression, gave the election to Harrison.

G. The Second Party System Matures

Between 1836 and 1840, the number of people who voted increased by 60 percent. This rapid increase in voter interest was caused by popular campaign techniques, strong contrast and competition between rival parties, and controversial issues like tariffs and banking, all of which characterized the mature second party system.

IV. *The Rise of Popular Religion*

A. Introduction

In the 1820s and 1830s, Americans turned to preachers who rejected the Calvinist belief in predestination. Just as politics was becoming more democratic, so was religious doctrine. The primary message was that any individual could be saved through his or her own efforts and faith. This democratic transformation was produced in part by a series of religious revivals known as the Second Great Awakening.

B. The Second Great Awakening

From New England the Second Great Awakening moved rapidly to frontier areas where thousands gathered at religious camp meetings. These frontier revivals helped to promote law and order and diminish the violence prevalent in new western areas.

C. Eastern Revivals

By the 1820s the center of religious revivals had moved east again and was particularly strong in an area of western New York known as the Burned-Over District. The revivalist leader Charles G. Finney preached that, rather than being naturally depraved, humans were capable of living without sin once they experienced an emotional religious conversion.

D. Critics of Revivals: The Unitarians

In New England the educated and wealthy were often repelled by the emotional excesses of revivalism and turned instead to Unitarianism. This denomination preached that goodness should be cultivated by a gradual process of character building and by emulating the life and teachings of Jesus. Although the Unitarians were critical of the revivalists, both shared the belief that humans could shape their own destiny and improve their behavior.

E. The Rise of Mormonism

Joseph Smith started Mormonism in the 1820s in the Burned-Over District. He and his followers founded a model city at Nauvoo, Illinois, but when they began the practice of polygyny, they were prosecuted by authorities and attacked by a mob that murdered Smith. The Mormons continued to make converts, however, many of whom followed their new leader, Brigham Young, to the Great Salt Lake area of Utah. There they created an independent, cooperative republic, the State of Deseret.

F. The Shakers

Started by Mother Ann Lee, the Shakers also founded cooperative religious communities. The Shakers and Mormons were unusual in that they rejected economic individualism and tried to withdraw from American society. Most of the religious revivalists encouraged their followers to get ahead economically, stay in society, and improve it and themselves. This message inspired many of the reformers of the period.

V. *The Age of Reform*

A. Introduction

The reform movements were strongest in New England and in areas of the Midwest settled by New Englanders.

B. The War on Liquor

The temperance movement began by preaching moderation in the use of liquor. With the formation of the American Temperance Society, however, the movement began to demand total abstinence and prohibition laws. Most members of temperance societies were middle class, though in the 1840s the Washington Temperance Societies attracted workers. The movement was successful in cutting per capita consumption of alcohol in half between the 1820s and 1840s.

C. Public School Reform

Secretary of the Massachusetts Board of Education Horace Mann advocated many educational innovations. These included state tax support of schools, grouping pupils into classes by age and level of competence, longer school terms, use of standardized textbooks, and compulsory attendance laws. Despite opposition from various groups, many northern states adopted these reforms because they were backed by three powerful constituencies: businesses that needed disciplined, literate workers; workingmen's groups that saw education as a road to social mobility; and native-born Americans who viewed public schools as an instrument for assimilating immigrant children.

D. Abolition

Opposition to slavery in the 1820s came mostly from black Americans. Not until 1831, when William Lloyd Garrison started publishing *The Liberator*, was there a militant white abolitionist movement. Most northern whites in the 1830s and 1840s, however, were hostile to the abolitionists. Moreover, the American Anti-Slavery Society, founded in 1833, suffered from internal quarrels between its Garrisonian wing and its New York and western wings. The main points of dispute were whether to support rights for women as well as blacks and whether to take abolitionism into politics. Despite hostility and internal division, the abolitionist movement kept the issue of slavery alive, put the South on the defensive, and gained supporters for the side issue of the constitutional rights of free expression and petition.

E. Women's Rights

Many of the women's rights leaders began their reform careers in the abolitionist movement. When women were denied full participation in that movement, Elizabeth Cady Stanton and Lucretia Mott in 1848 called a women's rights convention in Seneca Falls, New York. The convention adopted a Declaration of Sentiments, which launched the feminist movement. Thereafter, women gained a few rights, but they did not get the vote until 1920.

F. Penitentiaries and Asylums

In the 1820s and 1830s, religious revivalists and reformers came to believe that crime, poverty, and deviancy were caused by failures of parental guidance that could be mended by institutions providing the proper discipline and environment. Following that belief, reformers created penitentiaries and workhouses for criminals and the indigent. Dorothea Dix fought for the establishment of insane asylums to treat the mentally ill.

G. Utopian Communities

A few reformers founded "ideal" or "utopian" communities to demonstrate ways of life that they thought were superior to those prevailing in antebellum America. Among these model communities were New Harmony, Hopedale, and Brook Farm. Most of these settlements were short-lived.

VI. Conclusion

In the 1820s and 1830s politics and religion responded increasingly to the common man. The enlarged electorate, seeing Andrew Jackson as the champion of the ordinary American, swept him into the presidency. However, Jackson's stands on federally financed internal improvements, protective tariffs, nullification, and the national bank divided citizens and led to the rise of the second party system—Democrats versus Whigs. The Panic of 1837 furthered the partisan split. Meanwhile reformers offered a variety of proposals to unleash the basic goodness of humans and perfect society. Though initially avoiding "corrupt" politics, reformers by the 1840s were starting to enter the political arena to advance their particular aims.

Vocabulary

The following terms are used in Chapter 10. To understand the chapter fully, it is important that you know what each of them means.

suffrage   the vote; the right to vote

nullify   to render or declare legally void or inoperative

itinerant   one who travels from place to place

utopian   founded upon or involving perfection in law, politics, and human relations

deviancy   behavior differing from the normal, accepted behavior and/or morality of society

indigence   neediness, poverty

Identifications

After reading Chapter 10, you should be able to identify and explain the historical significance of each of the following:

Henry Clay and the American System

second American party system

spoils system

"Tariff of Abominations," 1828

John C. Calhoun and the *South Carolina Exposition and Protest*

Compromise of 1833

Nicholas Biddle and the Bank of the United States

"pet banks"

Specie Circular

Long Cabin campaign, "Tippecanoe and Tyler too," and the election of 1840

Second Great Awakening

Burned-Over District

Charles G. Finney and "perfectionism"

William Ellery Channing and Unitarianism

Joseph Smith, Brigham Young, and Mormonism

Lyman Beecher and the American Temperance Society

Horace Mann

William Lloyd Garrison, *The Liberator*, and the American Anti-Slavery Society

Frederick Douglass

Sojourner Truth

James G. Birney and the Liberty party

Angelina and Sarah Grimké

John Quincy Adams and the "gag rule"

Elizabeth Cady Stanton, Lucretia Mott, the Seneca Falls convention, and the Declaration of Sentiments

penitentiaries and the "Auburn and Pennsylvania systems"

Dorothea Dix

Robert Owen and New Harmony

Transcendentalists, Brook Farm, and *The Dial*

John Humphrey Noyes and Oneida

Skill Building: Maps

On the map of the New York and New England, on the following page, locate each of the places listed below. How is each connected with the religious and reform movements of the Age of Jackson?

Burned-Over District

Albany

Buffalo

Erie Canal

Hudson River

Lake Erie

Seneca Falls

Oneida

Boston

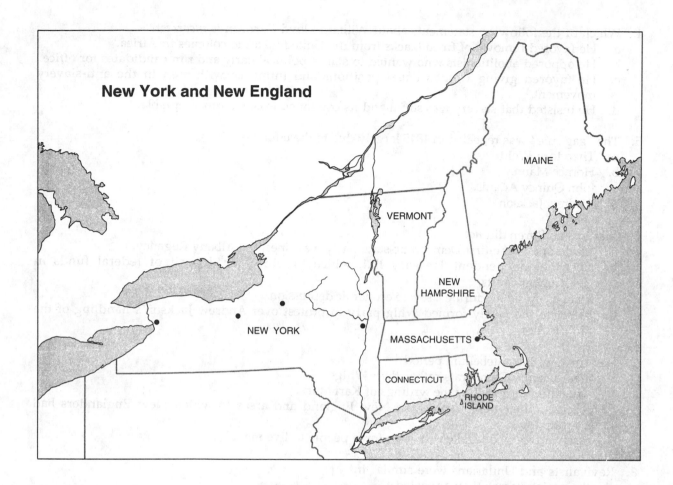

Multiple-Choice Questions

Circle the letter of the item that best completes each statement or answers the question.

1. The immediate result of Jackson's distribution of federal funds to state banks was to
   a. bring about rapid economic expansion, speculation, and inflation.
   b. increase the power of the Second Bank of the United States.
   c. make the purchase of land more difficult.
   d. increase the effectiveness of the Specie Circular.

2. The *South Carolina Exposition and Protest* was drawn up in opposition to the
   a. Missouri Compromise.
   b. spoils system.
   c. "Tariff of Abominations."
   d. Compromise of 1833.

3. All of the following were founded as utopian communities *except*
   a. New Harmony, Indiana.
   b. Oneida, New York.
   c. Brook Farm, Massachusetts.
   d. Rochester, New York.

4. Which of the following statements about William Lloyd Garrison is *incorrect*?
   a. He favored removal of freed blacks from the United States to colonies in Africa.
   b. He opposed abolitionists who wanted to start a political party and run candidates for office.
   c. He favored giving women equal positions and influence with men in the anti-slavery movement.
   d. He insisted that slavery was sinful and its continued existence unacceptable.

5. The "gag rule" was repealed in 1845 largely due to the efforts of
   a. Theodore Weld.
   b. Horace Mann.
   c. John Quincy Adams.
   d. Andrew Jackson.

6. Martin Van Buren did *not*
   a. create one of the first Democratic state party machines, the Albany Regency.
   b. sign the Independent Treasury Bill, which provided for deposit of federal funds in government vaults.
   c. serve as president during a severe economic depression.
   d. defect to the newly formed Whig party in protest over Andrew Jackson's handling of the nullification crisis.

7. Reformers of the antebellum period
   a. were usually Democrats rather than Whigs.
   b. were often inspired by the writings of Karl Marx.
   c. received their best response in New England and areas to which New Englanders had migrated.
   d. rarely advocated legal coercion to force people to live morally.

8. Revivalists and Unitarians were similar in
   a. the social classes they appealed to.
   b. their emotionalism.
   c. their belief that human behavior could be changed for the better.
   d. the cities and towns where most of their followers lived.

9. Which of the following quotations is *not* correctly paired with its source?
   a. "Our Union: It must be preserved." John C. Calhoun's *South Carolina Exposition and Protest*
   b. It makes "the rich richer and the potent more powerful." Andrew Jackson's veto message of the recharter of the Bank of the United States
   c. "I will not equivocate—I will not excuse—I will not retreat a single inch—AND I WILL BE HEARD." William Lloyd Garrison's *The Liberator*
   d. "All men and women are created equal." The Declaration of Sentiments of the Seneca Falls Convention

10. The Seneca Falls Declaration of Sentiments called for
    a. state tax support for public schools.
    b. equal rights for women.
    c. immediate abolition of slavery.
    d. humane treatment of the mentally ill and establishment of insane asylums for their care.

Short-Answer Questions

1. Explain the ways in which politics became more democratic in the 1820s and 1830s. What were the effects of greater popular participation in politics on parties and politicians?

2. Why were John Quincy Adams and Henry Clay accused of entering into a "corrupt bargain" in the election of 1824? How did that charge affect Adams's presidency?

3. Explain why the South disliked high tariffs and what John C. Calhoun proposed to do about such protective import duties.

4. Discuss the role Henry Clay played in the Compromise of 1833. Did the compromise settle the nullification question?

5. Why did Andrew Jackson hate the Second Bank of the United States? What actions did he take to destroy it?

Essay Questions

1. Andrew Jackson deserves to be ranked among America's greatest presidents. Accept or refute this statement and back up your position with a discussion of Jackson's policies and actions as president.

2. Discuss the origins and development of the second party system. Which parties were involved? Who supported each of them? What, if anything, did they stand for? What impact did their actions have on voter interest and participation in politics?

3. Discuss the reform movements of the antebellum period. Who participated? What inspired the reformers? What assumptions did they make? What were their aims and accomplishments?

4. Discuss the rise of "popular religion" in antebellum America. In what ways did religious doctrine become democratized? What assumptions did the new theologies make? How did these assumptions affect religious, social, and political life?

5. Compare and contrast the positions of Jacksonian Democrats and Whig supporters of Henry Clay's American System on the issues of the proper role of the federal government, protective tariffs, internal improvements, and banking. How do you account for their similarities and differences?

CHAPTER 11
Life, Leisure, and Culture, 1840–1860

Outline and Summary

I. Introduction

In the 1840s and 1850s most Americans believed God had ordained that man should progress, morally and materially. The means to progress of both kinds was through technology, which Americans defined as "the application of science to improve the conveniences of life." Chapter 11 covers the changes in the everyday lives of ordinary citizens brought about by the new technology of the period 1840 to 1860 as well as looking at the ways people responded to those transformations. After reading the chapter you should be able to answer the following questions: (1) How did technology transform life in the United States between 1840 and 1860? (2) In what ways did technology unite and in what ways divide the nation? (3) How did new technology and an expanded marketplace affect artistic and intellectual life in America? (4) Which aspects of technological change did artists and intellectuals applaud and which did they condemn?

II. Technology and Economic Growth

A. Introduction

The steam engine, cotton gin, reaper, sewing machine, telegraph, and use of interchangeable parts in manufacturing transformed American life in the pre–Civil War decades. This new technology increased productivity and eased travel and communication, which in turn brought down costs and prices. As a result, most Americans between 1840 and 1860 enjoyed improved standards of living. But the new technology hurt other Americans. The cotton gin encouraged expansion of the plantation-slave economy. Sewing machines and new manufacturing techniques rendered traditional crafts and the artisans who practiced them obsolete.

B. Agricultural Advancement

Between 1830 and 1860 settlers moved onto the grasslands of Indiana, Michigan, and Illinois, where John Deere's steel-tipped plow, developed in 1837, aided them in breaking the tough prairie sod. When Cyrus McCormick started to mass-produce mechanical reapers in 1847, farmers could harvest grain seven times faster than before, with half the labor. This made wheat the dominant crop of the Midwest. Although Americans quickly adopted these laborsaving inventions, they generally farmed wastefully, rapidly depleting soil and then moving to virgin land. Only in the East did some farmers introduce fertilizers to increase their yields to the point where they could compete with those of the new western fields.

C. Technology and Industrial Progress

Americans of the antebellum period readily invested in new technology. A most important advance was Eli Whitney's principle of using interchangeable parts. Manufacturing such parts was greatly facilitated by improved machine tools. Readiness to invest in innovations, interchangeable parts, and better machine tools resulted in rapid acceptance, mass production, and use of new inventions such as Samuel Colt's revolving pistol, Elias Howe's sewing machine, and Samuel F. B. Morse's telegraph.

D. The Railroad Boom

The desire to conquer time and space with technology encouraged Americans to invest heavily in railroad development. By 1860 the United States had thirty thousand miles of track, more than the rest of the world combined. Most of the new rail lines linked the East and Midwest. As a result, much of the produce of the Midwest, which had formerly been shipped downriver and out of the port of New Orleans, was now shipped via railroads radiating from Chicago eastward. These railroads stimulated settlement of the Midwest; growth of wheat farming there; and the development of cities, towns, and industry. As America's first big business, the railroads pioneered new forms of financing in the 1850s, particularly the sale of stock and other securities. Many of the transactions were handled through Wall Street, making New York the nation's leading capital market.

E. Rising Prosperity

Technological improvements reduced the price of commodities to consumers, which in turn contributed to an average 25 percent rise in the real income of American workers between 1840 and 1860. The increased annual income of working families also was attributable to the use of steam power, which allowed factories to operate in all seasons and therefore offer more work to laborers. Furthermore, the growth of towns and cities that accompanied industrialization opened new employment opportunities for women and children, who often had to work to supplement the inadequate wages of the husband and father. These economic opportunities, plus the comforts and conveniences of urban life, attracted a steady stream of Americans to cities.

III. *The Quality of Life*

A. Introduction

Technological advances improved the quality of life for those in the middle class. They now enjoyed luxuries formerly reserved to the rich, but these changes were slower to reach the poor. Medical knowledge lagged behind the strides made in industry and agriculture, leaving Americans to look to popular health fads for the prevention and cure of illness.

B. Dwellings

In the cities the typical dwellings of the period were row houses. The row houses that the middle class lived in became increasingly elaborate, while the poor were forced into crowded row houses that were further subdivided by several families and boarders. The worst of these were called tenements. On the frontier, one-room log cabins were common. These were replaced by the much more comfortable balloon-frame houses as the community matured and prospered.

The upper and middle classes, between 1840 and 1860, favored ornate home furnishings in the rococo style. The wealthy imported such furniture from Europe, but the middle class bought mass-produced imitations from new furniture manufacturing centers like Cincinnati and Grand Rapids.

C. Conveniences and Inconveniences

Industrialization and improved transportation affected home heating, cooking, and diet. By the 1840s coal-burning stoves were replacing fireplaces for heating and cooking. Although these stoves were more convenient and made it possible to cook several dishes simultaneously, coal burning contributed to fouling the urban environment. Railroads brought fresh produce to city dwellers, but only the rich could afford fruits out of season. Because home iceboxes were rare before 1860, most Americans still ate meat preserved by salting rather than fresh meat.

By the 1840s and 1850s, cities such as New York began to construct aqueducts, reservoirs, and water works. These brought pure water to street hydrants, but the majority of houses were not yet hooked up to the water mains. As a result, Americans of the period bathed infrequently. Because few cities had sanitation departments and most people used outdoor privies, American cities often stank.

D. Disease and Health

American cities also were racked by recurring epidemics of cholera, yellow fever, and other diseases. By the 1850s most big cities had established municipal boards of health to try to prevent these outbreaks, but the boards had almost no power. Furthermore, the medical profession, which was divided and uncertain about the causes and cures of epidemic diseases, was held in low esteem. In the 1840s the development of anesthetics by Crawford Long and William T. G. Morton advanced the field of surgery, but the achievements of surgeons were still blighted by their failure to recognize the importance of disinfection.

E. Popular Health Movements

Since neither public-health boards nor doctors seemed able to prevent disease, many Americans put their faith in various popular therapies, such as hydropathy and the Grahamite regimen.

F. Phrenology

Phrenology was the most popular of the scientific fads of the antebellum period. Its claim that a skilled phrenologist could make an accurate analysis of an individual's character by examining the contours of his skull appealed to Americans for the same reason that they turned to popular cures. All promised to teach the principles of life and give the individual control over his or her own fate.

IV. Democratic Pastimes

A. Introduction

New technology transformed leisure as well as work in the years 1830–1860. Imaginative entrepreneurs used new inventions and advances in manufacturing to sell the kinds of entertainment they believed the public wanted.

B. Newspapers

James Gordon Bennett, publisher of the *New York Herald,* was one of the first journalists to take advantage of new techniques in paper making and printing and the invention of the telegraph. He realized that a newspaper could make money by building mass circulation. He and other publishers slashed the price of their papers to a penny and used newspaper boys to sell hundreds of thousands of copies daily. The penny papers filled their columns with human-interest stories of crime and sex. Bennett's *New York Herald* and Horace Greeley's *New York Tribune* also pioneered in modern financial and political reporting.

C. The Theater

Antebellum theaters were filled with large, rowdy audiences from all social classes. People liked best romantic melodramas, although William Shakespeare's plays were performed more often than those of any other single dramatist.

D. Minstrel Shows

Starting in the 1840s, minstrel shows—performances of songs, dances, and skits by white men in blackface—became popular with white working-class audiences. These shows catered to and reinforced the prejudices of whites by depicting blacks as stupid, comical, musical, and irresponsible.

E. P. T. Barnum

P. T. Barnum, with his display of curiosities, flair for publicity, and development of the American Museum in New York, was the ultimate "entrepreneur of popular entertainment" in the antebellum period.

V. The Quest for Nationality in Literature and Art

A. Introduction

Europeans in the early nineteenth century looked down on American writing, while Americans pointed with pride to the achievements of Washington Irving, who by 1820 had published his famous stories "Rip Van Winkle" and "The Legend of Sleepy Hollow." By the 1820s and 1830s two things furthered the writing of fiction in the United States: the transportation revolution, which opened a nationwide market for books, the favorite being the novel; and the spread of the romantic movement, the American offshoot of which was called transcendentalism. Romanticism, with its stress on feelings rather than learning, suited fiction well. For that reason, women, still not admitted to most colleges, could publish best-selling romantic novels, such as Harriet Beecher Stowe's *Uncle Tom's Cabin*. Ralph Waldo Emerson, a leading transcendentalist, called on Americans of all classes to "trust the prompting of their hearts," and he encouraged U.S. writers to explore our own unique character as a nation, instead of imitating European writing and ideas.

B. The American Renaissance

Emerson's call for a new American creativity coincided with a flowering of distinctively national literature, often referred to as the American Renaissance. In his novels, James Fenimore Cooper introduced the uniquely American character, the frontiersman. Emerson, in his essays, searched for his inborn truth by following his feelings. His disciple Henry David Thoreau not only expressed his radical insights in his writing, but lived them. He went to jail rather than pay taxes to support what he considered the evil Mexican War and defended the right to defy unjust government policies in his essay "Civil Disobedience" (1849). Another Emerson follower, Margaret Fuller, combined transcendentalism and feminism in her *Woman in the Nineteenth Century* (1845). Walt Whitman, in *Leaves of Grass*, broke new ground with "lusty" and "bold" poetry in free verse that celebrated the American common man.

C. Hawthorne, Melville, and Poe

These three authors did not answer Emerson's call to write about the American scene or distinctly American characters. Rather, they were more interested in analyzing moral dilemmas and probing psychological states. Unlike Emerson and Whitman, who were essentially optimistic, Hawthorne, Melville, and Poe shared an "underlying pessimism about the human condition."

D. Literature in the Marketplace

Most nineteenth-century U.S. authors hoped to gain recognition and a living from their writings. Poe sold short stories to popular magazines. Emerson, Thoreau, and Melville made money by lecturing for lyceums. While most lyceum speakers were men, women could and did earn excellent livings by turning out sentimental novels, such as Susan Warner's *The Wide, Wide World*. Although neither the writers nor most of the female readers who consumed the sentimental novels were active feminists, many of the works did illustrate the moral that "women could overcome trials and make the world a better place."

E. American Landscape Painting

American artists between 1820 and 1860 sought to depict their native land, especially in its primitive grandeur before pioneers deforested and plowed it. George Catlin, for example, in hundreds of pictures portrayed Indians as "noble savages" doomed by the "march of progress." Others, like Thomas Cole, painted allegorical scenes on themes of importance to a young republic.

Many of the artists belonged to the Hudson River school, which included Thomas Cole, Asher Durand, and Frederic Church. Their works, which subordinated realism to emotional effect, reflected the romanticism of the period. The designers of New York's Central Park, Frederick Law Olmsted and Calvert Vaux, also shared a romantic view of nature. In their plan they aimed to refresh the souls of harried urbanites by creating for them an idealized pastoral landscape in the midst of the city.

VI. *Conclusion*

New technology changed the lives of millions of Americans between 1840 and 1860. Advances in transportation and manufacturing improved the American diet, made a greater variety of necessities and luxuries available at lower prices, transformed leisure pursuits, and encouraged efforts to diffuse and popularize culture. Technological progress also produced negative effects. It increased the gap between the lifestyles of the reasonably affluent and the poor and between middle class men and women. It led to assaults on America's beautiful natural environment. That despoliation troubled writers such as Thoreau and artists such as the painters of the Hudson River school. Nor did material progress and political democracy liberate man from the dark places in his own soul, Hawthorne's and Melville's fiction demonstrated.

Vocabulary

The following terms are used in Chapter 11. To understand the chapter fully, it is important that you know what each of them means.

despoliation   stripping of riches or resources; ruining

machine tools   machines that shape metal products

real income (real wages)   how much one's income or wages will purchase, given the prices at the time

tenements   subdivided houses or apartments in the poorer, crowded parts of large cities

celerity   speed

rococo   a style of architecture and decoration, originating in France about 1720, that was distinguished by abundant and elegant ornamentation

precepts   rules of action or conduct

stereotype   characteristics, usually negative, attributed to all members of a group

poll tax   a tax that must be paid to exercise the right to vote

allegory   a figurative or symbolic treatment of an abstract idea or spiritual concept

Identifications

After reading Chapter 11, you should be able to identify and explain the historical significance of each of the following:

Cyrus W. Field

John Deere's steel-tipped plow and Cyrus McCormick's mechanical reaper

American system of manufacturing, or interchangeable parts

Samuel F. B. Morse

Catharine Beecher, *A Treatise on Domestic Economy*

contagion theory versus miasm theory

Crawford Long and William T. G. Morton

hydropathy

Sylvester Graham

phrenology

James Gordon Bennett, the *New York Herald,* and the penny press

P. T. Barnum and the American Museum

Horace Greeley and the *New York Tribune*

Astor Place riot

minstrel shows

Washington Irving

James Fenimore Cooper

Edgar Allan Poe

American Renaissance

Henry David Thoreau

Ralph Waldo Emerson and "The American Scholar"

transcendentalism

Margaret Fuller

Nathaniel Hawthorne

Walt Whitman

Herman Melville

Thomas Cole, Asher Durand, Frederic Church, and the Hudson River school

lyceums

Frederick Law Olmsted and Calvert Vaux

Skill Building: Maps

1. Locate on the map on the following page each of the important railroad hubs and/or terminal cities listed below:

   Chattanooga, Tennessee

   Atlanta, Georgia

   Chicago, Illinois

   Buffalo, New York

   Pittsburgh, Pennsylvania

Baltimore, Maryland

Wheeling, Virginia (later West Virginia)

2. Trace on the map the routes of each of these main antebellum railroad lines:

   New York Central

   Erie

   Pennsylvania

   Baltimore and Ohio

   Illinois Central

3. What economic, social, and political effects did the building of these railroads have on the United States?

Eastern United States

Historical Sources

Pages 304–305 in Chapter 11 describe the deplorable sanitation and periodic epidemics that plagued America's antebellum cities. How do historians know about these conditions? Our most valuable sources on this are the investigative reports made to early municipal health boards by city inspectors. One of the most thorough of these, *The Sanitary Conditions of the Laboring Classes* (1845), was written by New York's crusading city inspector Dr. John H. Griscom.

Historians also try to learn about the attitudes, values, and interests of people in the past by reading what they read. Although many Americans today still read the works of Whitman, Hawthorne, Melville, and Poe, few but historians wade through the popular novels of the antebellum period, like Susan Warner's *The Wide, Wide World*. What did the author of Chapter 11 learn about American life and values from this and other popular novels, as well as the penny press and story newspapers?

Now look at "A Place in Time: Frances Trollope Invents Popular Culture in Cincinnati." What does the historian's description of the exhibits Trollope helped plan for the Western Museum (or for that matter the exhibits in Barnum's American Museum) indicate about antebellum American values, interests, and levels of sophistication?

Multiple-Choice Questions

Circle the letter of the item that best completes each statement or answers the question.

1. The 1840s and 1850s in the United States were characterized by all of the following *except*
   a. heightened literary and artistic output and inventiveness.
   b. advances in medical knowledge that lessened the danger and frequency of epidemics.
   c. improvements in transportation and increases in productivity that raised the standard of living for the middle class.
   d. building of municipal water works in many of the big cities to supply the needs of urban dwellers.

2. All of the following were inventions of the antebellum period that were mass-produced and/or widely used in the 1840s and 1850s *except*
   a. Alexander Graham Bell's telephone.
   b. Cyrus McCormick's mechanical reaper.
   c. Samuel F. B. Morse's telegraph.
   d. Elias Howe's sewing machine.

3. Which of the following cities declined in importance as a commercial center because of the railroad building that took place in the 1840s and 1850s?
   a. Atlanta
   b. Chicago
   c. Pittsburgh
   d. New Orleans

4. An urban middle-class home in the 1850s would probably *not* have
   a. several stories.
   b. indoor faucets supplying hot and cold running water.
   c. conspicuously ornamented furniture.
   d. a coal-burning stove for cooking and heating.

5. James Gordon Bennett was the
   a. founder of the American Museum.
   b. inventor of the cylindrical steam-driven press.
   c. founder of the penny press.
   d. founder of the lyceums.

6. Which of the following statements about transcendentalism is *incorrect*?
   a. It was an American form of romanticism.
   b. It claimed that knowledge of God and truth were born in each individual.
   c. It claimed that great literature must conform to universal standards of form and beauty.
   d. It claimed that a new democratic republic could produce art and literature as great as the old traditional societies of Europe.

7. In designing New York's Central Park, Frederick Law Olmsted and Calvert Vaux
   a. copied the lay-out of English formal gardens.
   b. tried to create the look of the countryside and screen out the surrounding city.
   c. celebrated the excitement and vitality of urban America by including museums, sports arenas, and other entertainment facilities.
   d. catered to the tastes and interests of the upper class by making the park resemble the grounds of the Palace of Versailles.

8. Which of the following writers introduced into fiction the character of the American frontiersman and the theme of conflict between primitive life in the wilderness and the advance of civilization?
   a. Herman Melville
   b. Edgar Allan Poe
   c. James Fenimore Cooper
   d. Nathaniel Hawthorne

9. Which of the following writers defended the right to disobey unjust laws, criticized the materialism of American society, and doubted the beneficial effects of technological advances?
   a. Walt Whitman
   b. Henry David Thoreau
   c. John Greenleaf Whittier
   d. James Fenimore Cooper

10. Which of the following statements about the Hudson River school of painters is *incorrect*?
    a. Its members painted only landscapes of the Hudson River and its vicinity.
    b. Its member subordinated realism to heighten emotional effect through the use of color and composition.
    c. It included Thomas Cole, Asher Durand, Frederic Church, and about fifty other painters.
    d. Its members sought to capture on canvas the natural grandeur of the American landscape.

Short-Answer Questions

1. Why were interchangeable parts and improved machine tools extremely important in the growth of American manufacturing?

2. How was most American railroad building in the 1850s financed? What role did New York City play in this financing?

3. Why did Americans' real and annual income increase between 1840 and 1860?

4. Why did antebellum American cities make little headway against recurring epidemics of cholera, yellow fever, and other diseases?

5. Explain the beliefs of American transcendentalists, such as Emerson and Thoreau.

Essay Questions

1. In the 1830s Ralph Waldo Emerson called for a probing exploration of American nationality in literature and art. To what extent did the writers and painters of the American Renaissance answer that call?

2. What technological advances were made in agriculture, industry, and transportation between 1830 and 1860? How did these affect the daily lives of antebellum Americans? What impact did these have on the environment?

3. "The bright possibilities rather than the dark potential of technology impressed most antebellum Americans." To what extent did Americans' lives and experiences between 1830 and 1860 justify that attitude?

4. Discuss the rise of popular culture in the period 1830–1860, including the penny press, the sentimental novel, theater and minstrel shows, and popular health and science movements. How did technological advances of the period affect popular culture?

5. How did new technology and an expanded marketplace affect artistic and intellectual life in American between 1840 and 1860? How did artists and intellectuals feel about these changes?

CHAPTER 12

The Old South and Slavery, 1800–1860

Outline and Summary

I. Introduction

Nat Turner's rebellion (August 1831), in which more than sixty whites were killed, touched off panic among whites about slave insurrections. Whites took indiscriminate revenge on blacks, and the Virginia legislature, in the winter of 1831–1832, came close to passing an emancipation bill. After the failure of that bill, however, white opposition to slavery in Virginia and throughout the South gradually disappeared. The Upper South relied less on slavery and cotton growing than the Lower South and seceded from the Union more hesitantly, but from 1832 on what united and created the region the "Old South" was its defense of slavery, its "peculiar institution."

Chapter 12 covers the economy and society of the Old South from 1800 to 1860. After reading it, you should be able to answer these questions: (1) What classes and class divisions existed in the Old South? (2) Why did most nonslaveholding whites come to support the "peculiar institution"? (3) What type of distinctive culture developed among the slaves and why did it develop?

II. King Cotton

A. Introduction

The main cash crop of the colonial South, tobacco, declined in the late eighteenth century. Cotton culture revived southern agriculture and encouraged its rapid expansion southward and westward. Cotton growing was stimulated by growth of the British textile industry, development of the cotton gin, and removal of Indians from southern and western lands.

B. The Lure of Cotton

The climate of the Lower South was ideal for growing cotton. Cotton could be grown profitably on any scale, with or without slave labor. However, cotton cultivation and the institution of slavery did increase side by side. Cotton and corn were often grown together so that the South did not have to spend money on imported food.

C. Ties Between the Lower and Upper South

The Upper South identified with the Lower South rather than with the free states because many Lower South residents had migrated from the Upper South; all southern whites benefited from the three-fifths clause in the Constitution; almost all southerners resented the criticism from northern abolitionists; and the residents of the Upper South enjoyed a large, profitable business in the sale of slaves to the Lower South.

130

D. The North and South Diverge

While the North was rapidly industrializing and urbanizing, the South remained primarily rural and agricultural. Slaves could be and were employed in southern factories, but much of the South's capital was tied up in slave ownership and, therefore, not available for investment in industrial development. Southerners believed that raising cash crops through slave labor would continue to be profitable, and hence they lacked the incentive to switch their capital from land and slaves to financing of industry.

The Old South made less provision for public schools than the North. School attendance was not compulsory for southern whites, and the law forbade teaching slaves to read and write. The South's agricultural, slave economy did not require a high rate of literacy.

E. Cotton and Southern Progress

"Rather than viewing the Old South as economically backward, it is better to see it merely as different."

III. Social Relations in the White South

A. Introduction

Southern white society showed a mixture of aristocratic and democratic elements. There were great differences in wealth between classes, but most whites did own land. Planters were overrepresented in state legislatures but did not always pass the laws they wanted.

B. The Social Groups of the White South

In 1860 only one-quarter of southern whites owned slaves; 1 percent of southern whites owned one hundred or more slaves. The whites of the Old South fit into four classes (although there was considerable variation within each category): (1) planters—owners of twenty or more slaves; (2) small slaveholders; (3) yeomen—nonslaveholding small family farmers; (4) people of the pine barrens.

C. Planters and Plantation Mistresses

Characterized by a high degree of division of labor, the plantation was almost a factory in the field. The planters' income depended on profits from the sale of a cash crop. The pursuit of profit led planters to look constantly for additional and more fertile land, organize their slave crews as efficiently as possible, and seek favorable merchant-banker connections to market their crops and extend needed credit. Psychological strains that plantation agriculture placed on planters and their wives included physical isolation from other whites of their class; frequent moves; crude living conditions, especially for the many who lived on the new frontier; and responsibilities of running a major economic enterprise. An additional stress on planters' wives was the sexual double standard that accepted illicit sexual relations between masters and their bondswomen, while demand absolute sexual purity from white females.

D. The Small Slaveholders

There were many more small slaveholders than planters. "In 1860, 88 percent of all slaveholders owned fewer than twenty slaves." In the upland regions, the small slaveholders tended to identify with the more numerous yeomen, while in the low country and delta, they identified with the planters and aspired to rise into that class, which they sometimes did.

E. The Yeomen

These nonslaveholding family farmers were by far the largest group among southern whites. Those with the least fertile land tended to be subsistence farmers, but most yeomen grew at least some crops for sale. Their farms ranged in size from fifty to two hundred acres. The yeomen farmers were congregated in the upland, hilly, and less fertile regions. They were, on the whole, a proud and self-sufficient group.

F. The People of the Pine Barrens

They made up about 10 percent of the white population and owned neither slaves nor land. They typically squatted on unfenced land, on which they grazed hogs and cattle and grew corn for their subsistence. Able to survive in this manner, they refused to work as hired help for others.

G. Conflict and Consensus in the White South

Planters and yeomen inclined toward opposing political parties, the elite being Whigs; the small farmers, Democrats. Other characteristics of the Old South, however, minimized conflict: the four main social groups clustered in different regions and often had little contact, both yeomen and planters were independent landowners, and whites rarely worked for other whites. Although planters dominated state legislatures, all white men had the right to vote by the 1820s; therefore, the planters could not ignore the desires of the yeomen majority.

H. Conflict over Slavery

There was a potential for conflict between slaveholders and nonslaveholders. The majority of nonslaveholding southerners, however, supported slavery. Why? (1) Some hoped to become slaveholders; (2) they feared freedmen would demand social and political equality with whites; (3) southern whites shared racist beliefs about blacks and feared that emancipation would be followed by a race war, which would endanger the lives of all whites.

I. The Proslavery Argument

The proslavery argument also was used as a tool to unite southern whites behind the institution. The argument, which was constructed by southern intellectuals between 1830 and 1860, claimed that slavery was a positive good rather than a necessary evil. It claimed that slavery was sanctioned by history and religion and that southern slaves were better treated than northern factory "wage slaves." By the 1830s most southern churches had adopted this proslavery position.

In addition to persuading themselves of the righteousness of their "peculiar institution," southerners increasingly suppressed all public criticism of slavery. They seized and destroyed abolitionist literature mailed to the South, smashed the presses of southern antislavery newspapers, and mobbed anyone who dare to question.

IV. Honor and Violence in the Old South

A. Violence in the White South

During the colonial and pre–Civil War periods, violence was more prevalent among southern whites than it was among the white population of the North.

B. The Code of Honor and Dueling

Behind much southern violence was an exaggerated notion of personal pride. White men must "react violently to even trivial insults in order to demonstrate that they had nothing in common with slaves." Among gentlemen this pride took the form of a code of honor. Any intentional insult to one's reputation had to be redressed by a challenge to a duel.

C. The Southern Evangelicals and White Values

The code of honor was potentially in conflict with the values preached by southern evangelical churches, such as humility and self-restraint. From the 1830s on, evangelical religion grew in influence to the point that some southern gentlemen, while clinging to the value of reputation in the eyes of others, did denounce drinking, gambling, and dueling as un-Christian practices.

V. Life Under Slavery

A. Introduction

Slavery was an exploitative institution that took by force the life and labor of one race for the profit of another.

B. The Maturing of the Plantation System

The institution of slavery changed between 1700 and 1830. In the earlier period, the majority of the black population were recent African or Caribbean arrivals, disproportionately young males who spoke little English and were isolated on small farms. By 1830 there was a more even balance between males and females. Most were American-born and English-speaking and worked on large plantations. These changes facilitated a more rapid natural increase in the black population.

C. Work and Discipline of Plantation Slaves

No other nineteenth-century Americans worked as many hours under as harsh discipline as slave field hands. Slave craftsmen and domestics on the plantations had higher status and easier work but also were subjected at times to physical brutality.

D. The Slave Family

The slave family was not recognized or protected by southern law. Slave families were disrupted by sale; physical separation of husbands and wives and of parents and children; and sexual demands made on black females by masters and other white men. Despite these hazards, the black family did not dissolve but evolved in ways that were different from those of middle-class whites.

E. The Longevity, Diet, and Health of Slaves

Slaves in the Old South lived longer and reproduced faster than those in Brazil or the Caribbean because of a more even sex ratio among U.S. blacks and a more adequate diet. On the other hand, southern slaves had a higher mortality rate than their white countrymen.

F. Slaves off Plantations

Although the majority of slaves worked on plantations, the Old South also used slaves in mining, lumbering, manufacturing, and performing a variety of skilled artisan jobs in cities and villages.

G. Life on the Margin: Free Blacks in the Old South

Not all blacks in the Old South were slaves; there were more than a quarter million free blacks in 1860. The position of the free blacks in the South deteriorated from the 1830s on. Southern law forbade teaching blacks, free or slave, to read. Obstacles were put in the way of manumission, and free blacks were barred from entering or remaining in many states. Nonetheless, many of the post–Civil War black leaders came from this group.

H. Slave Resistance

Nat Turner's 1831 rebellion was the only one in which whites were killed. Two earlier planned insurrections, Gabriel Prosser's (1800) and Denmark Vesey's (1822), were betrayed before they got underway. On the whole, the Old South experienced far fewer uprisings than did South America and the Caribbean because slaves did not form a large majority anywhere in the South, whites had all the weapons and soldiers, blacks were reluctant to endanger their families, and they rarely had allies in southern Indians and never in nonslaveholding whites. An alternative way to freedom was to try to escape to the North. Black abolitionists such as Frederick Douglass, Harriet Tubman, and Josiah Henson were escaped former slaves, some of whom returned repeatedly to the South to help others escape, giving rise to the legend of the Underground Railroad. Relatively few slaves, however, made it to the North successfully. More than by either running away or violent revolt, blacks resisted slavery by furtive means: theft, negligence, arson, and work stoppages and slowdowns.

VI. *The Emergence of African-American Culture*

A. Introduction

American blacks under slavery developed a distinctive culture that drew on African and American cultures but was "more than a mixture of the two."

B. The Language of Slaves

Blacks in the antebellum South developed an English pidgin.

C. African-American Religion

The first Africans brought to the South were Muslims or followers of a variety of indigenous African religions. By 1800 many had been converted to Christianity, especially as Methodists or Baptists. Masters hoped that by preaching Christian humility and acceptance to their slaves, they could make blacks docile and obedient. This did not necessarily work, since the rebels Gabriel Prosser, Denmark Vesey, Nat Turner, and many of their followers were devout Christians who were inspired by their interpretation of the Bible. While Christianity did not turn most slaves into revolutionaries, it did serve as a unifying force among blacks, as well as a source of hope and comfort. Few blacks accepted the white preachers' message that slavery was right in God's eyes.

D. Black Music and Dance

Compared to the cultural patterns of upper-class whites in the Old South, the culture of blacks was "extremely expressive." Blacks expressed their feelings in shouts, music, and dance. They composed work songs and religious songs, later known as spirituals.

VII. *Conclusion*

Slavery is what unified the Old South. Though the majority of white southerners owned no slaves, they had become convinced that the perpetuation of the "peculiar institution" was in the best interests of the entire South. Northerners, on the other hand, believed that slavery made the South backward and bankrupt. Southern whites reacted to outside criticism by defending slavery as a benevolent way to handle the innate inferiority of the black race. Few slaves agreed. While most of them did not revolt or escape successfully, they did engage in covert resistance. White masters hoped black conversion to Christianity would render their slaves submissive. However, when blacks accepted Christianity, they read into it the message that slavery was a gross injustice.

Vocabulary

The following terms are used in Chapter 12. To understand the chapter fully, it is important that you know what each of them means.

yeoman   nonslaveholding family farmers, the Old South's most numerous white class

malapportioned   unfairly divided and assigned, as when seats in a legislature are divided to give one group or geographical area more than its fair share of representation

portico   a structure consisting of a roof supported by columns, usually attached to a building as a porch

social structure   the classes or groups that make up a society and their relations with each other

planters   large landholders, especially those who owned twenty or more slaves, who were a small elite class of the Old South

alluvial soil   soil built up by the mud deposits of flowing rivers, usually very fertile, the best cotton-growing land

evangelical   referring to certain movements and/or denominations within the Protestant churches that stress the importance of personal experience of guilt for sin and of reconciliation to God through Christ

pidgin   a simplified language, with no original, native speakers, in which people of different native languages can communicate

Identifications

After reading Chapter 12, you should be able to identify and explain the historical significance of each of the following:

Nat Turner's rebellion

debate in the Virginia legislature over slavery, 1831–1832

three-fifths clause of the Constitution

J. D. B. De Bow

Tredegar Iron Works

Whig party

Democratic party

Hinton R. Helper, *The Impending Crisis of the South*

proslavery argument

George Fitzhugh

southern code of honor

northern "character"

Gabriel Prosser

Denmark Vesey

Henry "Box" Brown

Frederick Douglass
Harriet Tubman
Josiah Henson
Underground Railroad

Skill Building: Maps

On the map of the South, locate each of the areas listed below. In what states do you find these geographical areas? What was the historical significance of each?

Upper South
Lower (Deep) South
tidewater
pine barrens
piedmont
Mississippi Delta
uplands

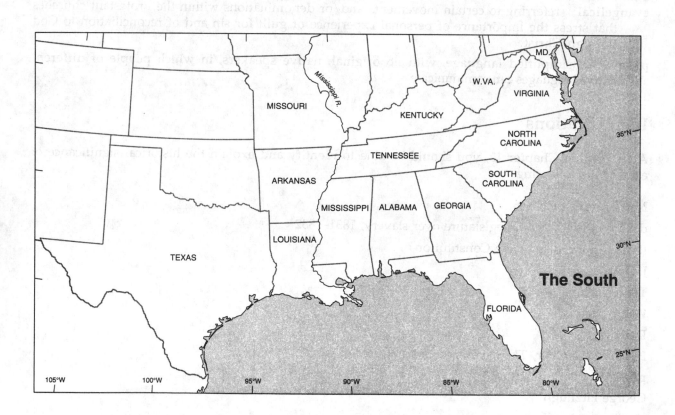

Historical Sources

The author of Chapter 12 has relied on many and varied historical sources to try to achieve a balanced and accurate account of life in the Old South. To see slavery as the bondsmen and bondswomen experienced it, the author has turned to accounts of former slaves, written or oral. Probably the most famous of the published narratives are those of black abolitionist, writer, and political leader Frederick Douglass, including his *Narrative of the Life of Frederick Douglass: An American Slave, Written by Himself* (1845); *My Bondage and My Freedom* (1855); and *Life and Times of Frederick Douglass* (1881). On pages 338, 340, and 348 the works of Frederick Douglass are referred to and/or quoted. How has the author used these historical sources in each instance? Another of the well-known written narratives, Solomon Northup's *Twelve Years a Slave* (1854), also is quoted. What does the author illustrate with this quotation? Northup was a free black living in New York who was kidnapped in 1841 and sold into slavery on a Louisiana cotton plantation. Find other places in the chapter where the memories of former slaves are cited. Many of these stories come from interviews that were conducted by unemployed writers and researchers who, during the depression in the 1930s, worked for the WPA Federal Writers Project. The government hired these persons to seek out elderly black people who had been slaves as children, ask them about their experiences, and record their answers. A sampling of these interviews, edited by Benjamin A. Botkin, was published in 1945 in a book titled *Lay My Burden Down*.

Historians have learned much about the life and attitudes of the planter class from letters and diaries. One of the most informative of these is the diary kept by Mary Boykin Chesnut, wife of a South Carolina planter. On page 330, of Chapter 12, she is cited on the "sorrows of plantation mistresses," many of whom were reminded daily of their husbands' infidelities by the features of the mulatto children in the slave quarters. The historian can find confirmation of this charge against planters and see how one bondswoman felt about the unwanted advances of her master by looking at the narrative of escaped slave Harriet A. Jacobs, *Incidents in the Life of a Slave Girl, Written by Herself* (1861).

Chapter 12 also lets us see the Old South as it appeared to visitors from the outside. On pages 338, 344, and 347 the author refers to and/or quotes from Frederick Law Olmsted's books *A Journey in the Seaboard Slave States* (1856), *A Journey Through Texas* (1857), and *A Journey in the Back Country* (1860). Olmsted, who later became one of America's foremost landscape architects and designer of New York's Central Park, took a fourteen-month tour of the slave states in the 1850s on a journalistic assignment from the *New York Times*. Olmsted's mostly critical observations about the Old South and its "peculiar institution" were different from the glowing defense of black slavery that historians encounter in the writings of its southern defenders. Chapter 12 cites the works of two such defenders, James Henry Hammond's "Letters on Slavery" in *The Pro-Slavery Argument* (1853) and George Fitzhugh's *Sociology for the South* (1854). What arguments did these books present in favor of black slavery?

Historians also conduct intensive studies of local records to gain insights into both regional and national history. Look at the account of the Edgefield District, South Carolina. What generalizations about the Old South does it seem to bear out?

Multiple-Choice Questions

Circle the letter of the item that best completes each statement or answers the question.

1. The majority of white men in the antebellum South were
   a. planters.
   b. small slaveholders.
   c. nonslaveholding family farmers.
   d. merchants or shopkeepers.

2. All of the following were true of planters *except*
   a. they searched constantly for more and better land.
   b. they were often in debt to Northern bankers and brokers.
   c. they usually managed their own estates.
   d. they almost always built mansions on their plantations for their families.

3. The yeomen farmers of the Old South
   a. were congregated in the upland and hilly regions.
   b. did not grow cash crops for market.
   c. did not have the right to vote.
   d. were generally tenants rather than landowners.

4. In 1857 a book calling on nonslaveholding southern whites to abolish slavery in their own interest was published by
   a. James Henry Hammond.
   b. Hinton R. Helper.
   c. George Fitzhugh.
   d. Gabriel Prosser.

5. As compared to the North, the Old South had a higher
   a. literacy rate.
   b. proportion of its people living in cities.
   c. murder rate.
   d. proportion of its white population working for other whites.

6. Southern evangelical churches generally preached against all of the following *except*
   a. slavery.
   b. gambling.
   c. dueling.
   d. intemperance.

7. The black family under slavery
   a. received no legal recognition or protection.
   b. disintegrated.
   c. copied the customs and patterns of white families.
   d. was protected against separation of young children and mothers.

8. Why weren't there more slave revolts in the Old South?
   a. Blacks were outnumbered by whites almost everywhere in the South and lacked allies and guns.
   b. Blacks had no strong desire for freedom, which they did not understand.
   c. Blacks had no inspired leaders.
   d. Blacks were restrained by strong bonds of loyalty to masters who treated them fairly.

9. Most blacks in the antebellum South
   a. rejected Christianity as the religion of their slave masters.
   b. accepted the preaching of white clergy that slavery was divinely sanctioned.
   c. drew from Christianity the view that slavery was an affliction to test their faith and for which masters would be punished.
   d. became obedient and docile because of the Christian promise of reward in heaven for faithful servants.

10. Which of the following statements about white people of the pine barrens is *incorrect*?
    a. They generally "squatted" on their land rather than owning it.
    b. They usually favored the institution of slavery, though they owned no slaves.
    c. They usually worked for the planters as tenant farmers, sharecroppers, or overseers.
    d. They carried on subsistence farming.

Short-Answer Questions

1. Explain the differences between the Upper and Lower South. What tied them together?

2. Explain why the Old South failed to industrialize.

3. Summarize the proslavery argument developed by southern intellectuals to defend the "peculiar institution."

4. Discuss the free black population of the Old South. How many were there by the eve of the Civil War? Where did most of them live? Under what economic and legal constraints did they exist?

5. Describe the "furtive resistance" of slaves in the Old South.

Essay Questions

1. Compare and contrast economic, social, and political developments in the North and South between 1800 and 1860. How do you account for the divergence between the two sections?

2. Discuss the white social structure of the Old South. How egalitarian was it? What social classes or groups existed? What was their relationship to each other and to the institution of slavery?

3. The great majority of white southerners never owned a single slave, yet the majority supported the institution of slavery. Write an essay explaining why.

4. Was slavery in the South essentially a paternalistic institution in which most slaves were treated reasonably well, or was it primarily an exploitative institution? Back up your conclusions by citing as much evidence as possible.

5. Discuss the emergence of African-American culture in the Old South. In what ways did it draw on African experiences? In what ways did it incorporate the American slave experience? How did it differ from white southern culture and values?

CHAPTER 13

Immigration, Expansion, and Sectional Conflict, 1840–1848

Outline and Summary

I. Introduction

In the 1840s many Americans believed it was the "manifest destiny" of the United States to possess North America from coast to coast. Acting upon that belief, the administration of James K. Polk, between 1845 and 1849, annexed Texas; divided the Oregon Territory with Great Britain; and fought the Mexican War, resulting in the conquest of California and New Mexico. Also, in the 1840s and 1850s a rising tide of new immigrants entered the country. Expansion and immigration were linked. The overwhelmingly Democratic immigrant vote helped elect President Polk, an ardent expansionist. Many Democratic party leaders saw acquisition of more land and a return to a republic of self-sufficient farmers as a way of relieving growing class, ethnic, and sectional conflicts. Adding Oregon would please the North; Texas, the South. In fact, westward expansion had the opposite effect; it sharpened sectional strife, split the Democratic party, and set the nation on the path to the Civil War. As you read about these events in Chapter 13, try to find the answers to the following questions: (1) Why did the Whig party decline? (2) What were the main issues in the election of 1844, and why was its outcome particularly important? (3) How did the Mexican War lead to heightened intersectional conflict and Democratic party splintering?

II. Newcomers and Natives

A. Introduction

Between 1840 and 1860, 4.2 million immigrants entered the United States. The two biggest groups came from Ireland and the German states.

B. Expectations and Realities

Immigrants came in hope of improving their economic condition. Few of the Irish immigrants possessed enough capital to acquire farms. Instead they settled heavily in northeastern cities, where they took jobs in construction and railroad building. Germans and Scandinavians, on the other hand, tended to concentrate in Illinois, Ohio, Wisconsin, and Missouri. Although more of them entered farming than did the Irish, they too were drawn to cities. By 1860 the Irish and Germans accounted for approximately 50 percent of the population of cities such as St. Louis, New York, Chicago, Cincinnati, Milwaukee, Detroit, and San Francisco.

C. The Germans

The German immigrants were quite diverse, including people of different social classes and religions, but they were bound together by their common language and often settled in German neighborhoods. They prospered and built many ethnic institutions: German-language newspapers, voluntary associations, and schools. Native-born Americans criticized them for being clannish.

D. The Irish

Between 1815 and 1844 almost 1 million Irish entered the United States, most of them Catholic, poor, and seeking greater economic opportunity. From 1845 to 1855, another 2 million arrived, now overwhelmingly Catholic and fleeing the potato famine that was ravaging their homeland. They usually entered the urban work force at the bottom, competing for jobs with equally poor blacks. The competition led to animosity between the two groups and made most Irish hostile to abolition and abolitionists. Those Irish who rose to the level of skilled and semiskilled workers competed against native-born, white, Protestant mechanics, again producing ethnic and religious hostilities.

E. Anti-Catholicism, Nativism, and Labor Protest

The antagonism of white, Protestant, native-born workers took the form of anti-Catholic and anti-immigrant outbursts and organizations. Such sentiments and organizations were behind the founding of the Know-Nothing (or American) party, which played a significant political role in the 1850s. Labor also responded to low wages and job competition by advocating land reform (including free 160-acre homesteads in the West for all who wanted them) and by forming unions and waging strikes. Unions won a few gains, but their growth was limited by government and employer opposition and by the deep splits along ethnic and religious lines in the antebellum working class.

F. Labor Protest and Immigrant Politics

Almost all Irish and German immigrants became supporters of the Democratic party. They saw it as an antiprivilege party, more sympathetic to the common man than the Whigs were. The Irish and Germans also resented Whig connections with the temperance movement and nativism. The Irish suspected the northern Whigs of antislavery views, and since the Irish feared economic competition from emancipated slaves, they wanted no part of abolitionism.

III. *The West and Beyond*

A. The Far West

In the 1820s, 1830s, and 1840s Texas and the present-day southwestern regions of the United States belonged to Mexico. The Oregon Territory (including what are now the states of Oregon, Washington, and Idaho and parts of Wyoming, Montana, and Canada) was under joint occupation by Britain and the United States.

B. Far Western Trade

The earliest Americans to enter the Far West were fur trappers and traders. They blazed trails, such as the Santa Fe; introduced eastern manufactured goods in exchange for beaver pelts or Mexican silver; and set up encampments and trading posts. They also spurred the interest of pioneer farmers with their tales of favorable climate and fertile soil in the Far West.

C. The American Settlement of Texas

In the 1820s the Mexican government gave generous land grants to Americans and encouraged their settlement in Texas as a way to guard against Indian attacks and hasten the economic development of the province. So many came, primarily from the southern states, that the Mexican government in the 1830s attempted to end American immigration and prohibit slavery in Texas. Its efforts antagonized the Americans but failed to stop the flood of immigrants that by 1836 had raised the American population in Texas to thirty thousand whites and five thousand slaves. Meanwhile, in 1834 the new president-dictator of Mexico, Santa Anna, started to tighten his hold on Texas. The Americans in the province rebelled.

D. The Texas Revolution

In 1836 Santa Anna led an army into Texas to suppress the uprising. The Mexicans defeated the Americans at the Alamo and at Goliad. Under the leadership of Sam Houston, however, the Americans in April at San Jacinto routed the Mexicans, took Santa Anna prisoner, and forced him to sign a treaty granting Texas independence. The Mexican government later refused to ratify the treaty, but Texas remained independent.

E. American Settlements in California, New Mexico, and Oregon

The Mexicans also initially welcomed American colonists to California. By the 1840s a growing number were settling in the Sacramento Valley, where they lived apart from the Mexicans. In the 1830s American missionaries entered Oregon's Willamette Valley to convert the Indians there. The missionaries' glowing reports of the territory's climate and resources aroused keen interest back in the United States.

F. The Overland Trail

In the 1840s, despite faulty maps and guidebooks, fears of Indian attacks, and other real and imagined dangers, more than fourteen thousand Americans joined wagon trains on the Overland Trail headed for Oregon or California.

IV. *The Politics of Expansion*

A. Introduction

At the start of the 1840s western expansion was not an important political issue. Only after politicians failed to deal effectively with troubling economic issues did some of these leaders seize on expansion as a primary goal.

B. The Whig Ascendancy

The Whig party won the election of 1840 with William Henry Harrison. The party planned to enact Clay's American System of a new national bank, protective tariffs, and federal aid for internal improvements. These plans were thwarted, however, by Harrison's death after only one month in the White House. This brought Vice President John Tyler into office. Tyler, a states' right Virginian, vetoed all the economic measures the congressional Whigs passed.

C. Tyler and the Annexation of Texas

At odds with his party on economic issues, Tyler attempted to gain popularity by achieving success in foreign policy. He supported U.S. annexation of Texas and appointed John C. Calhoun as his secretary of state to draw up a treaty. Calhoun wrote undiplomatically that one reason for annexation was to provide more territory for the expansion and protection of slavery. This added fuel to already existing northern suspicions that acquiring Texas was part of a southern conspiracy to expand slavery, and the Senate therefore rejected Tyler and Calhoun's annexation treaty.

D. The Election of 1844

The annexation of Texas became an important issue in the 1844 election. The Whig nominee, Henry Clay, wavered on annexation, first opposing it as sectionally divisive, then softening his opposition, and finally opposing it again. His shifts lost southern votes to the Democrats and northern antislavery votes to the Liberty party. The Democrats nominated the ardently expansionist James K. Polk, who called for admitting Texas immediately. Many Irish and other recent immigrants voted for Polk because they disliked the Whigs' association with nativism, temperance, and anti-Catholicism. Polk won in a close election.

E. Manifest Destiny

The election demonstrated, among other things, that expansionism had become a popular cause by the 1840s. Many expansionists repeated journalist John L. O'Sullivan's claim that it was the "manifest destiny" of the United States to spread its experiment in liberty and self-government from coast to coast. Others eyed the excellent harbors of California and Oregon as the natural outlets for American trade with Asia. Expansionists argued that acquiring additional fertile soil would safeguard the U.S. future as a democratic republic of self-sufficient farmers and combat the social stratification and class strife that accompanied industrialization and urbanization. These ideas, carried in the penny press, strongly appealed to struggling immigrants in the cities.

F. Polk and Oregon

In his 1844 presidential campaign, Polk had called for American ownership of all the Oregon Territory as well as the annexation of Texas. After he entered the White House, neither the British nor the United States wanted a war, and so they settled for a compromise treaty that split Oregon at the forty-ninth parallel. The Senate ratified the treaty in 1846.

G. The Origins of the Mexican War

In February 1845 Congress passed a joint resolution to annex Texas, although Mexico had never recognized the independence of the province. After Polk was inaugurated, he backed the Texan claim that its southern boundary was the Rio Grande as opposed to Mexico's contention that it was the Nueces River, one hundred miles to the northeast. This support encouraged Texas to accept annexation on July 4, 1845.

Polk also wanted to gain California and New Mexico, and he sent John Slidell to Mexico with an offer to buy them for $25 million. After Mexico refused, Polk ordered American troops under General Zachary Taylor into the disputed region south of the Nueces, hoping to provoke a war that would give the United States a chance to seize California and New Mexico. When Mexican troops clashed with Taylor's, Polk told Congress that Mexico had forced war with the United States. A minority in Congress accused Polk of aggressive, proslavery actions, but the majority supported the war.

H. The Mexican War

In February 1847 Zachary Taylor defeated an army commanded by Santa Anna at the Battle of Buena Vista. Colonel Stephen Kearny took New Mexico, and California fell to combined naval and land assaults under commodores John D. Sloat and David Stockton and army officers Kearny and John C. Frémont. Mexico surrendered in September 1847 when an American force led by General Winfield Scott conquered Mexico City. Under the terms of the Treaty of Guadalupe Hidalgo, Mexico accepted the Rio Grande boundary and ceded to the United States almost all of the present-day U.S. Southwest in return for $15 million and a promise by the U.S. government to pay claims of U.S. citizens against Mexico.

I. Intensifying Sectional Divisions

Despite the patriotism generated by the war, sectional conflict grew between 1846 and 1848. The Polk administration angered the North and West by lowering tariffs and vetoing federal aid for internal improvements. Most important, arguments began over expansion of slavery into the Mexican cession. Northern Democrats worried that the western expansion of slavery would close out opportunities for free laborers in the West and worsen class antagonism in the East.

J. The Wilmot Proviso

A northern Democratic congressman, David Wilmot, in 1846 tacked on to an appropriations bill an amendment that would bar slavery from the new territory acquired from Mexico. With much northern support, the so-called Wilmot Proviso passed the House but not the Senate. Extremist southerners led by Calhoun claimed it was unconstitutional for Congress to forbid slavery in any territory.

K. The Election of 1848

The Whigs nominated Zachary Taylor for president. The Democrats chose Lewis Cass, who tried to solve the sectional controversy by proposing squatter or popular sovereignty, giving the settlers who lived in a territory the right to decide whether to permit slavery. Not satisfied with this position, a faction of Democrats called Barnburners joined antislavery "conscience" Whigs and Liberty party abolitionists to create the Free-Soil party. It nominated Martin Van Buren, who ran on a platform opposing any further spread of slavery. Taylor, a military hero whose position on slavery was unknown, won the election. The good showing of the Free-Soilers in the North, however, demonstrated the popular appeal of keeping slavery out of the West and using it as a place of opportunity for poor white men.

L. The California Gold Rush

Just before the signing of the Treaty of Guadalupe Hidalgo, an American carpenter living in California discovered gold near Sacramento. The news, which soon reached the East, produced a rush of prospectors. California's population surged, and the weak military government proved unequal to containing the violence and disorder of the gold fields and mining boom towns. Californians demanded a civilian state government. This brought to a head the issue of slavery in California and the rest of the Mexico cession.

V. Conclusion

After winning the election of 1840, the Whigs were unable to enact their platform of national banking and protective tariffs because of the death of President William H. Harrison and his replacement by Vice President John Tyler, who espoused Democratic, not Whig views. In the election of 1844, the Whig candidate, Henry Clay, fell before the ardently expansionist Democrat, James Polk. Polk, during his one term, nearly led the United States into a war against Britain and did fight Mexico. The issue of the spread of slavery into the territories taken from Mexico fanned sectional strife and split the Democrats, as many northern members joined others in creating the Free-Soil party. The California gold rush made decisions about slavery in California and about statehood imperative.

Vocabulary

The following terms are used in Chapter 13. To understand the chapter fully, it is important that you know what each of them means.

steerage   the section of a ship, originally near the rudder, providing the cheapest accommodations for passengers

freethinker   one who has rejected authority and ritual, especially in religion, in favor of rational inquiry and speculation

nativism   dislike and suspicion of immigrants; the policy of protecting the interests of native inhabitants versus those of immigrants

secularize   to transfer control or ownership of something from the church or religious authorities to civil authorities, such as the government

allegiance   a feeling of duty, obligation, or faithfulness to a person, idea, country, or government

dark horse   a little-known or unlikely political figure who unexpectedly wins nomination and/or election

proviso   a clause in a statute, contract, or the like by which a condition is introduced; a stipulation or condition

Identifications

After reading Chapter 13, you should be able to identify and explain the historical significance of each of the following:

Know-Nothing, or American, party

George Henry Evans

Commonwealth v. *Hunt* (1842)

Spanish missions and presidios

Stephen F. Austin and American *empresarios* in Texas

Antonio López de Santa Anna

the Alamo

Sam Houston

Overland Trail and the Donner party

John Tyler

John C. Calhoun

Henry Clay

James K. Polk ("Young Hickory")

John L. O'Sullivan and manifest destiny

Zachary Taylor ("Old Rough and Ready")

Winfield Scott

John C. Frémont and the Bear Flag Republic

Treaty of Guadalupe Hidalgo

Wilmot Proviso

squatter or popular sovereignty

Martin Van Buren and the Free Soil party

Skill Building: Maps

On the map of the West on the following page, locate each of the following and explain its historical significance:

forty-ninth parallel
Great Plains
Rocky Mountains
Oregon Territory
54°40' latitude
St. Louis
Santa Fe
Santa Fe Trail
Texas and the Mexican cession
Sacramento Valley
Columbia River
Vancouver Island
Rio Grande
Nueces River
San Francisco
36°30' latitude

Western United States

Multiple-Choice Questions

Circle the letter of the item that best completes each statement or answers the question.

1. The two biggest sources of immigration to the United States between 1840 and 1860 were
   a. Italy and Eastern Europe.
   b. China and Japan.
   c. Ireland and the German states.
   d. Britain and Scotland.

2. In the case of *Commonwealth* v. *Hunt* (1842), the Massachusetts Supreme Court ruled that
   a. slavery was unconstitutional in Massachusetts.
   b. labor unions were not necessarily illegal combinations or monopolies.
   c. Massachusetts tax money could not be used to support an unjust war against Mexico.
   d. segregated schools for blacks in Massachusetts did not violate the U.S. Constitution.

3. Squatter or popular sovereignty meant
   a. allowing residents of a territory to decide whether to permit slavery there.
   b. extending the right to vote to all male settlers in the Far West.
   c. deciding the ownership of a territory by vote of its residents.
   d. the right of the native Indian peoples to keep the lands they were already cultivating.

4. Which of the following statements about President Polk's actions is *incorrect*?
   a. He sent John Slidell to Mexico with an offer to buy California and New Mexico.
   b. He ordered Zachary Taylor to keep his troops north of the Nueces River to avoid a confrontation with Mexico.
   c. He agreed to split the Oregon Territory with the British at the forty-ninth parallel, although he had demanded all of it during his presidential campaign.
   d. He signed a bill lowering the tariff and vetoed one giving federal aid for internal improvements.

5. The expansionist phrase *manifest destiny* was first coined by
   a. George Henry Evans.
   b. Horace Greeley.
   c. John C. Frémont.
   d. John L. O'Sullivan.

6. All of the following people or groups were nativist and anti-Catholic *except*
   a. the Know-Nothings.
   b. Martin Van Buren.
   c. Samuel F. B. Morse.
   d. Lyman Beecher.

7. The fate of the Donner party best illustrates
   a. the hazards faced by pioneers traveling west on the Overland Trail.
   b. the lack of appeal of abolitionism to the majority of immigrants.
   c. the widespread lack of interest among Americans in Henry Clay's American system by the 1840s.
   d. the vicious attacks on Catholics and immigrants that took place in the 1830s and 1840s.

8. The Senate rejected the treaty annexing Texas that was drawn up by Secretary of State John Calhoun because
   a. he defended annexation as a way to protect and defend slavery.
   b. the Texans made it clear that they were not yet ready to give up their independence and join the United States.
   c. the British threatened to break off diplomatic relations if the United States took the territory without compensating them.
   d. Mexico threatened to declare war on the United States if it stole her province.

9. The Wilmot Proviso called for
   a. annexation of Texas.
   b. prohibiting slavery in any territory acquired from Mexico.
   c. drawing the Missouri Compromise line of 36°30' to the West Coast.
   d. legislation to limit immigration into the United States.

10. Presidios were
    a. agents who contracted with the Mexican government to bring American settlers into Texas.
    b. Mexicans who owned huge ranches worked by enslaved Indians.
    c. Franciscan priests who endeavored to convert the Indians to Christianity.
    d. forts constructed by the Spanish to protect their missions in the Southwest.

Short-Answer Questions

1. In the antebellum period, why did Irish and German immigrants generally favor the Democratic party over the Whig party?

2. Why did Polk first demand all of the Oregon Territory from Britain and then agree to a compromise? What were the terms of that compromise?

3. Why did many northern Democrats who were not abolitionists favor the Wilmot Proviso?

4. What was the platform of the Free-Soil party in the election of 1848? How well did the party do in the election? Why was its showing significant?

5. Describe the impact of the gold rush on the sleepy Mexican village of San Francisco.

6. How did the California gold rush bring to a head the issue of slavery in the Far West?

Essay Questions

1. Discuss immigration to the United States in the 1840s and 1850s. Who came? Why did immigrants come? Where did they settle? What economic and political roles did they play?

2. Discuss the rise of anti-Catholic and nativist sentiment and movements in the United States in the 1840s. What caused them? Who supported such groups? What impact did these groups have on American politics?

3. What did expansionists mean by the term *manifest destiny*? What arguments did they use to justify expansion? To whom did these arguments appeal? Why?

4. Discuss the causes of the Mexican War. To what extent did the United States provoke the confrontation? Why did some members of Congress and the public oppose the war?

5. Explain the following statement with as much illustrative evidence as possible: "[E]xpansion brought sectional antagonism to the boiling point, split the Democratic party in the late 1840s, and set the nation on the path to the Civil War."

CHAPTER 14

From Compromise to Secession, 1850–1861

Outline and Summary

I. Introduction

The decade of the 1850s opened with a compromise that was supposed to settle sectional differences, but it quickly came undone. Instead, the 1850s lurched from one sectional crisis to the next. The most devastating of those occurred on October 16, 1859, when John Brown and eighteen followers seized the federal arsenal and armory at Harpers Ferry, intending to arm southern white and black dissidents in a holy war against slavery. Brown's failed raid convinced southerners that they had barely survived a northern plot to get them all murdered in a slave insurrection. Northerners, while initially disavowing Brown, came, during his trial, to sympathize with him. The whole incident set the stage for civil war. As you read about the events of the 1850s in Chapter 14, try to find answers to the following questions: (1) Why did the Compromise of 1850 come apart so quickly? (2) How did the Fugitive Slave Act and the election of 1852 contribute to the unraveling of the compromise? (3) What effects did the Kansas-Nebraska Act and the fighting in Kansas have on the Whig, Democratic, and Republican parties? (4) How did the Republicans' free-soil stance bring northerners together in opposition to the South? (5) Was the Civil War "inevitable"?

II. The Compromise of 1850

A. Introduction

When the treaty ending the Mexican War was signed in 1848, a delicate balance existed between free and slave states: there were fifteen of each. All the proposed solutions for handling slavery in the Mexican cession—whether to prohibit it, open the whole area to slaveholders, extend the Missouri Compromise line to the Pacific, or apply popular sovereignty—were controversial. Other issues also divided the North and South. Then, California and Utah asked Congress for admission to the Union as free states.

B. Zachary Taylor at the Helm

President Taylor had encouraged California to make this request for statehood. Believing that the majority of its residents opposed slavery, he urged Congress to welcome it into the Union as a free state. Southerners were horrified, however, at the prospect of losing the balance of power in the Senate by admitting California and perhaps next New Mexico as free states. In protest nine southern states sent delegates to a convention at Nashville.

C. Henry Clay Proposes a Compromise

Senator Clay proposed a compromise to settle the territorial problem and other sectional controversies:

1. Admit California as a free state.

2. Divide the rest of the Mexican cession into the New Mexico and Utah territories, with the future of slavery in each left up to its residents.

3. Settle the border dispute between Texas and New Mexico in New Mexico's favor.

4. Compensate Texas by having the federal government pay off the state's past public debt.

5. Allow slavery to continue in Washington, D.C., but ban slave trading there.

6. Pass and enforce a tough new fugitive-slave law.

After heated debate and much maneuvering, the compromise passed.

D. Assessing the Compromise

The compromise did not settle the underlying differences between the sections. The one clear advantage that the South gained, the passage of the stringent Fugitive Slave Act, backfired.

E. Enforcement of the Fugitive Slave Act

The law, which was blatantly stacked against black people and sent federal marshals all over the country looking for runaways, aroused widespread opposition in the North. Northern mobs attacked marshals to rescue arrested fugitives, vigilance committees helped runaways escape to Canada, and nine states passed personal liberty laws designed to interfere with enforcement of the act. Whereas the act embittered northerners against the South, southerners resented the North's refusal to live up to the terms of the compromise.

F. *Uncle Tom's Cabin*

The publication of Harriet Beecher Stowe's *Uncle Tom's Cabin* and the many dramatizations of it further aroused anti-southern feelings and sympathy for slaves in the North.

G. The Election of 1852

The Whigs nominated war hero General Winfield Scott to run against Democrat Franklin Pierce for president. The Democrats rallied behind the compromise and popular sovereignty in the territories. Pierce and the Democrats trounced the Whigs, whose northern and southern wings were being torn apart by the sectional controversy.

III. *The Collapse of the Second Party System*

A. Introduction

During Pierce's administration the second party system—Whig against Democrat—collapsed. In the 1850s the issues that had been the main focus of partisan politics (banking, internal improvement, tariffs, temperance) were pushed from center stage by the debate over slavery's extension. The Whig party, more internally divided on the question than the Democrats, disintegrated when Stephen A. Douglas's Kansas-Nebraska bill threw the future of slavery in the territories wide open.

B. The Kansas-Nebraska Act

Passage of this act in 1854 dealt a shattering blow to the second party system and renewed the sectional strife that the compromise aimed to quiet. Stephen A. Douglas was eager to advance settlement of Kansas and Nebraska and promote the building of a transcontinental railroad through the area. To accomplish these goals he needed to organize a territorial government for the region, but he was running into southern opposition because the area was north of the Missouri Compromise line and would therefore be free. To gain southern support, Douglas introduced the Kansas-Nebraska bill, which repealed the Missouri Compromise, organized two territories, and left the question of slavery in both Kansas and Nebraska up to popular sovereignty. That gave the South a chance to gain at least Kansas (adjacent to the slave state of Missouri) for the "peculiar institution."

C. The Surge of Free Soil

Douglas was surprised at the angry reaction in the North, where many regarded the law as part of an atrocious southern plot to spread slavery into Kansas, the rest of the Louisiana Territory, and even into the North. Free-soil sentiment had grown tremendously in the North, not primarily because of sympathy for black slaves—many free-soilers were racists—but because northerners wanted the territories to be the place where upwardly mobile, enterprising, poor Americans could become independent, self-employed farmers and businessmen. If slavery invaded the territories, it would discourage and drive out free labor.

D. The Ebbing of Manifest Destiny

Enthusiasm for expansion, which had unified the Democratic party, waned in the free states as northerners saw in each southern move to acquire territory a plot to gain additional slave states. This northern attitude became so pronounced that President Pierce had to repudiate southern-backed plans to buy or seize Cuba.

E. The Whigs Disintegrate

Southern Whigs had joined Democrats in voting for the Kansas-Nebraska Act. Northern "conscience" Whigs, led by Senator William Seward, and free-soil Democrats reacted angrily against both of the major parties. In the elections of 1854 and 1855 many of the disaffected voters turned first to the American, or Know-Nothing, party and later increasingly to the new Republican party. As a result of these moves the Whig party fell apart.

F. The Rise and Fall of the Know-Nothings

The American party (Know-Nothings) evolved out of a secret nativist society called the Order of the Star-Spangled Banner. In the North the party combined hatred of Catholics, immigrants, and slavery-extension. It took a conspiratorial view of the world in which the Pope and the Slave Power were both plotting to extinguish the American democratic republic. In 1854 and 1855 the Know-Nothings scored major victories in northern states such as Massachusetts. However, the party declined rapidly thereafter because, like the major parties, it was pulled apart by the slavery-expansion issue. Its southern adherents supported the Kansas-Nebraska Act, a position unacceptable to northern nativists, who deserted to the emerging Republicans.

G. The Origins of the Republican Party

The Republican party first appeared in several northern states in protest against the Kansas-Nebraska Act. As the Know-Nothings waned by 1856, the Republicans became the main opposition party to the Democrats. The Republicans were basically a coalition of former northern Whigs and

Democrats who wanted to restore the Missouri Compromise, Liberty party abolitionists, and free-soilers. Little united them at first except their opposition to the Kansas-Nebraska Act. However, the subsequent fighting in Kansas between proslavery and antislavery forces greatly strengthened the party and its free-soil stand.

H. Bleeding Kansas

Both proslavery and antislavery settlers rushed to Kansas. In 1855, when the first election for a territorial legislature took place, thousands of proslavery Missourians invaded Kansas for the day and voted illegally. This fraud produced a rabidly proslavery legislature, which from its capital in Lecompton, Kansas, passed repressive laws aimed at squelching the free-soilers. The free-soilers, considering the Lecompton legislature a sham, organized a rival government in Topeka. After the sack of Lawrence and John Brown's Pottawatomie massacre, civil war broke out in Kansas between the two governments and their followers. Popular sovereignty had not worked. Instead it caused angry debate between Pierce, who recognized the fraudulent Lecompton government, and dismayed northern Democrats and Republicans. It also spread violence to Congress with Preston Brooks's attack on Senator Charles Sumner.

I. The Election of 1856

The Republicans nominated John C. Frémont, whose platform called on Congress to exclude slavery from all remaining territories. The Democrats nominated James Buchanan and backed popular sovereignty. Millard Fillmore ran as a Know-Nothing. Buchanan won, but the Republicans did remarkably well in the North. Had Frémont carried Pennsylvania and either Illinois or Indiana, he would have been elected despite receiving almost no southern votes.

IV. The Crisis of the Union

A. The Dred Scott Case

Two days after Buchanan's inauguration, the Supreme Court entered the controversy over slavery in the territories with its *Dred Scott* decision. A court composed mostly of southerners ruled that blacks, slave or free, were not citizens of the United States and that the Missouri Compromise had always been unconstitutional because Congress had no right to exclude slavery from any territory. To do so violated the Fifth Amendment protection of property and property holders. The Republicans denounced the decision and prepared to ignore it.

B. The Lecompton Constitution

In Kansas the proslavery Lecompton legislature proposed a state constitution that protected slaveholders and gave the settlers the right to vote only on whether to allow more slaves into Kansas. President Buchanan backed the Lecompton constitution and called on Congress to grant Kansas statehood under it. Stephen Douglas, author of the Kansas-Nebraska Act, broke with Buchanan and denounced the actions of the Lecompton legislature. Northern Democrats and Republicans applauded Douglas; southern Democrats applauded Buchanan.

C. The Lincoln-Douglas Debates

In 1858 Douglas ran for reelection to the Senate. His lesser-known Republican opponent, Abraham Lincoln, challenged Douglas to a series of debates. In the debates Lincoln attacked slavery as morally evil but denied that Congress had the right to abolish it in the South or that he favored equality for blacks. Rather, he stuck to his position of barring slavery from the territories. Lincoln also forced Douglas into making his Freeport Doctrine statement, which pleased northern Democrats but made

Douglas and his views unacceptable to the South. Although Douglas won the Illinois Senate seat, the election further split the Democratic party. It also made Lincoln "famous in the North and infamous in the South."

D. The Legacy of Harpers Ferry

John Brown's raid touched off a wave of fear and hysteria in the South. Southerners believed Brown had the backing of abolitionists and Republicans who were plotting to incite more slave rebellions. These fears played into the hands of southern extremists.

E. The South Contemplates Secession

Southerners began to speak of secession as the only way to protect themselves. They regarded northern opposition to the Fugitive Slave Act and to slavery in Kansas as unconstitutional and an offense to the South, which wounded southern pride. Some argued that separation from the Union also would permit the South to seize more territory in the Caribbean and the West for slavery.

F. The Election of 1860

The Republicans broadened their appeal in the free states in 1860 by supporting a protective tariff, federal aid for internal improvements, and a homestead act. For president they nominated the Illinois moderate, Lincoln. The northern and southern Democrats, unable to agree on a platform, split. Northern Democrats nominated Douglas, who still advocated popular sovereignty. Southern Democrats selected John C. Breckenridge, who insisted that Congress must pass laws protecting slavery in all territories. The Constitutional Union party, with appeal mostly in the border states and Upper South, ran John Bell. Lincoln won a majority in the electoral college, but only 39 percent of the popular vote.

G. The Movement for Secession

Believing that a Republican president would unleash more John Browns upon them, the states of the Deep South began to secede even before Lincoln took office. South Carolina led the way in December 1860, followed by Alabama, Mississippi, Florida, Georgia, Louisiana, and Texas. On February 4, 1861, delegates from these seven states met in Montgomery, Alabama, to form the Confederate States of America. The states of the border and Upper South hesitated to secede and join the Confederacy for a number of reasons.

H. The Search for Compromise

Kentucky senator John Crittenden proposed a compromise to bring the Deep South back into the Union. It included constitutional amendments that guaranteed the federal government would never interfere with slavery in the South and that drew the Missouri Compromise line across the remaining territories, with slavery permitted south of the line in all present and future U.S. territory. Lincoln rejected the Crittenden plan because he would not abandon the free-soil promise on which he had been elected. He regarded the plan as an invitation to the South to seize territory in the Caribbean for slavery. He also felt that he had won an honest election and that giving in to a losing minority would damage the American tradition of majority rule.

I. The Coming of War

The Confederacy began to take over federal forts within its region. Soon after Lincoln's inauguration, it bombarded Fort Sumter in Charleston's harbor, thus firing the first shot. Lincoln responded by proclaiming that a rebellion existed in the Lower South and calling for seventy-five thousand militia volunteers from the loyal states to subdue it. Rather than send their troops to fight against sister southern states, Virginia, North Carolina, Arkansas, and Tennessee seceded and joined the Confederacy. The North was now aroused and ready to fight to save the Union, though not yet ready to abolish slavery.

V. Conclusion

At no time prior to the Civil War did the majority of Americans call for the end of slavery in the South. Rather, in the decade of the 1850s the gulf between North and South widened over the spread of slavery into the territories. Northerners believed their freedom to pursue economic opportunity would be denied if they had to compete against slave labor in the West. Southerners claimed that to curtail slavery in the territories violated their constitutional right to use their property (slaves) as they saw fit. Attempts to enforce the Fugitive Slave law, the Kansas-Nebraska Act's repeal of the Missouri Compromise, the subsequent fighting in Kansas, the *Dred Scott* decision, and John Brown's raid all further embittered intersectional conflict. National political parties collapsed under the strain; the Whigs disintegrated; the Democrats divided into northern and southern wings. A new strictly northern party, the Republican, emerged. By the end of the 1850s northerners were convinced the South meant to impose slavery through the nation. Southern states were ready for secession as the only way to protect their peculiar institution from a North that they saw as intent upon destroying slavery even in the South.

Vocabulary

The following terms are used in Chapter 14. To understand the chapter fully, it is important that you know what each of them means.

omnibus bill   a bill including numerous items or subjects

defector   one who withdraws allegiance from a political party, group, or country

stalwart   a steadfast or uncompromising political party supporter

conspiracy   a secret agreement to perform an evil or unlawful act; a secret plot

naturalization   the legal process that confers the rights and privileges of citizenship upon an immigrant

capital crime or offense   a crime or offense punishable by death

doughface   in the 1850s, a northern politician whose views were acceptable or even sympathetic to the South

plaintiff   one who brings suit in a court

referendum   the procedure of submitting legislative measures directly to the voters for approval or rejection

insurrection   an armed uprising or other open resistance against a government or other established authority; a revolt

lynch   to put a person to death for some alleged offense by the actions of a mob or group having no legal authority

vigilantes   members of extralegal citizen groups organized to maintain order and punish offenses

Identifications

After reading Chapter 14, you should be able to identify and explain the historical significance of each of the following:

John Brown's raid on Harpers Ferry

doctrines of free soil and free labor

William H. Seward and irrepressible conflict

popular (squatter) sovereignty

Daniel Webster

Henry Clay's omnibus bill and the Compromise of 1850

Millard Fillmore

Fugitive Slave Act of 1850 and personal-liberty laws

Harriet Beecher Stowe, *Uncle Tom's Cabin*

American (or Know-Nothing) party

Stephen A. Douglas and the Kansas-Nebraska Act

Gadsden Purchase

John A. Quitman, William Walker, and filibustering

Ostend Manifesto

"Bleeding Kansas"

Lecompton versus Topeka legislature and the Lecompton constitution

sack of Lawrence and Pottawatomie massacre

Charles Sumner and Preston Brooks

John C. Frémont

James Buchanan

Roger B. Taney and *Dred Scott* v. *Sandford*

Lincoln-Douglas debates and Douglas's Freeport Doctrine

Panic of 1857

John C. Breckenridge

John Bell and the Constitutional Union party

Jefferson Davis and the Confederate States of America

Crittenden compromise

Fort Sumter

Skill Building: Maps

On the map of the United States, locate and draw in each of the following. How is each related to sectional conflict and the coming of the Civil War?

Missouri

Kansas and Nebraska territories

30°30' latitude

New Mexico Territory

Utah Territory

California

Gadsden Purchase

states that seceded by February 1861 (Lower South)

states that seceded after fighting at Fort Sumter (Upper South)

border slave states that did not secede

Charleston, South Carolina

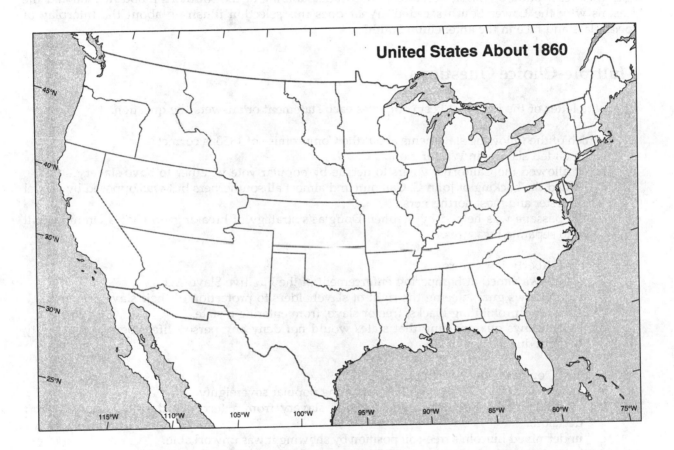

Historical Sources

Chapter 14 concentrates on the widening gulf between North and South on the questions of slavery and its extension into western territories. How do historians attempt to understand what northerners and southerners felt and believed in the 1850s? One historical source that the author of Chapter 14 uses is literary works published during the period, as well as the letters and comments of well-known poets and novelists. The most famous and influential piece of fiction in the 1850s was Harriet Beecher Stowe's *Uncle Tom's Cabin*. Look at the discussion of the novel on pages 384–385. By analyzing that novel, what does the historian learn about its emotional appeal to antebellum northerners? How did it touch their family values? Despite its abolitionist position, how did the book reflect the negative stereotypes about blacks that were prevalent among white northerners?

The historian can see the differing reactions to the novel in the North and South by reading reviews of it that appeared in northern and southern periodicals. For example, in December 1852 in a magazine called the *Southern Literary Messenger*, the historian can read a scathing denunciation of *Uncle Tom's Cabin*, which, according to the reviewer, criminally prostitutes the "high functions of the imagination to the pernicious intrigues of sectional animosity, and to the petty calumnies of willful slander."

The author of Chapter 14 also quotes a poem by John Greenleaf Whittier on page 384. Why does the author cite this 1850s writer? The historian can read an equally impassioned defense of the southern way of life and its planter elite in the poems, letters, and novels of the South Carolinian writer William Gilmore Simms.

Another way to gauge feelings in the Deep South on the eve of the Civil War is by taking a close look at a single city of the region. Turn to "A Place in Time: Charleston in the Secession Crisis." How does this description of Charleston add to our understanding of the southern mood in 1860 and the reasons why the Lower South seceded? What does this selection illustrate about the interplay of social class and race in the antebellum South?

Multiple-Choice Questions

Circle the letter of the item that best completes each statement or answers the question.

1. Which of the following statements about the Compromise of 1850 is correct?
    a. It ended slavery in Washington, D.C.
    b. It allowed the California voters to decide by popular vote whether to have slavery.
    c. It had the backing of John C. Calhoun and almost all southerners but was opposed by Daniel Webster and most northerners.
    d. Its passage was helped by Stephen Douglas's strategy of breaking up Clay's Omnibus bill into separate measures.

2. Personal-liberty laws were
    a. state laws aimed at hampering enforcement of the Fugitive Slave Act.
    b. federal laws guaranteeing the right of slaveholders to protection of their slave property.
    c. state laws prohibiting blacks, free or slave, from entering a state.
    d. federal laws guaranteeing that states would not deny any person life, liberty, or property without due process of law.

3. Stephen Douglas's Freeport Doctrine
    a. angered northern Democrats by repudiating popular sovereignty.
    b. pointed out how settlers could exclude slavery from a territory despite the *Dred Scott* decision.
    c. undermined Lincoln's free-soil position by showing it was unworkable.
    d. helped to unify the Democratic party for the election of 1860.

4. Which is the most valid statement describing the Republican party position in the election of 1860?
    a. There should be immediate, complete emancipation of slaves in the South.
    b. A program of gradual, compensated emancipation should be started.
    c. There should be no further extension of slavery into the territories.
    d. The principle of popular sovereignty should be applied honestly in the remaining territories.

5. What did the South gain from the Compromise of 1850?
    a. a stronger fugitive slave law
    b. a slave code for the territories
    c. the right to bring slaves into all territories taken from Mexico
    d. a lower tariff

6. The Lecompton constitution would have provided
   a. a policy for the Supreme Court to follow in cases involving slavery.
   b. an independent country in Africa for freed slaves.
   c. a permanent compromise on slavery for future states.
   d. a proslavery government for Kansas.

7. The Ostend Manifesto pertained to
   a. Cuba.
   b. California.
   c. Mexico.
   d. Florida.

8. The *Dred Scott* decision declared that Congress could *not*
   a. admit new slave states.
   b. prohibit slaveholders from taking slaves into northern states.
   c. bar slavery in the territories.
   d. pass a fugitive-slave law.

9. The secession of southern states began immediately after
   a. announcement of the *Dred Scott* decision.
   b. civil war in Kansas.
   c. Lincoln's inauguration.
   d. Lincoln's election.

10. The Crittenden compromise was not acceptable to Lincoln for all of the following reasons *except*
    a. he would not abandon the promise of free soil on which he had been elected.
    b. he had decided soon after his election to issue the Emancipation Proclamation.
    c. he believed that loyal southerners would soon overturn secession.
    d. he thought the plan would encourage southerners to seize more territory for slavery in the Caribbean.

Short-Answer Questions

1. Discuss the provisions of the Fugitive Slave Act of 1850. How did northerners attempt to prevent its enforcement?

2. What were the provisions of the Kansas-Nebraska Act? Why did it anger and alarm many northerners?

3. What brought about civil war in Kansas in 1856?

4. Explain Lincoln's position on slavery when he ran for the Senate in 1858 and for president in 1860.

5. Explain the impact of John Brown's Harpers Ferry raid on the South's mood and thought.

6. Discuss the political impact of the Confederacy's seizure of Fort Sumter.

Essay Questions

1. Imagine that you are a Virginia cotton planter or planter's wife. Compose a letter to a friend in New York explaining why your state has just seceded from the Union.

2. Repeated sectional compromises in 1820, 1833, and 1850 held the Union together and averted civil war. Why did compromise fail in 1860–1861?

3. Although the Compromise of 1850 postponed secession and civil war for a decade, it also contributed to embittered feelings in each section toward the other. Discuss and illustrate this statement.

4. Discuss the birth of the Republican party. How and why did it come about? Who supported it and why? What did it stand for? How and why did it broaden its appeal in the late 1850s?

5. Discuss the demise of the second party system. How is its breakdown related to immigration, nativism, slavery, and the spread of slavery into the West?

CHAPTER 15

Freedom Reborn: Civil War, 1861–1865

Outline and Summary

I. Introduction

Immediately after Fort Sumter's fall volunteers flocked to the Union and Confederate armies. Filled with loyalty and patriotism for their respective sides, neither soldiers nor politicians foresaw the long, bloody war ahead. As the Civil War dragged on and on and one out of every five soldiers who fought in it died, both the Union and Confederate governments were forced to impose the draft and adopt other coercive policies not dreamed of in 1861. Most important, the Union, which entered the fray with no objective beyond stopping secession, discovered that in order to in the war it also had to emancipate the slaves. As you read about the Civil War in Chapter 15, try to answer these questions: (1) How did both the Union and Confederate governments adapt in order to fight the war, and which administration adapted more successfully? (2) How and why did the Union finally commit itself to ending slavery? (3) Why did the North win the war? (4) In what lasting and meaningful ways did the Civil War transform the nation?

II. Mobilizing for War

A. Recruitment and Conscription

Initially, local governments and private citizens recruited volunteers for the armies, but their efforts proved insufficient. The Confederacy in April 1862 was the first to pass a conscription law. The act exempted from the draft people in several occupations, including those who owned or oversaw twenty or more slaves. The 20-Negro law led nonslaveholders to complain that this was "a rich man's war but a poor man's fight." The South managed to procure the arms it needed but was less successful in providing its troops with food and clothing. Therefore, in 1863 it imposed the Impressment Act, which allowed government agents to take food supplies from farmers at a set price and seize slaves to work for the army. This law was hated even more than the Conscription Act.

In 1863 the North passed the Enrollment Act, making all able-bodied white males aged twenty to forty-five eligible for the draft. The northern law also granted exemptions. Most resented were the provisions that permitted men to buy substitutes to serve in their places and excused those who paid the government a $300 commutation fee.

B. Financing the War

Both sides sold war bonds and printed unbacked paper money. The Union's greenbacks did not depreciate unduly in value because the federal government made greenbacks legal tender and imposed stiff new taxes to keep the government solvent. The South, which was reluctant to impose and collect new taxes and tried to pay its bills by printing more and more paper money, saw its currency depreciate drastically. The North also passed the National Bank Act, permitting federally chartered banks to issue national bank notes, backed by the federal government.

C. Political Leadership in Wartime

Lincoln faced opposition from northern Democrats, who disliked the National Bank Act, the draft, and emancipation of slaves, as well as from the Radical Republicans. Led by Salmon Chase, Charles Sumner, and Thaddeus Stevens, the Radicals pressed Lincoln to end slavery and, after 1863, criticized his lenient reconstruction plans. By his political skill, however, Lincoln held his party together. Jefferson Davis, president of the Confederacy, was less successful in containing factionalism. He was embroiled in destructive fights with his vice president, Alexander Stephens, and other states' rights southern leaders. The absence of an opposition party in the South further contributed to the factionalism of the southern Democrats.

D. Securing the Union's Borders

Because loss of the border states to the Confederacy would endanger Washington, D.C., and make fighting the war tougher, Lincoln took extraordinary measures. He occupied those states militarily and suspended the writ of habeas corpus there. The Supreme Court in *Ex parte* Merryman ruled Lincoln's actions unconstitutional, but he defied the Court and, with his emergency measures, kept Maryland, Delaware, Kentucky, and Missouri in the Union.

III. In Battle, 1861–1862

A. Armies, Weapons, and Strategies

Northern advantages over the South included a larger population, many more white men of fighting age, and control of 90 percent of the country's industry and two-thirds of its railroad track. The South's advantages were fighting a defensive war on its home territory and, with a slave labor force to carry on nonmilitary activities, being able to use a larger percentage of its white men for fighting.

The improved bullets and Springfield and Enfield rifles used during the Civil War increased the infantry's firepower, which in turn reduced the effectiveness of cavalry, encouraged the digging of trenches, and put a premium on the element of surprise in an attack.

At the start of hostilities the Union adopted the Anaconda plan, which called for sealing off the South with a blockade of its coastline and cutting it in two by gaining control of the Mississippi River. In 1861 the Union did not yet have enough ships and troops to carry out this plan. Instead, west of the Appalachians Union soldiers occupied Kentucky and moved southward into Tennessee, while in the eastern theater the North made repeated, futile attempts to capture Richmond.

B. Stalemate in the East

After the Confederates routed the Union at the first Battle of Bull Run (First Manassas), General George McClellan tried to take Richmond from the South, moving his army up the York Peninsula. Robert E. Lee's smaller Confederate army stopped McClellan, and Lincoln called off the Peninsula campaign. Then Lee and Stonewall Jackson headed north, defeated the Union at the Second Battle of Bull Run (Second Manassas), and continued into western Maryland. Lee hoped with this invasion to seize needed food; threaten Washington, D.C.; increase peace sentiment in the North; and convince Britain and France to recognize the Confederacy. At the bloody Battle of Antietam (Sharpsburg) in September 1862, Union forces under McClellan halted Lee's advance and forced him to retreat southward. After Antietam Lincoln issued his preliminary Emancipation Proclamation. Another Union attempt to take Richmond, under General Burnside, failed miserably at the Battle of Fredericksburg.

C. The War in the West

The western theater saw important Union victories. In 1861–1862 Ulysses S. Grant secured control of Missouri and Kentucky and then moved into Tennessee, capturing two key forts. Next he headed south toward Mississippi. Confederate attempts failed to stop him at the bloody Battle of Shiloh in southern Tennessee. Meanwhile a naval force under Admiral David G. Farragut captured New Orleans and pushed northward on the Mississippi. A second Union flotilla moving southward captured Memphis. By 1863 the North controlled the entire river except for a two-hundred-mile stretch between Port Hudson, Louisiana and Vicksburg, Mississippi.

Fighting also broke out in the Trans-Mississippi West, where northern and southern forces were joined by Mexican-Americans and Indians. After defeating the Confederates, much of the Union army in the Southwest and on the Great Plains turned to the final conquest of Native Americans.

D. Ironclads and Cruisers: The Naval War

The Union gradually tightened its blockade. It further disrupted foreign trade vital to the Confederacy by capturing its ports and coastal areas. Confederate attempts to break the stranglehold with an ironclad ship led to the battle of the *Merrimac* and the *Monitor,* the first clash of ironclads, but did not disrupt the blockade. The South inflicted serious damage on northern shipping with commerce raiders, but this did not hinder the Union's winning the war.

E. The Diplomatic War

The Confederacy tried to convince Britain and France that it was in their interests to extend diplomatic recognition. It even expected active help from the British, who, desperate for the South's cotton, might be counted on to break the Union blockade. There was tension between the Union and the British over the *Trent* affair and over the commerce raiders and rams built for the Confederacy in England, but the South's "cotton diplomacy" failed. The British had stockpiles of cotton on hand at the start of the war and then found alternative sources of supply. Lincoln's Emancipation Proclamation, which turned the struggle into a war against slavery, won British sympathy for the Union.

IV. *Emancipation Transforms the War*

A. From Confiscation to Emancipation

In his inaugural address Lincoln proclaimed that he had no intention of interfering with slavery in the South. Whenever Union armies approached, however, slaves fled to them. Some commanders, calling these people contraband of war, refused to return them to their masters. In August 1861 Congress backed this policy with the First Confiscation Act but stopped short of freeing the slaves. Lincoln at first resisted calls for emancipation because he did not want to push the border slave states into secession; further, he knew many northerners feared that freedmen might come north and compete for jobs. Radical Republicans, however, demanded immediate emancipation and pointed out that the South's use of slave labor was helping it militarily. After early Union defeats, many northerners agreed that it was necessary to strike a blow against slavery to beat the Confederacy. In July 1862 Congress passed the Second Confiscation Act, which authorized freeing slaves who came within Union lines and using blacks as soldiers. Lincoln hesitated a while longer to enforce this law, but when he failed to persuade the loyal slave states to accept voluntary, federally compensated abolition, he drafted his Emancipation Proclamation. The Proclamation stated that, as of January 1, 1863, all slaves in areas then in rebellion were "forever free." Since it applied only in areas not controlled by the Union, the Proclamation at first freed no slaves, but issuing it was a masterful move. It satisfied the Radicals, appealed to antislavery sentiment in Britain and France (forestalling their recognition of the Confederacy), and encouraged slaves to run away and join the Union army.

B. Crossing Union Lines

By 1865 about half a million former slaves were in Union territory. Some worked for the army. Others worked for loyal planters or on abandoned plantation lands. Many Union soldiers were bitterly prejudiced against blacks but began to change their attitudes as black spies and scouts helped them. Freedmen's aid societies in the North sent agents into the South to distribute relief and open schools. In March 1865 Congress created the Freedmen's Bureau to educate, dispense relief to, and find employment for the former slaves.

C. Black Soldiers in the Union Army

After Lincoln issued the Emancipation Proclamation, large numbers of blacks were accepted in the Union army. By 1865, 186,000 blacks had served, making up approximately one-tenth of all Union soldiers. The black troops suffered much discrimination. Placed in segregated regiments and commanded by white officers, they received less pay and suffered a higher mortality rate than whites. Despite unfair treatment, they served well.

D. Slavery in Wartime

Southerners attempted to maintain control over their slaves by stepping up patrols, telling slaves horror stories about the Yankees, and moving slaves far from Union lines. Nonetheless, blacks ran to Union camps. Others remained on the plantation doing little or no work.

E. The Turning Point of 1863

In the summer and fall of 1863 the Union scored important victories. Lee's invasion of the North was turned back at Gettysburg in July. Simultaneously, Grant took Vicksburg and Port Hudson fell to another Union force. The North then controlled the whole Mississippi River. In September the North also routed the Confederacy from Chattanooga, leaving the way clear for Union troops to invade Georgia.

V. War and Society, North and South

A. The War's Economic Impact: The North

War-related industries and the railroads boomed. The Republican-dominated Congress enacted measures that encouraged further business development: raising tariffs, chartering and granting land and loans to the Union Pacific and Central Pacific railroad corporations to build a transcontinental line, and creating a new national banking system. Other legislation benefited the West particularly, such as the Homestead and the Morrill Land Grant acts (1862). Everyone did not benefit equally from the rising economy. While manufacturers and speculators made fat profits, workers' wages lagged behind inflation. Women, who increasingly replaced drafted men, received even less pay than males. Workers protested their economic lot by forming national unions.

B. The War's Economic Impact: The South

The war destroyed the South's economy, wrecking its railroads and cutting its cotton and food production. Food shortages worsened the South's already rampant inflation and caused such hardships for soldiers' families that many Confederates deserted to try to provide for their wives and children.

C. Dealing with Dissent

The Union and the Confederacy both faced internal dissent. In the South nonslaveholders with Unionist sentiments and states' rights politicians denounced Jefferson Davis's government. On the whole the Confederate government took little action against these dissidents. In the North peace Democrats (Copperheads) criticized the Emancipation Proclamation and demanded an immediate peace settlement with the South. Peace Democrats had their strongest following in the border states, in the Midwest, and among immigrant workers in northeastern cities. Attempts to begin drafting men in July 1863 sparked riots in New York City that had to be quelled by federal troops. Lincoln suspended the writ of habeas corpus and imposed martial law more frequently than Jefferson Davis did. Although Lincoln was hardly the despot his opponents charged, his actions did lead to the Supreme Court case *Ex parte* Milligan (1866), in which the justices ruled that civilians cannot be tried by military tribunals when the regular civil courts are open.

D. The Medical War

Northern citizens formed the U.S. Sanitary Commission, a civilian organization that raised money for medical supplies and distributed extra food and medicine to army camps. Some thirty-two hundred women volunteered their services as nurses to either the Union or Confederate army. Nevertheless, limited medical knowledge about sanitation and germs led to a frightful death toll from disease and infected wounds. Conditions in prisoner-of-war camps were particularly grim. The Confederate prison camp at Andersonville, Georgia was the most notorious.

E. The War and Women's Rights

Feminists hoped that the war would win equality for women as well as blacks. Elizabeth Cady Stanton and Susan B. Anthony organized the National Woman's Loyal League in 1863 to campaign for amendments ending slavery and granting blacks and women the vote. The Civil War, however, did not change women's inferior political status.

VI. *The Union Victorious, 1864–1865*

A. The Eastern Theater in 1864

In 1864 Lincoln put Grant in command of all Union armies. Grant moved his headquarters to the eastern theater and proceeded to attack Lee in Virginia. At the same time, he ordered Sherman to invade Georgia. Despite heavy casualties at the Battles of the Wilderness, Spotsylvania, and Cold Harbor, Grant pressed forward, forcing Lee to pull back to trenches outside Petersburg and Richmond. Grant dispatched another Union force under Philip Sheridan, which devastated and conquered the Shenandoah Valley.

B. Sherman in Georgia

While Grant battled Lee in the Wilderness, Sherman advanced relentlessly into Georgia. Confederate forces had to evacuate Atlanta, which fell to Sherman in September 1864.

C. The Election of 1864

Lincoln faced a tough election fight first from the Radical Republicans, who would have preferred to nominate Salmon Chase, and then from the peace Democrats, who nominated George McClellan. To win the votes of prowar Democrats, Lincoln and the Republicans renamed their party the National Union Party and nominated a prowar Tennessee Unionist, Andrew Johnson, for vice president. Sherman's capture of Atlanta in September clinched Lincoln's victory in November. Following the election, Congress passed the Thirteenth Amendment, which was ratified by the end of 1865.

D. Sherman's March Through Georgia

After burning much of Atlanta, Sherman marched across Georgia to Savannah. His army lived off the countryside and seized or destroyed everything of possible military value. In December 1864 Sherman took Savannah and turned north to South Carolina. The destruction visited on that state was even greater and was climaxed with the gutting of its capital, Columbia. Sherman then continued into North Carolina.

E. Toward Appomattox

While Sherman swung north, Grant closed in on Lee's army. By spring 1865 Confederate morale had broken and men were deserting in droves. On April 3 Grant entered Richmond. Lee made a last attempt to escape from the Union armies but soon after surrendered to Grant at Appomattox Courthouse. Within a month all remaining Confederate resistance ended. On April 14 John Wilkes Booth shot Lincoln, who died the next day, bringing Andrew Johnson to the presidency.

VII. *Conclusion*

The Civil War killed some 620,000 Americans, more than any other war the nation has fought. It ruined the southern economy but stimulated industrialization and capital investment in the North. While the Civil war did not wipe out the states' rights doctrine, it did greatly strengthen the federal government: there would be no more attempts at secession. The war ended slavery, but it left undecided the future of 3.5 million freedmen and the form that reconstruction of the South would take.

Vocabulary

The following terms are used in Chapter 15. To understand the chapter fully, it is important that you know what each of them means.

conscription   compulsory enrollment of men for military or naval service; the draft

gross national product (GNP)   the sum, measured in dollars, of all goods and services produced in a given year

tithe   a tax amounting to one-tenth of income or agricultural produce due to the government or the church

writ of habeas corpus   a formal order requiring that an arrested person be brought before a judge or court and either charged with a specific crime or released (The right to such a writ is guaranteed in the U.S. Constitution.)

reconnaissance   a search in the field to uncover useful military information

flotilla   a group of small naval vessels; a subdivision of a fleet

emissaries   agents sent out on a mission, sometimes of a secret nature

belligerent   when used as a diplomatic term, as in this chapter, a state or nation at war

bigotry   intolerant attachment to a particular belief, prejudice, or opinion

dissent   to disagree with the opinions and policies of the government, church, or social majority

martial law   law imposed on an area by military forces when civil authority has broken down or been pushed aside

feminist   an advocate of equality for women in political, economic, and social life

Identifications

After reading Chapter 15, you should be able to identify and explain the historical significance of each of the following:

20-Negro law
bounty jumpers
Legal Tender Act and greenbacks
National Bank Act, 1863, and national bank notes
Jefferson Davis
Charles Sumner, Thaddeus Stevens, and the Radical Republicans
Ex parte Merryman, 1861, and *Ex parte* Milligan, 1866
Winfield Scott and the Anaconda plan
first and second battles of Bull Run (First and Second Manassas)
George B. McClellan
Thomas "Stonewall" Jackson
Robert E. Lee
Battle of Antietam (Sharpsburg)
Ulysses S. Grant
William T. Sherman
ironclads and the battle of the *Merrimac* and the *Monitor*
Trent affair
Charles Francis Adams, the *Florida, Alabama,* and Laird rams
cotton diplomacy
First and Second Confiscation Acts and Emancipation Proclamation
Fort Pillow massacre
Gettysburg
Vicksburg
Homestead Act, 1862
Morrill Land Grand Act, 1862
Copperheads and Clement L. Vallandigham
New York City draft riot
Elizabeth Cady Stanton, Susan B. Anthony, and the National Woman's Loyal League
National Union party and Andrew Johnson
surrender at Appomattox Courthouse

Skill Building: Maps

On the map of the South on the following page, locate each of the areas or places listed below. What is the political and/or military importance of each in the Civil War?

western theater
eastern theater
Appalachian Mountains
Mississippi River

Montgomery, Alabama

Richmond, Virginia

Washington, D.C.

Shenandoah Valley

Maryland

Missouri

Kentucky

Memphis, Tennessee

Vicksburg, Mississippi

Gettysburg, Pennsylvania

Atlanta, Georgia

route of Sherman's march to the sea

Port Royal, South Carolina

Southeastern United States

Skill Building: Graphs and Charts

Look at the bar graphs under the title "Brothers in Combat: The Opposing Armies of the Civil War" on page 408. These graphs present in a kind of visual shorthand many historically important facts. By glancing at them, you should be able to answer the following questions, among others:

1. In which of America's wars, from the Revolution to Vietnam, did the United States suffer the greatest number of deaths? How do you account for this?

2. How significant an advantage did the Union have over the Confederacy in the size of the army it was able to put into the field?

3. Which side had the greater percentage of its army made up of volunteers? Which had more draftees and substitutes?

4. Given the size of their respective armies, which side suffered the greater percentage of deaths? Why do you think that might be? Which side had the greater percentage of desertions? How do you explain that?

5. New York City draft rioters in 1863 complained that the Civil War was a rich man's war and a poor man's fight. Looking at the graph on draftees and substitutes, do you see any merit to their complaint?

Historical Sources

Among the many historical sources used in Chapter 15 are two particularly interesting ones: published personal narratives of participants in the Civil War and letters written by Union and Confederate soldiers and their families.

On page 423 the author quotes from Thomas W. Higginson's *Army Life in a Black Regiment.* Who was Higginson? What does the author intend to show by using his book? Why is Higginson's book a valuable historical source? Was Higginson an "objective" observer? Would there be any danger in a historian's relying on this source alone to learn about black soldiers in the Civil War?

Another personal narrative used is Ray Billington, ed., *The Journal of Charlotte Forten.* Charlotte Forten was a member of a wealthy, free black family from Philadelphia who went south during the Civil War and Reconstruction to teach and aid freedmen. What does her account on page 423a illustrate? Why is it a valuable historical source? Are there any dangers in using it as one's only source on the experiences and reactions of freedmen?

In many places in Chapter 15, letters of soldiers and their families are quoted. Find some of these and show how the historian uses them. Would these letters tend to duplicate what the historian can learn from William T. Sherman's *Memoirs*? Why or why not?

Multiple-Choice Questions

Circle the letter of the item that best completes each statement or answers the question.

1. Lincoln's Emancipation Proclamation
   a. freed the slaves in the slave states that remained in the Union.
   b. freed the slaves in the western territories.
   c. freed the slaves in areas in rebellion against the U.S. government.
   d. freed all slaves in the Union and Confederacy.

2. Which of the following Union military objectives proved the hardest and took the longest to accomplish?
   a. taking Richmond
   b. gaining control of the Mississippi River
   c. taking New Orleans
   d. seizing the sea islands off the South's Atlantic coast to strengthen the blockade

3. Andrew Johnson was nominated as Lincoln's running mate in 1864 to
   a. please the Radical Republicans.
   b. win the votes of prowar northern Democrats.
   c. influence the South to rejoin the Union, since he would be a southern vice president.
   d. reward Tennessee for remaining loyal to the Union.

4. Which of the following men, denouncing Lincoln's Emancipation Proclamation and suspension of the writ of habeas corpus, called for immediate peace with the Confederacy?
   a. Thaddeus Stevens
   b. Salmon Chase
   c. Clement L. Vallandigham
   d. Charles Sumner

5. Union capture of Vicksburg and Port Hudson was strategically important because
   a. it opened the way to Richmond.
   b. it completed Union control over the Atlantic coast.
   c. it gave Lincoln the victories he was waiting for to issue the Emancipation Proclamation.
   d. it gave the North control over the whole Mississippi River.

6. The Supreme Court ruled in *Ex parte* Milligan that
   a. civilians could not be tried by military tribunals when the civil courts were open.
   b. Lincoln had no constitutional right to free slaves in the Confederacy.
   c. the Union had no right to confiscate the property of rebel leaders.
   d. Congress rather than the president had the right to direct Reconstruction of the South.

7. Slaves during the Civil War
   a. mostly remained loyal to their masters and the South.
   b. often served as officers in the Union army over other blacks.
   c. ran to Union lines when they could and worked for or fought for the North.
   d. were never allowed to enlist as soldiers in either the Union or the Confederate army.

8. By 1865, African-Americans constituted about what portion of the Union army?
   a. 1/10
   b. 1/4
   c. 3/4
   d. 1/20

9. Which of the following statements about women in the Civil War is correct?
   a. Women were *not* allowed to enter army camps to nurse soldiers.
   b. Women replaced draftees in many of the industrial jobs in the North.
   c. Loyal Unionist women were allowed to vote and run for political office.
   d. Northern missionary and freedmen's aid societies refused to use women volunteers.

10. Which of the following statements is correct?
    a. Both the Union and the Confederacy printed unbacked paper money to help finance their war efforts.
    b. The Union had to resort to conscription to get enough soldiers, but the Confederacy recruited enough volunteers to avoid imposing the draft.
    c. Neither the Union nor the Confederacy exempted the wealthy from the draft.
    d. Both the Union and the Confederacy ruthlessly suppressed all internal dissent for the duration of the war.

Short-Answer Questions

1. Explain how President Lincoln kept the four border slave states in the Union.

2. Why didn't the British recognize the Confederacy as a nation? What help did the British give the South?

3. Who were the Radical Republicans? On what grounds did they criticize Lincoln during the Civil War?

4. How were African-Americans in the Union army discriminated against?

5. What caused the 1863 New York City draft riot?

Essay Questions

1. In his inaugural address in 1861 Lincoln said, "I have no purpose, directly or indirectly, to interfere with the institution of slavery in the states where it exists." In September 1862 he issued his preliminary Emancipation Proclamation. Explain why and how this marked change of policy took place.

2. Discuss the military advantages and disadvantages of each side at the start of the Civil War. Considering that the preponderance of advantages belonged to the Union, why did it take the North four years to defeat the South?

3. Compare and contrast the economic impact of the Civil War on the Union and the Confederacy.

4. The Civil War has been called a second American Revolution that significantly transformed the social, economic, and political fabric of the nation. Write an essay agreeing or disagreeing with that assessment and offer as much evidence as possible to back up your position.

5. Pretend that you are one of the following: a northern woman or young man working in a factory, the wife of a Confederate soldier, or a rank-and-file Confederate soldier. Write a journal or letter, based on the content of Chapter 15, explaining your attitudes, experiences, hardships, aspirations, and gripes.

CHAPTER 16

The Crises of Reconstruction, 1865–1877

Outline and Summary

I. Introduction

The ending of the Civil War and the Reconstruction period that followed constituted a "crucial turning point" in American history. Vital problems had to be solved, above all, how and under what conditions the South should be readmitted to the Union and what the rights and status of the 3.5 million freedmen should be. Chapter 16 discusses the challenges facing the nation between 1865 and 1877 and how those challenges were met or failed to be met. While reading the chapter you should consider the following questions: (1) How did the Radical Republicans gain control over reconstructing the South and what was the impact of their program on the ex-Confederates, other white southerners, and southern blacks? (2) How did freed blacks remake their lives after emancipation? (3) What brought about the end of reconstruction? Should it be considered a success or failure? Why?

II. Reconstruction Politics

A. Lincoln's Plan

Differences between President Lincoln and Congress on reconstruction of the Confederate states began as early as 1863. In December Lincoln issued a plan that would allow the formation of a new state government when as few as 10 percent of the state's voters took an oath of loyalty to the Union and recognized the end of slavery. This plan said nothing about votes for the freedmen. Lincoln hoped with this plan to win over southern Unionists and draw them into the Republican party. Republicans in Congress thought the plan inadequate and passed the Wade-Davis bill instead. This bill required that at least 50 percent of the voters take an oath of allegiance, and it excluded from participation in government all those who had cooperated with the Confederacy. Lincoln pocket-vetoed the bill, and at the time of his death he and Congress were at an impasse.

B. Presidential Reconstruction Under Johnson

President Andrew Johnson, who was unconcerned about the blacks but wished to promote the interests of the poorer whites in the South, announced his Reconstruction plan in May 1865. Johnson required whites to take an oath of allegiance to the Union, after which they could set up new state governments. These had to proclaim secession illegal, repudiate Confederate debts, and ratify the Thirteenth Amendment (abolishing slavery). Whites who had held high office under the Confederacy and all those with taxable property of $20,000 or more could not vote or hold office until they applied for and received a special pardon from the president. During the summer, Johnson undermined his own policy of excluding planters from leadership by handing out pardons to them wholesale. The new governments created under Johnson's plan were soon dominated by former Confederate leaders and large landowners. Some of the Johnson governments refused to ratify the Thirteenth Amendment, and all showed their intention of making black freedom only nominal by enacting "black codes." Horrified by such evidence of continued southern defiance, the Republican-dominated Congress, in December 1865, refused to recognize these governments or to seat the men they sent to the House and Senate.

C. Congress Versus Johnson

The Radical Republicans, who wished to give black men the vote and transform the South into a biracial democracy, were in a minority in 1866. The majority Moderate Republicans wanted only to get rid of the black codes and protect the basic civil rights of blacks. The Moderates attempted to accomplish these limited goals by continuing the Freedmen's Bureau and passing the Civil Rights Act of 1866. When Johnson vetoed both of these measures, he drove the Moderates into alliance with the Radicals, and together they overrode his vetoes. The now radicalized Republicans also moved to protect the provisions of the Civil Rights Act by embodying them in a constitutional amendment.

D. The Fourteenth Amendment

With the Fourteenth amendment, the federal government for the first time defined citizenship and intervened to protect persons from state governments. The amendment stated that all persons born in the United States or naturalized were citizens. No state could deny any person's rights without due process of law or deny equal protection of the law. States that refused black men the vote could have their representation in Congress reduced. Former Confederate officials were excluded from voting and officeholding until pardoned by a two-thirds vote of Congress. The southern states, except for Tennessee, refused to ratify the amendment and Johnson denounced it, but in the congressional elections of 1866 the Republicans won huge majorities, giving them a mandate to force ratification of the Fourteenth Amendment and proceed with congressional Reconstruction of the South.

E. Congressional Reconstruction

In 1867 and 1868 Congress enacted its Reconstruction program over Johnson's vetoes. The earlier Johnson governments, black codes, and all other laws they had passed were invalidated. All the former Confederate states except Tennessee, which had been readmitted, were divided into districts under the temporary rule of the military. Each state was required to write a new constitution enfranchising black men and to ratify the Fourteenth Amendment. When these things had been done, Congress could readmit the state to the Union. Congressional Reconstruction was more radical than Lincoln's or Johnson's, since it enfranchised blacks and temporarily disfranchised many whites. It did not, however, go as far as the Radicals wanted, since it failed to confiscate southern land and redistribute it to blacks and poor whites. Johnson, as commander in chief of the army, dragged his feet in enforcing congressional Reconstruction, thus convincing Republicans that he had to be dealt with.

F. The Impeachment Crisis

In March 1867 Congress passed laws aimed at reducing the president's power. Johnson violated one of them by firing Secretary of War Stanton, at which point the Republicans in Congress began impeachment proceedings. Some Republicans wavered, however, fearing that removal of Johnson would upset the constitutional balance of power. As a result, the vote to convict and remove the president fell one short of the necessary two-thirds of the Senate.

G. The Fifteenth Amendment

Congress passed a final amendment to complete its Reconstruction program. The Fifteenth Amendment stated that the right to vote could not be denied because of race, color, or previous condition of servitude. The Republicans hoped with this amendment to protect southern blacks, extend suffrage to northern blacks, and gain many new voters for their party. When Congress refused to include women's suffrage, some feminists denounced the amendment and its Republican sponsors. By 1870 the three new amendments—ending slavery, guaranteeing the rights of citizens, and enfranchising black men—were a part of the Constitution and Congress had readmitted all the former Confederate states. Thereafter congressional efforts at Reconstruction weakened.

III. Reconstruction Governments

A. A New Electorate

The Reconstruction laws of 1867–1868 created a new electorate in the South by enfranchising blacks and temporarily disfranchising 10 percent to 15 percent of the whites. This new electorate put in power Republican governments that were made up of a coalition of carpetbaggers (northerners who had come south for a variety of reasons), scalawags (cooperating southern whites), and blacks.

B. Republican Rule

The Republican Reconstruction governments democratized southern politics by abolishing property and racial qualifications for voting and officeholding, redistricting state legislatures, and making formerly appointive offices elective. They undertook extensive public works, offered increased public services, and established the South's first public schools. All of this cost money, and therefore taxes rose. Southern landowners bitterly resented the increased taxes and accused the state governments of corruption and waste. Some of their charges were true, but many were exaggerated.

C. Counterattacks

White southern Democrats refused to accept black voting and officeholding and launched a counterattack to drive the Republican Reconstruction governments from power. White vigilante groups began a campaign of violence and intimidation against blacks, Freedmen's Bureau officials, and white Republicans. Congress investigated this reign of terror and attempted to suppress it with the Enforcement Acts, but only a "large military presence in the South could have protected black rights" and preserved the black electorate. By the 1870s Congress and President Grant were no longer willing to use military force to remake the South.

IV. The Impact of Emancipation

A. Confronting Freedom

Freedmen, usually lacking property, tools, capital, and literacy, left the plantations where they had been enslaved and searched for family members from whom they had been separated. Once reunited many took the first opportunity to legalize their marriages so that they could raise their children and live an independent family life.

B. Black Institutions

The desire to be free of white control also led blacks to establish their own institutions. Most important were the black churches, which played major religious, social, and political roles. Many black schools were started with the help of the Freedmen's Bureau and northern philanthropists, including the earliest black universities: Howard, Atlanta, and Fisk. Segregation of all facilities in the South became a way of life despite Charles Sumner's Civil Rights Act of 1875, which was unenforced and later invalidated by the Supreme Court.

C. Land, Labor, and Sharecropping

Above all freedmen wanted to become landowning, independent farmers, but few did because the Republicans believed that property rights were too sacred to violate by confiscation and redistribution of white planters' land. Besides, blacks did not have the capital to buy land and agricultural tools. With the end of slavery, the planters continued to own the land but had no work force. Therefore, landless laborers and landholding planters developed the form of tenantry known as sharecropping. Many white small farmers also lost their land and became sharecropping tenants. By 1880, 80 percent of the land in the cotton states was worked by landless tenants.

D. Toward a Crop-Lien Economy

Rural merchants (often themselves landlords) sold supplies to sharecroppers on credit—with a lien on the tenants' share of the crop as collateral. Because interest rates were exorbitant, cotton prices low, and merchants often dishonest, sharecroppers fell deeper and deeper into debt. Southern law prohibited their leaving the land until they had fully repaid their debts. Thus sharecroppers were locked into poverty and "debt peonage."

V. New Concerns in the North

A. Grantism

The popular Civil War hero Ulysses S. Grant won the presidency in 1868 on the Republican ticket. His administration was marred by rampant corruption, as were many state and local governments of the time. In 1872 Republicans disgusted by the scandals broke with Grand and formed the Liberal Republican party.

B. The Liberals' Revolt

The Liberal Republicans nominated Horace Greeley for president, and the Democrats endorsed him as well. The regular Republicans renominated Grant, who won the 1872 election, but the split in Republican ranks seriously weakened Republican efforts to remake the South.

C. The Panic of 1873

During Grant's second term the nation suffered a financial panic and a severe economic depression. These produced business failures, mass unemployment, heightened labor-management conflict, and disputes over the country's currency system, all of which further diverted Republican attention from Reconstruction.

D. Reconstruction and the Constitution

The Supreme Court in the last quarter of the nineteenth century also undermined Republican Reconstruction. In a series of decisions, the Court interpreted the Fourteenth and Fifteenth amendments in a way that made them all but useless for protecting black citizens. It declared the Civil Rights and Enforcement acts unconstitutional and upheld state segregation laws.

E. Republicans in Retreat

By the 1870s the Republicans were abandoning their Reconstruction policy. Most of them were more interested in economic growth than in protecting black rights. The Radicals who were committed to biracial democracy in the South were dead or had been defeated in elections. Many northerners wanted to normalize relations with the white South. They shared the racial belief that blacks were inferior to whites, and the federal government could not force equality.

VI. Reconstruction Abandoned

A. Redeeming the South

After 1872 congressional pardons restored voting and officeholding rights to all ex-Confederates. These men and the South's rising class of businessmen led the Democratic party in a drive to redeem the South from Republican rule. Using economic pressure, intimidation, and violence, the Democrats had regained control of all the southern states but South Carolina, Florida, and Louisiana by 1876. Once in power the Democrats cut taxes and public works and services, and they passed laws favoring landlords over tenants. Some blacks responded to the deteriorating situation by migrating from the South, but most were trapped where they were by debt and poverty.

B. The Election of 1876

The Republicans nominated Rutherford Hayes; the Democrats, Samuel Tilden. Tilden won in the popular vote, but because of fraud and intimidation at the polls, the electoral votes in four states were disputed. A special electoral commission stacked in favor of the Republicans awarded all the disputed votes to Hayes. The Democrats refused to accept the finding until a compromise deal was worked out by southern Democrats and Republican supporters of Hayes. In exchange for southern acceptance of Hayes as president, the Republicans promised (1) to let Democrats take over the last Republican Reconstruction governments in Louisiana, South Carolina, and Florida; (2) to remove the remaining troops from the South; (3) to give more federal patronage to southern Democrats; and (4) to provide federal aid for building railroads and for other internal improvements in the South.

VII. Conclusion

By the end of the Reconstruction era the Republicans had firm support in the Northeast and Midwest; the Democrats were solidly entrenched in the South and would remain so for nearly a century. Many historians today look back on Reconstruction as a democratic experiment that failed partly because Congress did not redistribute land to freedmen, and without any property they were too economically vulnerable to hold on to their political rights. The Republicans also were unwilling to continue using military force to protect blacks and remake southern society. Reconstruction did, however, leave as a lasting legacy the Fourteenth and Fifteenth amendments. During that brief era, southern blacks reconstituted their families, created their own institutions, and for the first time participated in government.

Vocabulary

The following terms are used in Chapter 16. To understand the chapter fully, it is important that you know what each of them means.

suffrage   the vote; the right to vote

enfranchisement   the giving of the rights of citizenship and voting (the taking away of these rights is called disfranchisement)

allegiance   faithfulness and obligation to a person, idea, country, or government

amnesty   a general pardon for offenses against a government

partisan   a supporter of a political party or cause; having to do with actions motivated by support of a political party or cause

yeomen   nonslaveholding, small landowning farmers

status quo antebellum   the way things were before the war

referendum   the procedure of submitting legislative measures to the voters for approval or rejection

mandate   instruction about policy given or supposed to be given by the voters to a legislative body or government

confiscate   to seize private property by government authority

impeachment   the charging of a public official, such as a judge or president, with misconduct in office

vigilantes   members of extralegal citizens' groups organized to maintain order and punish offenses

electorate   the body of persons entitled to vote in an election

stereotype   a characteristic or set of characteristics, usually negative, attributed to all members of a group

coalition   a combination or alliance between different groups, parties, or states in support of a particular cause, individual, or purpose

mulatto   the offspring of one white and one black parent; a person of mixed black and white ancestry

mobilization   putting forces or resources into active service for a cause

writ of habeas corpus   a formal order requiring that an arrested person be brought before a judge or court and be charged with a specific crime or released; the right to such a writ is guaranteed in the U.S. Constitution

capital   wealth (especially money) that can be used to produce more wealth

segregation   the act of separating or setting apart from others, especially on the basis of race (the undoing of such separation is called desegregation or integration)

collateral   security or property pledged for the payment of a loan

debt peonage   the practice of holding someone in servitude or partial slavery until that person's debt is paid off

speculator   one who trades in commodities, securities, or land in the hope of making a profit from changes in their market value; a person who engages in business transactions that involve considerable risk but offer the chance of large gains

filibuster   to use delaying tactics, such as long speeches, to prevent a vote or action by a legislative body

Identifications

After reading Chapter 16, you should be able to identify and explain the historical significance of each of the following:

Charles Sumner, Thaddeus Stevens, and the Radical Republicans

Lincoln's 10 percent plan versus Wade-Davis bill

Thirteenth Amendment

black codes

Freedmen's Bureau

Civil Rights Act of 1866

Fourteenth Amendment

Reconstruction Act of 1867

Tenure of Office Act

Fifteenth Amendment

Elizabeth Cady Stanton and Susan B. Anthony

carpetbaggers and scalawags

Ku Klux Klan, Enforcement Acts (Ku Klux Klan Act)

Civil Rights Act of 1875

Jay Gould and Jim Fisk

Crédit Mobilier

William M. Tweed

"Seward's Ice Box"

Liberal Republicans and Horace Greeley

greenbacks and the Greenback party

Slaughterhouse cases

Mississippi Plan and redemption

"Exodus" movement

Rutherford B. Hayes, Samuel J. Tilden, and the Compromise of 1877

Skill Building: Charts

1. Look at the table titled "The Duration of Republican Rule in the Ex-Confederate States" on page 467 in the textbook.

   a. For how many years on average did Republicans control the governments of the ex-Confederate states?

   b. Can you explain why Republican rule lasted less than a decade in every one of them?

   c. Which state was readmitted to the Union before the start of congressional Reconstruction? After reading the chapter, can you explain why?

   d. In what three states did Republicans hold power the longest? Can you explain what brought about the return of the Democrats to power in those three states?

2. Look at the table titled "Percentage of Persons Unable to Write by Age Group, 1870–1890, in South Carolina, Georgia, Alabama, Mississippi, and Louisiana" on page 459 of the textbook.

   a. What percentage of whites in each age group were unable to write in 1870? After reading the textbook, can you explain why these figures are so high?

   b. Did the educational levels of whites improve by 1890? Can you explain why it did or did not?

   c. Was the educational level of blacks higher or lower than that of whites in 1870? What about 1890? How might a critic of Republican Reconstruction of the South use these figures?

   d. After reading the text, can you explain the reasons for the differences between whites and blacks?

Historical Sources

Among the many historical sources used in Chapter 16 are three that are often useful to historians writing political history: (1) law codes, statutes, and constitutional amendments passed by the states and the federal government; (2) records of congressional speeches, remarks, and votes, as found in the *Congressional Globe,* later named the *Congressional Record;* (3) records of congressional hearings and investigations that are printed and made public by the federal government.

Page 445 of the text refers to laws known as black codes passed by the ex-Confederate states. By studying these laws, what does the historian learn about the intentions and attitudes toward blacks among the governing whites? What other conclusions does the textbook come to on the basis of this source?

Find at least three places in Chapter 16 where remarks of congressmen or important votes in the House or Senate are discussed. In each example, analyze what the author is illustrating or proving with this evidence.

Page 456 of the text cites testimony about vigilante violence in the South that was given before a joint congressional committee. Why are records of hearings and investigations by congressional committees a rich source for historians? Could a historian get a distorted or biased view of a past situation by relying solely on such a source? Why or why not?

Studies that focus on a local area or single city also provide useful historical insights. Look at "A Place in Time: Atlanta Reconstructed." What light does this historical sketch of Atlanta during the Reconstruction period throw on some of the major points made in Chapter 16? For instance, how does the story of Atlanta illustrate the ways in which African-Americans reshaped their lives and built new institutions after emancipation? How does Atlanta's development show economic transformation during Reconstruction, as well as making clear the failure of Radical Republicans to "create a biracial democracy in the South"?

Multiple-Choice Questions

Circle the letter of the item that best completes each statement or answers the question.

1. Lincoln's plan of reconstruction
   a. required southern states to enfranchise blacks.
   b. required that 50 percent or more of white voters in an ex-Confederate state take an oath of allegiance to the Union before a new state government could be established.
   c. was intended to gain the support of southern Unionists and attract them to a southern Republican party.
   d. was eventually accepted by Congress.

2. Which of the following statements about Andrew Johnson is *incorrect*?
   a. He wanted to exclude planters from political leadership in the South, but then he undermined his intention by granting many pardons to this group.
   b. He cared deeply about obtaining just treatment for the freedmen.
   c. He was a lifelong Democrat with no interest in building the strength of the Republican party.
   d. He vetoed all of the congressional Reconstruction acts, only to have Congress override his vetoes.

3. The black codes
   a. were imposed by Congress on the ex-Confederate states.
   b. guaranteed such basic liberties as freedom of movement and employment, the right to testify in court, and the use of all public facilities.
   c. were seen by Thaddeus Stevens and other Radical Republicans as a necessary legal step to help blacks make the transition from slavery to freedom.
   d. were laws passed by the Johnson governments in the South to keep blacks as a semifree, cheap labor force.

4. Which of their plans did Radical Republicans persuade Congress to embody in the Reconstruction acts and in the Fourteenth and Fifteenth amendments?
   a. black suffrage, a period of military occupation of the South, temporary exclusion of ex-Confederates from voting and officeholding
   b. confiscation and redistribution of land in the South, imprisonment of ex-Confederate leaders
   c. forty acres and a mule for each freedman, temporary disfranchisement of whites, enfranchisement of blacks
   d. exile of Jefferson Davis and other ex-Confederate leaders, upholding of all Civil War debts, extending the right to vote to all citizens over age twenty-one

5. Andrew Johnson was impeached but not convicted because
   a. he proved that he had not violated the Tenure of Office Act.
   b. he resigned before the Senate voted on his guilt.
   c. seven Republicans, fearing that removal of the president would upset the balance of power among the three branches of government, voted "not guilty" with the Democrats.
   d. the Supreme Court ruled that he had not engaged in misconduct in office.

6. The Fifteenth Amendment
   a. defines citizenship and requires states to extend to all persons equal protection of the laws.
   b. states that no one shall be denied the right to vote because of race, color, or previous condition of servitude.
   c. extends suffrage to all citizens over twenty-one years of age.
   d. gives Congress the power to deny seats in the House to states that do not allow black men to vote.

7. In the Republican Reconstruction governments of the South, the group that held the most political offices consisted of
   a. carpetbaggers.
   b. scalawags.
   c. blacks.
   d. the planter elite.

8. The Republican Reconstruction governments of the South
   a. gave the region the most honest, efficient governments it had ever had.
   b. excluded almost all whites from officeholding and were run almost exclusively by blacks.
   c. created public-school systems, built and repaired roads and bridges, and opened institutions to care for orphans and the disabled.
   d. cut taxes and passed laws favoring the interests of landlords over those of tenants and sharecroppers.

9. The sharecropping and crop-lien systems that developed in the post–Civil War South
   a. contributed to soil depletion, agricultural backwardness, and southern poverty.
   b. reduced the portion of southern land owned and controlled by the planter elite.
   c. forced most black people out of agriculture and into southern cities.
   d. tied white planters and black tenants together economically but had no effect on white small farmers.

10. Most historians today view Radical Reconstruction as a democratic experiment that failed because
   a. it left blacks without property and thus economically unable to defend their political rights.
   b. it relied on excessive military force instead of political persuasion.
   c. it was unrealistic in its expectation that illiterate blacks could be turned into responsible citizens overnight.
   d. it was overly vindictive and harsh toward all white southerners.

Short-Answer Questions

1. What actions of President Johnson drove Moderate Republicans in Congress into cooperation with Radical Republicans?

2. Why did Elizabeth Cady Stanton, Susan B. Anthony, and some other feminists oppose the Fifteenth Amendment?

3. Why did the Liberal Republicans break with President Grant? What impact did the split have on Republican Reconstruction?

4. Explain how Supreme Court decisions in the 1870s and 1880s undermined Republican Reconstruction.

5. What were the terms of the Compromise of 1877? Which of the terms were actually carried out after the inauguration of Rutherford B. Hayes?

Essay Questions

1. Compare and contrast Lincoln's, Johnson's, and Congress' plans of reconstruction (as represented by the Reconstruction Acts of 1867–1868 and the Fourteenth and Fifteenth amendments). What were the objectives of each plan? Why did each fail to achieve its goals?

2. Discuss the transformation of southern agriculture during the Reconstruction period. Why did the sharecropping and crop-lien systems evolve? What were the consequences of those systems for the economy of the South and for white and black farmers?

3. Discuss the achievements and failures of the Republican Reconstruction governments in the South. Who supported and who opposed them? Why? Why and how were they driven from power?

4. Imagine that you are a Freedmen's Bureau agent in the South during the Reconstruction period. Using the information in Chapter 16, write an account of what you have seen black people doing and experiencing. As such an agent, how have you been involved with the blacks in your district?

5. Write an essay discussing the Grant administration. What were its policies on Reconstruction and the freedmen? What was meant by "Grantism" and Grant's "Great Barbecue"? What successes and failures did the administration have in foreign policy? Why did the Liberal Republicans break with Grant?

Preparing for the Final Examination: Prologue, Chapters 1 to 16

As you approach the end of part 1 of your American history course, you may well wonder how you are supposed to remember all those facts for the final. Here are some hints for preparing to take that semester exam: (1) do not wait until the night before the test (or even the last couple of days prior to it) to start your studying; (2) review the notes that you have taken on class lectures and assigned readings other than your textbook; (3) review the chapters of this study guide, rereading carefully the Outline and Summary portion of each; (4) as you do steps 2 and 3, look for issues and themes that seem to come up again and again. History, after all, is about change and continuity over time. Therefore, ask yourself as you review what things about American society changed between the colonial period and the end of Reconstruction and why. On the other hand, which things remained essentially constant or recurred periodically throughout those years? The following sample multiple-choice and essay questions are designed to assist you in pulling together all the facts and seeing more clearly the patterns of change and continuity over the first centuries of American history.

Multiple-Choice Questions

Circle the letter of the item that best completes each statement or answers the question.

1. Which of the following ended slavery everywhere in the United States?
    a. Lincoln's Emancipation Proclamation
    b. the Crittenden compromise
    c. the Thirteenth Amendment
    d. the Fifteenth Amendment

2. The statement "We hold these truths to be self-evident, that all men are created equal, that they are endowed by their Creator with certain unalienable rights . . ." is found in
    a. the Declaration of Independence.
    b. the U.S. Constitution.
    c. Lincoln's first inaugural address.
    d. all of the above.

3. Which of the following people is *incorrectly* matched with the reform he or she championed?
    a. Dorothea Dix—more humane treatment of the mentally ill
    b. Elizabeth Cady Stanton—women's rights
    c. Jonathan Edwards—separation of church and state and religious toleration
    d. William Lloyd Garrison—abolition of slavery

4. The convention held at Seneca Falls, New York, in 1848
   a. threatened that New England and New York would secede if peace were not made with England immediately.
   b. launched the feminist movement.
   c. was the first held by a political party to nominate its candidate for president.
   d. launched the abolitionist movement.

5. The forty-ninth parallel became the dividing line between
   a. northern and southern states.
   b. American and British parts of the Oregon Territory.
   c. Kansas and Nebraska
   d. the Mexican cession and the Louisiana Purchase.

6. The case of *Commonwealth* v. *Hunt* is significant in the long struggle of
   a. labor to win recognition of unions and the right to strike.
   b. women to gain equality in receiving an education.
   c. the federal government to increase its powers at the expense of the states.
   d. the abolitionists to end slavery in Washington, D.C.

7. Which of these statements comes closest to expressing Secretary of the Treasury Alexander Hamilton's views on the proper financial program for the federal government?
   a. A government should be frugal and avoid a standing debt.
   b. The government should repudiate the financial obligations incurred by the Continental Congress.
   c. The federal government should tie the monied classes of the nation to it by selling public securities at attractive rates of interest to them.
   d. The federal government should encourage the states to pay off their debts quickly by giving them matching grants.

8. Which of the following statements about the Era of Good Feelings is *incorrect*?
   a. It was a period of one-party politics.
   b. During these years the Republicans adopted much of the centralizing nationalism of the old Federalists.
   c. Congress passed a protective tariff and chartered a new national bank.
   d. The federal government began an extensive program of federally subsidized transportation improvements.

9. A typical western farmer in the 1830s and 1840s would probably favor all of the following federal policies *except*
   a. federal aid for internal improvements.
   b. renewing the charter of the national bank.
   c. easy land-purchase terms for squatters.
   d. the Indian Removal Act of 1830.

10. The influence of Puritanism was greatest and lasted the longest in
    a. New France.
    b. New England.
    c. New York and Pennsylvania.
    d. Virginia and Maryland.

11. During the colonial and Revolutionary War periods, the crop that most shaped the economy and society of the Upper South was
    a. sugar.
    b. cotton.
    c. tobacco.
    d. wheat.

12. Which of these was a slave uprising?
    a. Bacon's Rebellion
    b. Shays's Rebellion
    c. the Whiskey Rebellion
    d. Nat Turner's rebellion

13. Which of the following statements about slavery in colonial America is correct?
    a. Slavery existed in all thirteen English colonies.
    b. The slave population exceeded the free white population in most of the southern colonies.
    c. British attempts to outlaw slavery in her overseas colonies helped to incite the American Revolution.
    d. The majority of those enslaved were Indians rather than Africans.

14. In the eighteenth century most of the British colonies in America were governed by
    a. the elders of the established church.
    b. a governor, council, and assembly—all elected by the people.
    c. a governor appointed by the crown and an elected assembly dominated by the upper classes.
    d. a proprietor or appointed representatives of the company that had established the colony.

15. Thomas Jefferson was responsible for all of the following *except*
    a. framing the Virginia Statute for Religious Freedom.
    b. drafting the Declaration of Independence.
    c. drafting the U.S. Constitution.
    d. writing the Kentucky resolution.

16. The first systematic statement of the strict versus broad interpretation of the Constitution arose out of the debate over the
    a. tariff.
    b. chartering of a national bank.
    c. barring of slavery from new territory.
    d. purchase of the Louisiana Territory.

17. Which of these describes the Indian policy adopted during the Jacksonian era?
    a. to remove Indians to lands west of the Mississippi River
    b. to establish reservations for Indians in various sections of the country
    c. to force Indians to migrate to territory owned by Mexico
    d. to assimilate the Indians by breaking up the tribes and granting American citizenship to individuals.

18. For white males almost all property qualifications for voting had been abolished
    a. by the end of the American Revolution.
    b. with the ratification of the Constitution and the addition of the Bill of Rights.
    c. by 1800, when Jefferson was elected president.
    d. by the Jacksonian era.

19. The right of the federal courts to declare acts of Congress unconstitutional was first exercised in
    a. *Marbury* v. *Madison*.
    b. *McCulloch* v. *Maryland*.
    c. *Dred Scott* v. *Sandford*.
    d. *Ex parte* Milligan

20. The United States acquired these territories in which chronological order?
    a. Alaska, Florida, Louisiana Territory, Texas, California
    b. Louisiana Territory, Florida, Texas, California, Alaska
    c. Florida, Texas, Louisiana Territory, Alaska, California
    d. Florida, Louisiana Territory, California, Alaska, Texas

21. In the 1840s and 1850s many Americans believed that it was the manifest destiny of the United States to
    a. abolish slavery.
    b. become the world's leading industrial power.
    c. build a mighty overseas empire.
    d. spread its borders from coast to coast.

22. By the eve of the Civil War which groups accounted for roughly 50 percent of the population of cities such as New York, Chicago, St. Louis, and San Francisco?
    a. Italians and Eastern European Jews
    b. Irish and Germans
    c. Polish and Chinese
    d. Scandinavians and Hispanics

23. Which of these led directly to the formation of the Republican party?
    a. the Compromise of 1850
    b. the Fugitive Slave Law
    c. the Kansas-Nebraska Act
    d. the *Dred Scott* decision

24. Which of these did Lincoln *oppose* in the first year of the Civil War?
    a. abolishing slavery everywhere in the nation
    b. compensating the owners of freed slaves
    c. colonizing freedmen outside the United States
    d. fighting a war primarily to preserve the Union

25. Many historians believe that Radical Reconstruction was a democratic experiment that failed for all of the following reasons *except*
    a. Congress did not redistribute southern land, and without property the freedmen were too economically vulnerable to hold on to their political rights.
    b. the Republicans were unwilling to continue to use military force to protect blacks and remake southern society.
    c. freedmen failed to understand the responsibilities of citizens and showed little interest in voting and officeholding
    d. Republicans were willing to abandon the last of the Republican Reconstruction governments in 1877 to secure the election of their presidential candidate, Rutherford B. Hayes.

Essay Questions

1. The antebellum years saw the birth and development of the Federalist, Jeffersonian Republican, Democratic, Whig, and Republican parties. Discuss how and why each of these parties began.

Who founded each? To which groups did each one mainly appeal? What led to the demise of the Federalist and Whig parties?

2. Each of the following men was in some way involved in the sectional conflict that eventually led to the Civil War: Thomas Jefferson, John C. Calhoun, Daniel Webster, Henry Clay, and Stephen A. Douglas. Discuss the views and activities of these men regarding the sectional conflict.

3. Trace Abraham Lincoln's position on blacks and slavery from the time of the Lincoln-Douglas debates in 1858 to the time of his assassination in 1865. Why did he modify his stands?

4. Discuss the causes of the Civil War. Cite as many facts as possible to back up your analysis.

5. Compare and contrast Andrew Jackson's handling of South Carolina's nullification of federal law in 1832 and James Buchanan's handling of that same state's secession in 1860.

6. Explain the causes of the Mexican War and its impact on sectionalism.

7. Ralph Waldo Emerson once wrote, "There is no strong performance without a little fanaticism in the performance." To what extent could this observation be applied to the abolitionists and other antebellum reformers?

8. In 1820, 1833, and 1850 sectional compromises were agreed to and the Union was preserved. What accommodations were made each time, and why did the attempts to reach one more compromise in 1860–1861 fail?

9. If the enduring vision of America is embodied in the Declaration of Independence's statements about equality and universal rights to justice, liberty, and self-fulfillment, how much progress toward those ideals had blacks and women made by 1877? Back up your evaluation with as many specific facts as possible about the status of blacks and women at the end of Reconstruction.

10. In what respects was the Constitution of the United States as written and ratified in 1787 undemocratic? How was the American political system democratized between 1789 and 1877? What undemocratic features remained to be addressed? Give as many specific examples in your answer as possible.

Answers to Multiple-Choice Questions

Prologue

1. d
2. c
3. b
4. d
5. c
6. b
7. a
8. d
9. a
10. c

Chapter 1

1. c
2. c
3. b
4. c
5. b
6. a
7. c
8. d
9. c
10. a

Chapter 2

1. a
2. c
3. d
4. b
5. c
6. d
7. a
8. a
9. b
10. c

Chapter 3

1. b
2. c
3. a
4. d
5. c
6. a
7. d
8. b
9. d
10. b

Chapter 4

1. b
2. c
3. d
4. a
5. c
6. d
7. c
8. a
9. b
10. a

Chapter 5

1. a
2. c
3. b
4. a
5. c
6. d
7. c
8. b
9. d
10. c

Chapter 6

1. a
2. b
3. d
4. c
5. b
6. d
7. c
8. a
9. c
10. d

Chapter 7

1. d
2. c
3. c
4. a
5. a
6. d
7. b
8. c
9. b
10. b

Chapter 8

1. b
2. a
3. c
4. b
5. c
6. d
7. b
8. c
9. a
10. d

Chapter 9

1. c
2. b
3. d
4. a
5. b
6. d
7. c
8. c
9. a
10. c

Chapter 10

1. a
2. c
3. d
4. a
5. c
6. d
7. c
8. c
9. a
10. b

Chapter 11

1. b
2. a
3. d
4. b
5. c
6. c
7. b
8. c
9. b
10. a

Chapter 12

1. c
2. d
3. a
4. b
5. c
6. a
7. a
8. a
9. c
10. c

Chapter 13

1. c
2. b
3. a
4. b
5. d
6. b
7. a
8. a
9. b
10. d

Chapter 14

1. d
2. a
3. b
4. c
5. a
6. d
7. a
8. c
9. d
10. b

Chapter 15

1. c
2. a
3. b
4. c
5. d
6. a
7. c
8. a
9. b
10. a

Chapter 16

1. c
2. b
3. d
4. a
5. c
6. b
7. b
8. c
9. a
10. a

Preparing for the Final Examination

1. c
2. a
3. c
4. b
5. b
6. a
7. c
8. d
9. b
10. b
11. c
12. d
13. a
14. c
15. c
16. b
17. a
18. d
19. a
20. b
21. d
22. b
23. c
24. a
25. c